Getting Started as a Therapist

T0384995

Getting Started as a Therapist provides students and new therapists with a bridge between education and practice. Written for a transtheoretical audience, the book explores questions and struggles common to students and new therapist supervisees. Readers can find pointed guidance in 52 chapters, spanning five categories. Categories include:

- Establishing better therapeutic relationships.
- What to avoid saying to patients.
- Increasing diagnostic accuracy, understanding why diagnosis is not a dirty word, and how it is critical to a good outcome.
- Specialized topics like how to more effectively talk about self-injury and learning to use metaphors.
- Professional development such as making the most of supervision and how to limit liability.

The succinct chapters come alive with real-life examples and are often followed by suggestions for further reading and worksheets that help readers to refine their practice.

Anthony D. Smith is a licensed mental health counselor, certified juvenile court clinician, professor, clinical supervisor, and trainer with more than 20 years of experience. He maintains "Up & Running," a popular *Psychology Today* blog for new therapists.

"This is a very user-friendly book that's sure to become a guiding light for students and new therapists who want to stand out from the start! Highly recommended."

Bill O'Hanlon, *Oprah-featured author of 41+ books, including* In Search of Solutions *and* Do One Thing Different

"In a wise and thoughtful manner, Anthony Smith has crafted a remarkable book of effective strategies for conducting psychotherapy and growing professionally. Beginners and seasoned professionals alike will benefit from his perspective on best therapeutic practices."

Richard P. Halgin, PhD, ABPP, *Professor Emeritus of Psychology, University of Massachusetts Amherst, and textbook author*

"This book is so comprehensive and well-written. I wouldn't hesitate to recommend it to seasoned mental health practitioners and graduate-level instructors for their use with students who have an eye on clinical practice."

Joseph W. Shannon, PhD, *teacher, consultant, and psychotherapist in private practice in Columbus, Ohio*

"In the style of a metaphor-making storyteller with the clear-thinking, staccato delivery of someone with decades of experience, Anthony Smith has crafted a delightfully provoking and informative resource for new therapists and supervisors alike."

Emma E. Redfern, MA, *psychotherapist, supervisor, author, workshop presenter, and podcast co-host*

Getting Started as a Therapist

50+ Tips for Clinical Effectiveness

Anthony D. Smith

Routledge
Taylor & Francis Group

NEW YORK AND LONDON

Designed cover image: Vertigo3d © Getty Images

First published 2025
by Routledge
605 Third Avenue, New York, NY 10158

and by Routledge
4 Park Square, Milton Park, Abingdon, Oxon, OX14 4RN

Routledge is an imprint of the Taylor & Francis Group, an informa business

© 2025 Anthony D. Smith

The right of Anthony D. Smith to be identified as author of this
work has been asserted in accordance with sections 77 and 78
of the Copyright, Designs and Patents Act 1988.

Library of Congress Cataloging-in-Publication Data
Library of Congress Cataloging-in-Publication Data
Names: Smith, Anthony D. (Mental health counselor), author.
Title: Getting started as a therapist : 50+ tips for clinical
effectiveness / Anthony D. Smith.
Description: New York, NY : Routledge, 2025. | Includes
bibliographical references and index. |
Identifiers: LCCN 2024016491 (print) | LCCN 2024016492
(ebook) | ISBN 9781032623467 (hardback) | ISBN
9781032623436 (paperback) | ISBN 9781032631400 (ebook)
Subjects: LCSH: Psychotherapy—Vocational guidance. |
Psychotherapy—Practice.
Classification: LCC RC465.5 .S55 2025 (print) | LCC RC465.5
(ebook) | DDC 616.89/14023—dc23/eng/20240501
LC record available at https://lccn.loc.gov/2024016491
LC ebook record available at https://lccn.loc.gov/2024016492

ISBN: 9781032623467 (hbk)
ISBN: 9781032623436 (pbk)
ISBN: 9781032631400 (ebk)

DOI: 10.4324/9781032631400

Typeset in Galliard
by codeMantra

With much love to my parents, Dennis and Phyllis Smith, for unwavering support through so much.

Contents

SECTION V
Professional Development   191

Acknowledgments

Much gratitude is extended to:

Derek Paar, PhD, my graduate school advisor, and Richard Halgin, PhD, both of whose wisdom, friendship, and encouragement has been, and remain, foundational in my professional development.

Bill O'Hanlon, MS, who very early on inspired me to cultivate myself in this field and provided the initial spark to write and teach. Along with Bill, Joseph Shannon, PhD, fanned the flames of my desire to teach, along with shaping my clinical interests.

My dear friend Robert Roose, MD, my niece, Alyssa Wright, and my friendly colleagues Sheryl Waxler, PhD, Michael Mantz, MD, and Emma Redfern, MA. All parties offered moral support and/or helpful brainstorming throughout.

Anna Moore at Routledge, who saw promise in my proposal and encouraged this project to happen, then patiently guided me through this first book-publishing process.

Also the copyeditor, Sue Cope, who saw to it the manuscript shined.

The patients, students, and supervisees of the past 20-something years who provided the experience needed to assemble this volume for current and future students, supervisees, therapists, and *their* patients.

Introduction

If you were to have met me 30 years ago, you'd have said, "There's no way he's ever going to interact much with others, let alone have a career in a social science, work with the most difficult inmates, teach, provide trainings, or write a book." I guess this book is just part of the natural progression of a series of serendipitous events.

When I was a teen, my psychiatrist, who had for years been treating me for Tourette's Syndrome, obsessive-compulsive disorder, and social anxiety, suggested that my parents apply for disability assistance for me. Apparently, I wasn't on a great trajectory. Apparently, too, mom and dad knew better, watching me, like water on the ground, find my way, and didn't bother disabling me.

During all of the above, I had taken to making fishing flies, an activity known as fly tying, to give me something to do since I wasn't very social. After a few years, this hobby began to open doors. Ironically, the thing I took to because I feared socializing literally opened the world to me, and probably saved my life. It got to the point where if I wanted to improve, I needed to interact with people, and eventually I mustered the guts to attend shows and ask the guys I saw in books and magazines what they thought of my work.

Results were favorable. Those years in the basement churning out flies led to talent that impressed, and, by age 17, I had befriended some big names in the fly-fishing world. This boosted my confidence, *made* me socialize, for their company was rewarding, and one thing led to another until I was happily globetrotting, demonstrating at shows and for private clubs.

Amidst this transformation, I had entered college and studied psychology, inspired by my own struggles. I figured I'd be a therapist (at the time, I wasn't aware of any other career with the degree), putting my empathy for, and understanding of, mental illness, to good use. During my master's degree training, I was intrigued by an opportunity to intern at the local house of correction and was awarded the position.

DOI: 10.4324/9781032631400-1

Any remaining social angst began to be wrung out of me, perhaps my ultimate exposure therapy. Timidity or lack of confidence meant certain failure in a correctional environment, and the last thing I wanted was to jeopardize my internship, because I thoroughly enjoyed the work. I must have done OK, as within a month, I was offered a position there. For the next almost nine years I honed my clinical skills in this forensic environment. Interest flourished in personality, differential diagnosis, chronic/severe mental illness, developing an effective style of therapy, and the mental illness-legal nexus.

Despite enjoying the work, this period was not without waves of frustration. I soon came to realize that practice wasn't anything like sitting in a classroom. Memorizing facts, critical thinking about theories, and role playing is nothing more than a sliver of an introduction to the subject matter encountered in the field. In fact, book smarts seemed to have little to do with actual practice.

Wanting to excel, I often felt overwhelmed and on my own when I discovered that colleagues could really only be general guides. They couldn't imbue me with what I felt I needed or wanted to know; most didn't share my enthusiasm and weren't interested in the finer points of specific areas I wished to learn about. In some situations when I needed direction with an intervention, or encountered a diagnostic conundrum, I would receive simple advice such as, "You need to process that more with them" or "Diagnosis doesn't matter so long as you're treating symptoms."

At that point, I decided it was best to become dedicated to self-study and attending conferences. In 2007, I was closing in on my first licensure renewal and perusing catalogs for interesting seminars to get the last few continuing education credits I required. My interests and needs merged, for Bill O'Hanlon, a popular, solution-oriented psychotherapist and protégé of the late, revered psychiatrist Milton Erickson, was providing a day-long event with the number of credits I needed.

That seminar was a critical point in my budding career. While I enjoyed the material in the training, called "Resolving Trauma without Drama," I was most taken by Bill's excitement and ability to share on stage and in writing what he felt was important to help therapists refine. I was no longer just interested in being helpful to people one-on-one. I wanted to teach, to be like *that guy*. I collected my first professional hero, and, 16 years later, things came full circle as Bill kindly provided a review for this book. I've joked with Bill that he had to, for this book was really his fault.

My first impetus to teach was rooted in irritation about poor diagnostic habits I witnessed, complete with the damage they caused. It wasn't long ago I had sat in classes learning to carefully assess patients, yet I felt surrounded by impulsively diagnosed individuals. Women who pushed a boundary or sought attention were quickly assumed "borderline" or "histrionic;" difficult men were rendered "antisocial."

These assumptions implied incorrigibility. Colleagues opined such people shouldn't be engaged unless there was some unique circumstance like they arrived on psychotropic medications or were prone to self-injury. Personality-disordered or not, was it not possible they suffered and were causing a scene at times because that was the only way they knew how to communicate internal turmoil? Invalidating them by ignoring, or "intervening" by setting boundaries, and not examining the conflict often only made things worse for everyone.

Particularly irritating was hearing "bipolar" applied to any alteration in mood, as if it were as prevalent as the common cold. I knew that even liberal estimates placed the prevalence at perhaps 6 or 7 percent; how were they all ending up here? And how was it that, even though unmedicated and under inordinate stress, most of those thus diagnosed never exhibited actual manic/hypomanic/mixed episodes? The clientele didn't know any better and once arbitrarily diagnosed, unnecessarily considered themselves mentally ill. The savvy inmates would apply this idea to justify problematic behaviors, especially violence, perpetuating the idea that mental illness is dangerous. Other examples are found throughout the upcoming pages.

By 2011, it was all coming together when a colleague, Dr. Diane Hall, connected me with an adjunct teaching position at Baypath College (now University), where she was teaching. To my surprise, Dr. Kathy Stevens, the Psychology Department chairwoman, soon reached out with unexpected praise. She said I had the enthusiasm and positive student feedback of a good professor, and wanted me to teach abnormal psychology, for she knew my interest in differential diagnosis.

Over time, while teaching undergraduate students and supervising master's degree practicum students, and eventually professionals already in the field, I couldn't help but notice common themes of struggle and interest. Some of these matters were already familiar to me. Topics included being influenced by popular culture portrayals of mental illnesses, developing a style of psychotherapy, and how to talk about medications despite not being a physician.

Surely, I thought, these questions must be ubiquitous, and they're being asked about or struggled with so regularly because they are foundational matters that perhaps aren't being taught or sufficiently addressed in supervision. Subjects that were taught at the beginning of a program, such as diagnostic interviewing and attending skills, were, sometimes two years later, suddenly expected to be remembered and put to use in practicums, internships, and first jobs. There needed to be a bridge between education and practice.

With this in mind, during the 2020 Covid lockdown, I made use of the isolation by finding an outlet to reach an audience for this kind of material.

After some networking, I began writing for *Psychology Today*. My blog, "Up & Running," aimed at helping students and new therapists refine, and presenting information about misunderstood diagnoses to the consumer, has so far accrued four million hits.

Despite this resource, some students and supervisees began asking, "When are you going to write a book?" They explained that a compact resource of tips and further reading suggestions could serve as a good reference for reminders of what to strive for, or guidance between supervision sessions, as they entered the field. Sometimes emails arrived from Up & Running readers and agency education departments inquiring, especially, about further pointers or providing training on accurate diagnosing habits.

With encouragement from veteran psychologists and clinical supervisors Richard Halgin and Derek Paar, writers themselves, and my friends and mentors, I endeavored to make it happen. It was becoming clear that an upward trend of unprecedented numbers of students and new therapists was not stopping. With this would be an increase in the need for quality supervision that might not be available to help them refine. Therefore, the time was right, said Rich and Rick, for additional guidance around these perennial topics to be shared in an easily accessible, cross-theoretical reference.

Given the sheer number of topics and the limited space, I saw the necessity for a brief, but thorough, format. Taking a cue from famed psychiatrist Irvin Yalom's *Gift of Therapy*, a tome of 83 mini chapters, it indeed seemed possible to get useful information across with brevity. That said, this book is necessarily not exhaustive, either in scope of topics or breadth of particular items; most topics could be their own book.

Rather, this book was written to highlight common areas that present opportunities for improvement early in therapists' careers, provide tips for navigating the material, and pique curiosity to learn more. Further resources are provided in many chapters to encourage the latter. In fact, if teaching and supervising have taught me anything, it's that cultivating curiosity might be the most important thing of all, for it encourages a "never stop learning" mentality.

Readers will note that some topics trending in mental health care, like trauma, diversity, and technology, are not expounded upon. They are only included herein relative to particular hurdles someone early in their career might encounter. This is because such topics are given inordinate attention in modern therapists' education and workplace training. This considered, I felt the space would be better used for other important areas that could more covertly affect the practitioner.

On another note, as a therapist of integrative style, it's only natural that throughout the book examples span cognitive, existential, psychodynamic, and solution-oriented psychotherapy approaches. This is not to suggest that one approach is better than another. Each example simply happened to be an encounter from my own practice that adequately illustrated a point, or a trademark skill of a particular theory that I've noticed can be helpful across therapist styles.

That said, examples reflect my own experiences with patients, students, and supervisees. Thus, names and other potentially identifying material, including symptom details and, in some cases, gender, of patients, students, and supervisees have been altered.

Also, throughout the book I use "patient" as opposed to "client," "person served," or "consumer." Patient means "one who suffers" and people sit with us because they are suffering. The more distance we gain from the original term, the more potential there is to lose the meaning of our work. Are not the latter terms more reflective of business transactions than the intimate, interpersonal experience that is psychotherapy?

Whichever term a therapist decides to use is less important than how they provide for the people seeking their care. Social media and professional forums can make it seem as if such academic debate is more important than the actual work of psychotherapy. Concern yourselves with the practice of psychotherapy and fully encountering the people in front of you the best you can, and it will be an education like no other. It's my hope that the material herein helps students and new therapists to construct sturdy bridges across to the patients who, ultimately, are the best teachers.

Section I

Setting the Stage

Chapter 1

It's Not Like on TV

If you haven't encountered mentally-ill people, or been to successful therapy to witness what good therapy entails, beware. Mental health care *should not* be like most TV and movie portrayals, whether diagnosis or intervention.

Have clinical heroes, but please don't aspire to be a reality television interventionist or TV series psychologist. Remember, entertainment with drama sells. Real life therapy involves ethics and empathy, not putting people in their place. Nor should every session involve transferential dilemmas requiring chronic supervision. Further, not all patients are deeply disturbed and immensely challenging. Shows like *Hoarders* could imply that certain conditions should have rapid successes, but consider how much time has been cut out for TV timeframes.

Pop culture does not accurately depict mental health, whether it is diagnoses or treatment, and Hollywood is a leading cause of stigma. Movies like *Split* lend force to the idea that mentally-ill people are dangerous and scary. Influential people like Tom Cruise (Hausman, 2005) and Marianne Williamson have publicly minimized the seriousness of diagnoses and the effectiveness of psychotropic medications. The latter once went so far as to say depression is "such a scam" during a presidential campaign (Abrams, 2019).

TV and radio show therapists can seem to suggest that in order to get anything done, therapy must be a confrontational and aggressive activity. Their solutions are no more complicated than taking a stance of moral authority, telling patients to stop doing this or that, to make better choices, or to embarrass them and put them in their place. This could understandably scare people away who are considering therapy but TV and radio shows are their only reference point.

Further inaccuracies involve the portrayal of psychotherapy being either decades-long psychoanalysis with an old man saying "tell me more" or an aggressive, cognitive-behavioral therapist weeding out problems left and right. This can give the idea that therapy is supposed to be either painfully extended or forced and brief. The truth lies somewhere in between. Therapy, no matter the approach, takes time. Life naturally lends itself to perpetual

DOI: 10.4324/9781032631400-3

analysis, but that is not the agenda of an analytic therapist. Even this longer term, "depth" therapy averages only 3–8 years, not the oft-depicted lifetime (Werbart & Lagerlöf, 2022).

Alternatively, more "targeted" cognitive/behavioral interventions may engender rapid success, but are the improvements optimal or just enough to say "treatment goals have been met"? It's easy, for example, to show someone how to cope with anger. However, it will likely only provide tenuous stability if a character flaw, such as the belief one is entitled to special treatment, as in narcissism, isn't also addressed, which takes time.

It's a rare day that therapists do not apply for more sessions for their patients, and it's not to turn a profit. The lines out of the doors of clinics and private practices leave no want for business. It is because work is not complete.

People enter this field to help erase suffering, but, if they are not careful, some of their actions, influenced by popular culture, while well-intended, can discourage, stall, or add to problems. For instance, a new therapist could think they *must* get a traumatized person to discuss the trauma details because it's a popular belief. As a result, the patient never returns for it was too much, too fast. Endless questioning about history might somehow seem therapeutic because it "works" on TV. However, as detailed in Chapter 13, psychological archeology is not psychotherapy.

Lastly, adopting popular culture portrayals of mental illness as accurate summaries one can clinically rely on, as discussed in Chapter 19, is a dangerous practice. Attention-deficit hyperactivity disorder (ADHD), bipolar disorder, dissociative identity disorder (DID), obsessive-compulsive disorder (OCD), and schizophrenia have become grossly misrepresented. Unfortunately, without enough clinical experience, it is easy to rely on what one has otherwise been exposed to. These concerns will all be expanded on in the following chapters.

To be effective, remember your professional role was not born in Hollywood. For a good start, rely on your education and research, take continuing education seriously, and engage in sound supervision.

References

Abrams, A. (2019, August 6). Experts criticize Marianne Williamson's views on vaccines, depression and illness. *Time.* https://time.com/5644331/marianne-williamson-health-science-skepticism

Hausman, K. (2005, August 5). Cruise finds himself at sea after antipsychiatry tirade. *Psychiatric News, 40*(15). https://doi.org/10.1176/pn.40.15.00400007

Werbart, A. & Lagerlöf, S. (2022) How much time does psychoanalysis take? The duration of psychoanalytic treatments from Freud's cases to the Swedish clinical practice of today. *The International Journal of Psychoanalysis, 103*(5), 786–805. doi:10.1080/00207578.2022.2050463

Chapter 2

Be Yourself

Students of psychotherapy are reminded that, just as in their non-professional life, it's best to not try to be someone they are not. Being inauthentic makes therapy more of an act than a service. If someone is inspired by Carl Rogers, for example, but does not possess his grandfatherly demeanor, that doesn't mean they can't adopt his methods. There's no point in trying to alter your tone and cadence just to better emulate him. It's the therapy principles that count. If a therapist becomes fixated on their image, self-consciousness could become more central to sessions than the patients.

Supervisees have confessed to feeling a need to change personal quirks or flaws they feel might adversely affect their ability to be a solid treatment provider.

We can be our own worst critics and rapidly assume that others will view us similarly. Practicum supervisees, just getting their feet wet and tending to have the most performance anxiety, have wondered aloud if some characteristic ("flaw") of theirs could get in the way of being an effective therapist.

I ask if their "flaws" have ever hindered their ability to socialize effectively. More often than not, they say nobody ever pointed it out, or if they do, it's something likeable. Indeed, we tend to like uniqueness in people. Of course, there may be quirks of a nature that have received negative feedback, like a tendency to interrupt, which we'll return to in a later chapter.

The truth is, therapists and patients need to be good fits, and nobody fits everybody. If some characteristic of the therapist's consistently surfaces as a hindrance, it can always be worked on in supervision. Until then, try to practice naturally, just like you'd approach a social situation, without worrying about any potential flaws. In the following examples, it's clear that what we may see as flaws are quite possibly assets in patient care.

To begin, if you're energetic, let it flow. Don't be influenced by the overly analytic, serious, stereotypical therapist image and feel that is the essence of a practitioner. That's merely a relic ingrained in pop culture. Being energetic, of course, doesn't mean the therapist does most of the talking, or trying to be coercive. Rather, let your energy signify your enthusiasm.

DOI: 10.4324/9781032631400-4

If a practitioner is enthusiastic, does it not signify positivity to the patient? A couple of things that can be conveyed to a patient by a therapist's energetic nature include, "They're really invested in assisting me," or, "They're encouraging despite my real struggle, perhaps this is reassurance I *can* be helped."

Conversely, a new practitioner once worried that their matter-of-fact disposition might be a liability in that they were not "warm and fuzzy" as therapists tend to be portrayed. Such impassivity, however, can lend itself well to the occupation. Those of us who are more expressive may give away strong internal reactions like a sense of heightened concern, that a patient is being ingenuine, or frustration. In turn, the patient might shut down, become angered, or feel they are disappointing the therapist whom they look up to, adding to their poor self-image.

Another student once lamented they might be seen as "a hard ass" by future patients. I thought they were going to share foreseeing themselves telling patients they're not working hard enough. Upon exploration, the student described themself as not being a drill sergeant, but that they were assertive. Assertiveness is not synonymous with aggression. It is often that a person prefers to "take the bull by the horns" and be more direct in managing something that needs fixing. You can be firm and fair (empathic) at the same time. Having this characteristic can be beneficial in numerous ways. For example, many a patient has told me, "I need to be called on my bullshit." In addition, those who work with personality disorders must be quick to confront boundary violations and set limits.

Lastly, one supervisee always brought humor to our meetings. When I shared that I enjoyed her wittiness, she revealed a fear that her silly side could be perceived as not taking patients seriously, such as when she made a pun to take the edge off. Having a playful edge is a useful tool. Think about how scared many people are to enter a therapist's office. Breaking the "I'm going to be judged and analyzed" fear with a smile can show them it is not a hostile environment. It's not minimizing the patient or making fun of them, but it's important to be judicious because therapy is not a comedy show.

Whether a therapist is assertive, energetic, or silly, don't just see them as personality traits or characteristics. They can be tools for therapy work.

Chapter 3

Therapy isn't a Race

New therapists are eager to help, which can be a strength and a deficit. To gage supervisee or student mindsets, I ask, "What do you do in psychotherapy?" A common response is some form of, "People come in with problems. I need to have the solutions to make their problems go away." It's as if therapy is perceived as a special forces operation, picking off the bad guys.

It has been my experience that students and new therapists, when asked about their theoretical preference, express wanting to develop a cognitive-behavioral therapy (CBT) skill set. This is likely at least in part because it's what they are primarily exposed to in today's graduate programs. Further, I'm told, "It gets right to fixing the problem."

Upon further examination, their expanded definition is sometimes nothing more than identifying symptoms and providing coping skills. Psychotherapy is thus reduced to the fastest possible symptom reduction, as if it is a paint-by-number procedure. While seemingly efficient, there are inherent fatal flaws in this approach, perhaps most thoroughly examined by Enrico Gnaulati, PhD, in his book, *Saving Talk Therapy* (2018).

Over the years I've noticed an increasing assumption that therapy is not, or should not be, an exploratory process. Rather, there is an idea it should be neatly packaged solutions ostensibly remedying problems in short order. This is no doubt further fueled by the uptick in manualized, short-term (8–12 sessions) interventions, implying therapy is supposed to be short.

Despite the implication of these popular tools, psychotherapy is not a race. What's more, it does not take long in the field to realize that it's not unusual for any level of meaningful, lasting change to take six months to a year, regardless of the theoretical approach (Shedler & Gnaulati, 2020).

Sure, therapists wish to relieve patients' symptoms as soon as possible, but it's important to realize that ground must be broken to accomplish this. While therapists can offer immediate objective interventions, like diaphragmatic breathing to combat panic, or grounding techniques to interrupt dissociations, it is still necessary to examine the uniqueness of each person's experience. Do we not need to get to know the person, and allow the person to get to know themselves?

DOI: 10.4324/9781032631400-5

Getting to understand the meaning behind people's experiences can help unveil the foundational complication for ultimate resolution. This is not a Victorian relic, for modern psychoanalysts and existentialists operate thus, and traditional cognitive-behavioral therapists explore thought processes behind behaviors on the principle that thoughts drive feelings, which drive behaviors (Ellis & Harper, 1997; Burns, 1999).

From its inception, psychotherapy was an activity of exploration and allowing the patient to unfold. By helping a patient explore their being, we help them come to realizations, make painful or shameful confessions, and share intimate details that almost certainly have a bearing on the problematic feelings and symptoms that led to seeking therapy. It is then that the more substantial work may begin of pulling up the anchor of deeply seated dilemmas, and allowing the person to work towards sailing freely once again.

While symptom reduction is relieving, symptoms are just the fruit of a deeper-rooted conflict. I've yet to meet, for instance, someone with illness anxiety (hypochondriasis) who simply developed the symptoms, which in turn can simply be given replacement behaviors, and life goes happily on.

While working with patients on reducing their preoccupation with perhaps having a serious illness, I've many times discovered they have an unusually pervasive fear of death. This tends to be correlated with a feeling they are not living authentically and fear dying because they have not truly lived. In effect, the hypervigilance for serious medical illness serves as a check to catch any illness that may prematurely terminate their chance to live authentically. Clearly, helping this type of patient recover from illness anxiety also involves resolving the conflict driving it.

Even in this age of increasingly popular, ultra-brief CBT protocols, icons in the CBT field have illustrated that deeper exploration provides a foundation for more substantial work to begin. For example, Dr Jeffrey Young created the "Young Schema Questionnaire" to help such exploration. This is a standardized tool created to help patients with deep-seated maladaptive beliefs explore the troubling way they conceptualize their world and how that leads to their struggle (Yalcin et al., 2023). Thus, this insight becomes a springboard for patients to identify and accept what needs changing, and bolsters a collaborative intervention environment.

While people come to therapy for symptom relief, it's not always as easy as categorical symptom reduction with intensive exposure therapy or teaching them to be responsive and not reactive through a dialectical behavioral therapy (DBT) skills manual. Even DBT, considered a relatively quick and effective approach to borderline personality disorder, involves some deeper exploration for sustained success, and averages six months to one year of treatment (Cleveland Clinic, 2023).

While successful ultra-brief and single-session therapy does occur, and I've certainly conducted it at times, it's usually a very specific issue with a very motivated person that makes it successful. Most patients are going to need to unfold.

Perhaps the fastest way to psychotherapeutic success is taking the required time, which will vary amongst patients. Before deep work can begin, a therapeutic alliance must be forged, where patients come to trust that the therapist is interested and cares. It is necessary to establish a dynamic where patients may be vulnerable and reveal themselves to expose the conflicts to resolve that will ensure long-term symptom relief.

People in therapy are seeking lasting change. What is the point of quick symptom reduction if the therapist does not work with the person to make sure improvement is sustained, and this newfound way of being has not been woven into the fabric of their lives?

Suggested Resources

Readers interested in learning in-depth about how long meaningful, effective therapy often takes are encouraged to read Jonathan Shedler and Enrico Gnaulati's article "The Tyranny of Time: How Long Does Effective Therapy Really Take?" in *Psychotherapy Networker* (March/April, 2020). Expanding on the issue, in *Saving Talk Therapy* (2018, Beacon Press) Gnaulati unveils how the accelerating push for shortened therapy is at the detriment of patients' sustained stability and encourages critical thought about navigating patients' therapy needs.

References

Burns, D.D. (1999). *Feeling good: The new mood therapy*. Avon Health.

Cleveland Clinic (2023). *Dialectical behavior therapy (DBT)*. https://my.clevelandclinic.org/health/treatments/22838-dialectical-behavior-therapy-dbt

Ellis, A. & Harper, R.A. (1997). *A guide to rational living*. Wilshire Book Co.

Yalcin, O., Marais. I., Lee C.W., & Correia, H. (2023). The YSQ-R: Predictive validity and comparison to the short and long form Young Schema Questionnaire. *International Journal of Environmental Research and Public Health, 20*(3). https://doi.org/10.3390/ijerph20031778

Chapter 4

Don't Forget the Basics

Driven by the eagerness to resolve someone's suffering, it could be easy to "dive right in" and immediately start asking questions about symptoms and giving advice to make them go away. It's as if the goal is strictly to eradicate symptoms.

I'll never forget one student who, after exchanging pleasantries at our first meeting, struck a very serious tone. He proceeded to reveal that he was there to learn to have answers for patients and "fix" them as fast as possible. He continued that this meant giving them relevant homework and having profound things to say to them to help alter pathological mindsets.

After absorbing this proclamation, I asked him what constituted therapy. "Getting to know what the problem is, and making it go away," he replied. He was right, of course, on a rather basic level.

"How does that happen?" I wondered aloud.

"We ask questions," was the reply.

"So, we need to establish a talking relationship with the folks?"

"Of course."

"*Establish* a relationship," I emphasized.

Appearing puzzled, he said, "They're in your office talking to you, they want to have a relationship with you and feel better, right?"

I decided to change course. I like to ease into getting to know my students and supervisees, as I would with patients. Being too intense or formal can make an already nervous person more uptight. This involves, in as easy-going a way as possible, getting a feel for the people, what I can help with, and what they would like to accomplish. Simply guiding my student along in such a conversation, he became less rigid and more relatable.

After a while, I pointed out to him that his demeanor had changed, and inquired what accounted for it. "Well, we're just talking."

"Pretty comfortable, eh? Like no pressure, just getting a feel for one another ...?"

"Yeah. What are you getting at?" he inquired.

DOI:10.4324/9781032631400-6

"If you were a therapy patient, would you rather feel what's going on between us when you meet your therapist? Or would you rather feel interrogated and have advice slung at you right away when chances are you're not even understood yet?" He began to understand the exercise.

Therapy is so much more than a conveyor belt process of sitting on a couch, knocking off symptoms in checklist fashion, and sending patients on their way, though insurance companies would prefer it that way.

While I'm sure my student knew to utilize attending skills, like maintaining eye contact and showing interest in the patient, other basics were in absentia under his original idea of therapy. These included establishing a therapeutic alliance, what some have commented is perhaps *the* most substantial item of all (Ardito & Rabelino, 2011; Prusiński, 2022). Without such a trusting relationship, a person is not likely to share the personal material necessary for change. Perhaps they'll describe symptoms that can be managed with some coping skills, but as illustrated in the previous chapter, symptoms are manifestations of bigger, internal conflicts that must be explored and resolved.

Remember, many patients are managing deep inner conflicts, feel shameful or guilt-ridden. They might be seeking therapy as a last resort after having been shot down by trusted family members because their culture believes in "grinning and bearing it." The original complaint of "anxiety" may just be the word they best knew to assign to their experience to get in the door and have help exploring and navigating their complicated internal landscape.

While patients can present us with a well-defined problem, such as wanting to resolve matters related to early sexual abuse, they may feel too vulnerable to provide material to work with. Especially in abuse cases, trust has been shattered, and re-establishing the idea that trust can occur is sometimes the most important part of therapy.

It isn't unusual, for, say, someone with sexual trauma to complain of anxiety, sleep disruption, or moodiness as their need for treatment. Imagine a patient calling for an appointment and saying, "I was abused last week, I need therapy." It is not likely to happen. Understandably, a patient needs to see they can trust and rely on a therapist before baring themselves. An impatient therapist may feel the person is "treatment resistant" if, after three months, they've not given details. A wise therapist, however, knows to mine the interpersonal dynamic, for it's what will allow patients to want to relate to us the rest of the experience at the heart of their pain.

All of the above considered, it is not to say we cannot help alleviate acute problems at the outset, like cultivating sleep hygiene or dampening anger. However, think about what it takes to get to know someone socially or romantically, how long it takes to reveal the real you to them. A therapy relationship is a social interaction and similar rules are at play.

References

Ardito R.B. & Rabellino, D. (2011). Therapeutic alliance and outcome of psychotherapy: Historical excursus, measurements, and prospects for research. *Frontiers in Psychology*, 2(270). doi:10.3389/fpsyg.2011.00270

Prusiński, T. (2022). The strength of alliance in individual psychotherapy and patient's wellbeing: The relationship of the therapeutic alliance to psychological wellbeing, satisfaction with life, and flourishing in adult patients attending individual psychotherapy. *Frontiers in Psychology, 13*. https://doi.org/10.3389/fpsyt.2022.827321

Chapter 5

Forget About Being So Formal

Attending, or the presence the therapist creates for patients, is meant to cultivate an environment conducive to engaging them (e.g., bedside manner). In effect, attending skills are gestures to show interest and that the therapist is following the patient. If this dynamic is too methodical, however, it might do anything but.

Imagine being a patient and sitting across from a therapist who leans in intently with unflinching eye contact. Or picture a therapist sitting within an arm's length, leaning forward, elbows on knees, stereotypically nodding and smiling at each sentence, a bit too eager to prove they're following along. How about a therapist stopping to paraphrase every couple of minutes, or asking too many questions? What do these scenarios conjure up for you if you place yourself in the patient's shoes?

Showing interest with body language, acknowledging and showing understanding, and being inquisitive are all things therapists should do. Unfortunately, albeit well intentioned, there can be too much of a good thing. While formality encourages therapists to pay attention to their attending skills, if too ardent, it can detract from rapport building and putting a patient at ease.

Leaning in with unyielding eye contact can seem intimidating, no matter how friendly someone may be. It's also the body language equivalent of putting someone under a microscope. Patients, especially at the outset, are often playing it close to the vest and unfold naturally as they warm up to us. Feeling suffocated by attendance, or "too paid attention to," may make them feel the relationship is being forced, or too intimate too quickly. More than one practicum student has shared recorded sessions where they sat at attention, close to the patient, muttering "uh huh, uh huh," after every statement. As we review the recordings, some students have remarked that as they watched themselves do this it appeared unnatural, as if they were acting.

Attentiveness and summarizing are crucial qualities that should be used judiciously. Too frequent use can present roadblocks. While well intentioned

DOI: 10.4324/9781032631400-7

to let the patient know they were heard and confirm the therapist is understanding, utter devotion to the actions might disrupt the patient's flow of thought. Further, it could imply that the therapist is seeking constant reassurance they're following correctly, as if feeling unsure of themselves.

Showing interest is also an attending skill, of which asking questions is naturally a part. Reflecting on my own beginnings, and something I've noticed when working with supervisees, there can be a tendency to show curiosity by asking question after question to keep the ball in the air. This may seem like forward motion in that it propels one through the 50-minute session without silences, a matter addressed in Chapter 9. In reality, it makes a disorganized interaction, could render a feeling of interrogation, as detailed in Chapter 28, and opportunities to obtain important information are lost.

To illustrate, a recent student worked with a partner who complained of insomnia and poor concentration. After asking how long it went on for, the student began taking a family history. Upon reflection, the student concluded the detailed family history was irrelevant and it would have yielded better grist for the therapy mill to say things like, "Describe that for me," "Give me an inside-out view of that. What's it like for you?," and/or "How does that effect you?".

Curiosity is more important than questioning. A conversational "Tell me about that" might be expected to build a better relationship and yield more information than rote question asking. If attending skills were clothing, keep it business casual.

Chapter 6

Mastering Your Therapeutic Presence

Polished listening, the cornerstone of therapy, depends on three items that set the listening stage (Smith, 2021). These might seem like common sense, but directly facing the person, keeping eye contact, and being relaxed aren't necessarily common. You may have noticed this if you have visited your physician lately. Researchers have determined that patients often feel their doctors are having more intimate encounters with screens (Northwestern University, 2014; Martin, 2018).

As mental health care joined the paperless movement, it was hard not to notice this phenomenon budding here, too. No longer do therapists perform their intake session sitting with a clipboard, having a discussion, and periodically jotting information down on forms. Rather, they're forced to tap, click, and follow an electronic template during a crucial meeting.

Bruce Wampold, a psychologist who researches the ingredients of successful therapy, wrote: "The initial interaction between patient and therapist is critical, it seems, because more patients prematurely terminate from therapy after the first session than at any other point" (Wampold, 2015). Further, he explained that patients, during the initial meeting, rapidly assess whether the therapist is trustworthy, has the necessary expertise, and will take the time to listen and understand the presenting concern. This obviously becomes challenging when a screen is like a third person in the room.

For better patient experiences, effective therapists are obliged to consistently act as described in the following sections.

Face the Speaker

This is not Victorian Austria where our patients lay on the couch, the analyst behind them. Even modern psychoanalysts sit facing their patients; it just makes sense for a discussion. How often have you gone for a physical examination and the doctor sits perpendicular to you, at a computer? Does it feel as if they are carefully listening and interested, regardless of how much they look up and talk to you? It quickly becomes evident why psychotherapy, relying heavily on relationship-building, can't afford to cut corners.

DOI: 10.4324/9781032631400-8

Maintain Eye Contact

The philosopher Confucius advised: "Look into a person's pupils. He cannot hide himself." Eyes, and "look" convey a lot. Surely, you have "read" someone's intention by the look in their eyes. Were they genuine or was it mere lip service? Are they indeed caring and kind, or spewing scripted material?

Some emerging therapists may struggle with their own anxiety and find it difficult to maintain eye contact. They're also nervous about their new role as therapist and the lack of initial confidence can make it even harder to maintain a gaze with patients. Some supervisees have found the advice from a socially-anxious young adult I once worked with valuable.

When I complimented the individual on his ability to keep eye contact, he laughed, and said, "Well, I'm paying attention to your eyebrows." He learned that, if he looked towards my eyes, but pushed his *attention* upwards, "eye contact" was manageable. As someone who struggled with social anxiety early in life, this tactic was familiar to me. Periodic direct glances served as a sort of "exposure therapy" working towards more sustained, actual eye contact.

Establishing a relationship is dependent on eye contact. While a patient may have poor return eye contact, perhaps a cultural product or the result of anxiety, the practitioner has little excuse. Even if someone is not looking up at us, looking for opportunities to make eye contact models the importance of this basic communication skill and shows interest. Should someone notice the therapist staring at the floor, even with an eye contact-averse patient, it can come across as meek and unconfident, perhaps the very thing they're trying to overcome; "If the therapist doesn't have what I want, how are they going to help *me*?"

One caveat is if the patient is from a culture where eye contact in general is frowned upon. Some Asian cultures do not generally practice prolonged eye contact, and in Muslim cultures eye contact between men and women is restrained (Vishwakarma, 2023).

Conducting some research on cultural eye contact norms can help circumvent any culture clash. It may also be helpful to simply broach the topic; asking about their cultural norms shows you're interested in knowing them. The therapist's acceptance of the patient's experience can also send the message they're safe to share and be vulnerable.

Remain Calm and Relaxed

There will undoubtedly be alarming situations. Perhaps a patient confesses they are suicidal and scared, but don't want to go to hospital; an irate patient screams at you; someone has a panic attack in the middle of the session.

Depending on a therapist's experience and temperament, they could become visibly nervous with the suicidal patient, want to raise their voice in defense at the irate patient, or reflexively exclaim "What's happening!?" with the panicking person. Chances are that these reactions will only serve to escalate the respective situations.

Of similar concern, borderline, narcissistic, and antisocial individuals sometimes try to intimidate therapists. If the therapist is reactive and nervous, they're seen as someone who can be taken advantage of; if the therapist reacts as a hothead, the more litigious folks could complain to the licensing board.

Even if a therapist feels they are internally unraveling, maintaining their cool benefits everyone. Therapy can be a taxing job some days. If someone is already stressed, they are more prone to cave under pressure with a demanding patient. It pays for therapists to not only practice their wellness, elaborated on in Chapters 50 and 51, but to generally be prepared for high-stress situations. The following checklist can help:

- Take time to become grounded between patients, perhaps with a round of diaphragmatic breathing.
- Avoid caffeine during office hours.
- If a particular patient pushes the therapist's buttons, it might help to realize that any reactions are simply empowering them. Ideally, therapists have a grounding exercise prepared for if this occurs, and the reactive countertransference is discussed in supervision as discussion material for future sessions with the patient.
- If feeling defensive towards a patient, ask yourself, "Is what I'm about to say going to be productive?"
- Have a plan for managing suicidal patients in your office. If working at a facility, know the agency's protocol intimately, and know where to find a supervisor for consultation. If in private practice, therapists should have their own plan to reference and a trusted therapist peer or formal supervisor to reach out to.
- If one works in an environment with unusually challenging individuals, like corrections, *Coping with Difficult People Workbook*, by Leutenberg and Lipatk (2012) can provide a form of guidance to maintain equilibrium.

References

Leutenberg, E. & Liptak, J. (2012). *Coping with difficult people workbook*. Whole Person Associates, Inc.

Martin, K.L. (2018, April 10). Adding more "screen time" for physicians must come with caution. *Medical Economics*. https://www.medicaleconomics.com/view/adding-more-screen-time-physicians-must-come-caution

Northwestern University (2014, January 24). Do doctors spend too much time looking at computer screen? *Science Daily.* www.sciencedaily.com/releases/2014/01/140124115750.htm

Smith, A.D. (2021, August 11). In therapy: Listen better by mastering your presence – effective listening requires some physical etiquette. *Psychology Today.* https://www.psychologytoday.com/us/blog/and-running/202108/in-therapy-listen-better-mastering-your-presence

Vishwakarma, V.K. (2023). A review of non-verbal communication and cultural implications. *Journal of Namibian Studies: History Politics Culture, 34,* 1741–1754. https://doi.org/10.59670/jns.v34i.3417

Wampold, B.E. (2015). How important are the common factors in psychotherapy? An update. *World Psychiatry, 14*(3), 270–277. https://doi.org/10.1002/wps.20238

Chapter 7

Body Language Basics

Body language is defined as, "The movement and gestures of the body that communicate to another person non-verbally" (*Oxford Advanced Learner's Dictionary*, 2023).

This is another source of patient information therapists must "listen" to. While a straightforward concept, body language can be tricky to work with. For example, it's easy to make assumptions about patient body language and jump to conclusions. Also, therapists might infer information from patients' body language but not *do* anything with it. Further, a therapist may not realize what *their* body language is communicating to the patient.

It can prove useful to keep the following items about body language in mind while working with patients (Smith, 2021).

Things Aren't Always as They Seem

One of my supervisees, Bonnie, was convinced her patient was withholding information because of his folded arms:

"I've met with Jason a few times now, and he's always sitting with his arms crossed," said Bonnie. "The conversation flows, but I'm worried he might not be speaking honestly."

"Is he just comfortable?" I asked.

"Well, when people are 'crossed off' that's a sign they're withholding something, isn't it?"

"I've been sitting with my arms folded while we've been talking this evening, do you question my truthfulness?"

"No, but I don't know, it's different from a patient. He could be defensive about a topic that he feels vulnerable about and not really saying what's going on. His crossed arms are the giveaway. You and I are just talking," replied Bonnie.

I inquired, "How do you sit when you're with patients?"

"Relaxed in the chair, maybe cross my legs."

DOI: 10.4324/9781032631400-9

"So you're not leaning towards Jason in a stereotypical 'listening therapist' pose?"

"No."

"Does that mean you're not interested in the patient?"

"Certainly not."

I continued, "So is it possible you may be jumping to a conclusion?"

"I suppose," replied Bonnie.

"It's easy to do at the start," I went on. "You're working with all kinds of information and signals and may read too much into stuff, wanting to make sure you don't miss anything."

I finished, "Now, if Jason were sitting with arms folded and being tight-lipped, often lost eye contact, or seemed to change his story, then we'd have more reason to think he's closed off or disingenuous. For now, how about giving him the benefit of the doubt? You be comfy and relaxed in your chair, and he can sit with his arms folded. Without other evidence, there's no point in scratching where it doesn't itch. If you confront him about the arms being crossed, he could feel you're scrutinizing him, and it could fray the rapport."

Being analytical has its advantages, but keep in mind that observations are best contextualized before drawing a conclusion.

Working with Patients' Body Language

It's good to recognize body language, but if it's not *worked with*, it might be a wasted opportunity.

Body language may not be verbal, but that doesn't mean it's off limits to talk about. So often it seems that "working" with body language means noticing someone is getting tense or irritated, and taking that as a cue to back off about a topic. While that could be a good idea, it's also not a signal to do a 180 from the topic. If something is creating that response in a patient, it's clearly grist for the therapy mill. But how?

A good starting point is acknowledging the patient appears distressed. Then, just like a therapist would do if someone verbalizes distress, do some exploring. Therapists might be uncomfortable with a patient appearing in distress, or assume the patient isn't OK talking about the apparently distressing item further, so they decide to exit the topic.

However, the patient may wish to work through what's happening. If a therapist is reactive to their own anxiety about a patient's discomfort and comments, "I can see it's making you upset, we don't have to talk about it" and switches gears, it's possibly at the peril of good treatment. It can be helpful to think of patients' body language as an opportunity for exploration and a lesson in articulating internal experiences.

To continue, changing course might signal that it's not acceptable to show emotions or vulnerability. Second, it could cause a patient to lose faith in the therapist. They may be thinking, "They're supposed to help me work through this and learn how to deal with these feelings when they come out, and they can't deal with it." Instead, consider the following example of how to safely mine body language for therapeutic material:

> Justin, age 15, looked away and bit his lip as the therapist inquired what he meant by, "I can't get a lot of stuff out of my head." Then he turned red and his eyes welled up. "We don't have to keep talking about it," said the therapist; "Tell me how the new medication change has been for you."

A more effective approach would be working *with* Justin's presentation:

> "Justin, I can tell something is on your mind about that. When you're ready, what can you tell me about what's going on inside?" This response allows the therapist to stick with what's happening for Justin, but not seem interrogative about something clearly sensitive to him. The therapist shifts to focusing more on Justin's *experience*, which is likely going to be more revealing of what led to his presentation.

If Justin still struggled to articulate his experience, the therapist could reroute by noting, "Today's a tough session for you, thanks for sticking with it. I know you're trying to get something across to me, and it's challenging right now, but I do want to understand to help you move forward. If those emotions you're showing had words, what are they trying to explain to me?"

Therapist, Monitor Thyself!

It's foolish to think a therapist may not have to sneak in a yawn at the end of a long day, or restless individuals don't need to move a bit. However, frequent yawning, looking about the room, doodling, squirming, hand wringing, or playing with cuticles are red flags to patients. Though these activities may be innocent, they could convey boredom and discomfort with the patient or their material.

Even if a patient's material arouses angst in the therapist, as mentioned in the previous chapter, it's imperative they remain composed. If a patient sees a therapist become fidgety, they might stop sharing for fear of provoking negative reactions in the therapist, jeopardizing treatment. Bouncing legs or shaking a foot is often an unconscious habit, but how might you feel if, while sharing intimate material, the therapist seemed impatient? Of course, the hope is they may point it out to the therapist for discussion, but this is unlikely given the power differential, and the patient could feel the therapist is anxious to complete the session instead of focus on their needs.

Developing self-awareness is just as important as honing one's observational skills of others. The aim is for the therapist to become sufficiently aware of their own reactions and vulnerabilities and bring them to supervision if they feel they're hindering therapeutic interactions.

References

Oxford Advanced Learner's Dictionary (n.d.). Body language. Retrieved October 14, 2023. https://www.oxfordlearnersdictionaries.com/us/definition/american_english/body-language

Smith, A.D. (2021, August 25). In therapy: Understanding and working with body language – good listening requires attention to visual input. *Psychology Today*. https://www.psychologytoday.com/us/blog/and-running/202108/in-therapy-understanding-and-working-body-language

Chapter 8

How to Polish Your Summarizing

Maintaining a good physical presence and cultivating basic listening skills sets the therapeutic stage. Active empathic listening (AEL) takes listening to the next level by reflecting on what is heard to develop an understanding of the patient's experience and communicating that the therapist is attentive. The core of AEL regards paraphrasing and summarizing along with providing validation and acknowledgment.

Perhaps the most effective way of indicating someone is being heard in a clinical setting is to verbally reflect on what they say. To show that they're engaged and following along, therapists periodically offer quick synopses, or paraphrases, of what they're hearing and understanding throughout the session. It also allows patients to correct any possible misunderstanding.

Sometimes paraphrasing can be just a few words, while other instances require a more expansive summary. The following two examples illustrate effective formats of both.

1. *Patient:* "I need to talk to you about my sister. My parents don't believe me that she's relapsed with her bulimia. She was hospitalized for it a couple of years ago. She knows how to play them so well. I'm really worried!"

   Therapist: "You're worried she'll keep playing them and get sicker?"

2. *Therapist:* "Jenny, you've told me quite a bit so far about how your boyfriend has become increasingly smothering. Just to make sure I'm following accurately; he's never been good at spending time alone. Lately, if you simply want a day to yourself or to hang out with girlfriends, he accuses you of not appreciating him, maybe even cheating on him. When you try to talk about it, he breaks down, and you feel compelled to soothe him. The relationship feels draining some days, and you're not sure what to do. Did I hear all that right?"

DOI: 10.4324/9781032631400-10

Further, validation and acknowledgment help the therapist express to the patient that they realize what they're struggling with is real. It also shows the therapist is not being judgmental and can even help normalize what they're going through. A lot of people, for instance, think it's bad to exhibit certain emotions. Women may believe it's unladylike to feel angry or aggressive; males often believe it's emasculating to experience sadness/depression or anxiety. This need to contain their feelings compounds the stress of the emotional state.

Even if someone's reactions or emotions seem excessive, it doesn't mean that the patient is not experiencing it as dramatically as it's expressed. This is a particular concern when working with people with borderline personality disorder (BPD). Those with BPD can be dismissed as "overreactive," but they indeed feel extremely strong emotions. This is especially so with anger, given their inherent hypersensitivity of their amygdala, a part of the brainstem that dictates defensive responses (Goodman et al., 2014; Gu et al., 2020). Telling them to calm down or not acknowledging their strong emotions for fear of "feeding into them" only engenders further upset. Imagine having a storm surge of emotion only to be essentially told it isn't real.

Simply acknowledging that the strong emotions are their experience and are real to them can go a long way in rapport building when the patient is used to hearing others say they're too dramatic. In fact, this is a tenant of dialectical behavioral therapy (DBT), a popular, effective BPD treatment (Linehan,1997). The BPD experience of feeling disbelieved is poignantly covered in Bill Lichenstein's 2006 documentary *Back from the Edge*, featuring Marsha Linehan, the creator of DBT.

It's been my experience that patients generally feel that those of us who do validate their intense emotions are more understanding and thus better able to help them. To be an effective validator, two things must be kept in mind.

First, it's important to note that validation does not mean the therapist agrees with the person. What it means is the therapist is acknowledging that the patient is experiencing something. Second, effective validation is not simply quipping, "That's a valid way to feel." A patient may not understand what "valid" means. Further, it's a dead-end statement that isn't very conducive to patient response and further exploration. Consider "That's a valid way to feel" versus the following examples:

1. *Female patient:*   "I get so mad when they just keep passing the buck. I want to tell them how it's affecting me, but can't bring myself to say it. Whenever I'm ready to let it out, I feel guilty for being angry. I flash back to my mother saying, 'Little girls shouldn't act so mad' after that kid broke my favorite toy."

Therapist:	"If no one is taking responsibility, it'd be surprising if you *didn't* feel some level of anger."
2. *Parents:*	"We're worried that Johnny is falling into the wrong crowd since he began high school. He's keeping up academically, but has come home smelling like pot, and doesn't want to play soccer anymore. Our friends have said we're making too big a deal, that it's normal teen stuff. Their kids did the same and turned out OK, but we just don't have a good feeling about this."
Therapist:	"It's normal for teens to rebel to some degree and change interests, but you don't have a crystal ball and know if it'll continue. Naturally, you have some concern."

If these examples seem like they're also summarizing/paraphrasing, you're right. With practice, therapists can get two birds with one stone by adding a validating statement into their summarization. In these examples, the therapist gives details to show they're following along, while offering that the anger and concern is normal/valid.

This multifaceted kind of AEL might be considered an art unto itself. Thankfully, we can learn from one of the best. Carl Rogers, the creator of person-centered, or humanistic, therapy, participated in the recording, *Three Approaches to Psychotherapy*, also known as *The Gloria Tapes* (Shostrom, 1965), a video exhibition of three different approaches to therapy. His exemplary demonstration is available on YouTube, which my supervisees have invariably found a good reference.

References

Goodman, M., Carpenter, D., Tang, C.Y., Goldstein, K.E., Avedon, J., Fernandez, N., Mascitelli, K.A., Blair, N.J., New, A.S., Triebwasser, J., Siever, L.J., & Hazlett, E.A. (2014). Dialectical behavior therapy alters emotion regulation and amygdala activity in patients with borderline personality disorder, *Journal of Psychiatric Research*, 57, 108–116. https://doi.org/10.1016/j.jpsychires.2014.06.020

Gu, Y., Piper, W.T., Branigan, L.A., Vazey, E.M., Aston-Jones, G., Lin, L., LeDoux, J.E., & Sears, R.M. (2020). A brainstem-central amygdala circuit underlies defensive responses to learned threats. *Molecular Psychiatry*, 25(3), 640–654. doi:10.1038/s41380-019-0599-6

Lichenstein, B. (2006). *Back from the edge: A landmark documentary-style short film* [Video]. YouTube. https://www.youtube.com/watch?v=HNwNzXHcy9w

Linehan, M.M. (1997). Validation and psychotherapy. In A.C. Bohart & L.S. Greenberg (Eds.), *Empathy reconsidered: New directions in psychotherapy* (pp. 353–392). American Psychological Association. https://doi.org/10.1037/10226-016

Shostrom, E. (1965). *Three approaches to psychotherapy*. Psychological and Educational Films.

Chapter 9

Find Value in Silence

The poet Thomas Carlyle wrote, "Silence is the element in which great things fashion themselves together; that at length they may emerge, full-formed and majestic, into the daylight of Life, which they are thenceforth to rule" (Good Reads, 2023). It is no different in psychotherapy, but many therapists squirm in silence, and opportunities for things to emerge can get lost.

When I was new in the field, the most anxiety-provoking encounters in a session were periods of silence. I felt I *must* have something to say, lest I wasn't being helpful. Even worse, perhaps it painted me as inept in the eyes of the patient. In time, I learned this was mostly projection, or the assumption others perceived me the way I was viewing myself, as an insecure new therapist.

Today, I'm often reminded of how disquieting silences can be at the outset, as practicum students confess or demonstrate a similar fear. While reviewing student's practicum videos, palpable discomfort may follow the briefest silence, and there's a desperate attempt to fill the void. The follow-up supervisory meetings are always rich as the student digests their experience, only to be surprised to discover that filling the void can threaten the therapeutic process.

Once they have met their "silence threshold" a therapist might tell themselves, as an excuse to break the silence, that the patient's momentary quiet means they no longer want to discuss the topic. Panicked, the therapist offers impulsive commentary or abruptly changes the topic to have something to say. After all, who wants to see a therapist with nothing to offer?

Upon inspection, however, silence is not always indicative of, "It's your turn to talk." The patient could be contemplating something the therapist said. Perhaps, while silent, they are mustering the guts, or finding the words, to say something that requires attention. Can you think of a time, perhaps in a meeting, when you had something to say but weren't sure if you should, or how to say it? Now imagine having something critical to share, such as disclosure of abuse, or revealing something one feels ashamed of, and the space that could require to confess or articulate.

DOI:10.4324/9781032631400-11

If the therapist becomes talkative during such a pregnant pause, the patient might not try to bring up the topic again, at least not that session, when it seemed like the right moment; it was an uncomfortable item to bring to light, and any excuse to not have to might be capitalized on. Clearly, providing patients with an ample silence berth is a valuable gesture. With enough silence, they are more likely to crack and use the moment. Like a buried seed, once the shell breaks, new growth begins to emerge.

Indeed, try giving the silence an opportunity to resolve on its own. This will be less of a task with some patients than others, and become easier as you get to know them.

I frequently sat in silence for up to five minutes with Corrine, a patient I knew well. She would trail off and become contemplative, sometimes spontaneously. At the same time, she began to rhythmically draw her finger tips of one hand down her fingers of the other hand and across her palms in a self-soothing activity. I learned to let Corrine be, and focused on watching her hand motions for their hypnotic relaxing effect, which broke any of the silence discomfort I may have experienced as the minutes ticked away. More often than not, she would start to reflect on something poignant we had touched on immediately prior.

If she did not speak after some time, Corrine would look up and produce a pained smile. This was my cue to coax her. "If I know anything about you," I'd begin, "when you get quiet and play with your fingers this long, something is brewing inside, and you're either not sure how to say it or are a little afraid to." Merely getting her to acknowledge this was usually enough to spur her on. It was as if my reminder of how well we knew each other assured her it was safe to broach any concern. Being someone ashamed of her body who generally didn't think highly of herself, the material sometimes related to intimacy with her boyfriend. Other times, Corrine, afraid to disappoint me, struggled to let me know she had re-engaged in a self-destructive activity like drinking benders. Both items were important grist for the therapy mill, which would have been lost if Corrine was not allowed to engage in her process.

When a therapist is just getting to know a patient, it can be helpful to be especially careful not to force away silence. This might occur with an observation like, "What are you thinking about?" That could come across as you wanting to know too much, too fast. It is less confrontational to offer an observation, like, "It's been my experience that when someone sits quietly in here, there's something knocking that wants out." If affirmed, helping the patient partner with their silence can help the state of arrested expression. Posing the paradoxical question, "If that silence was words, what would it be telling me?" has been notably productive over the years.

Other scenarios that can generate patients' silence are if they are unused to talking about themselves, or are fearful of exposing themselves and appearing weak. This could be related to cultural matters, machismo, or fear of vulnerability. They might answer your questions as briefly as possible, and offer no spontaneous dialogue. Not surprisingly, this terse presentation is a common scenario in males, who are often socialized to feel negatively about help-seeking (Wendt & Schafer, 2016; Cole et al., 2018). Autistic people, given the inherent social deficits, can present similarly. It's important to know your audience, for, in these cases, prolonged silences that were beneficial for others could be very difficult to endure. A therapist would do well to seize these opportunities to teach a patient to interact and communicate.

In situations like this, the patient honestly may not know what to say, awaiting the therapist's prompts. To promote a forum of focused sharing, the therapist can be productive by blowing on the embers that have begun glowing with simple persuasion, like asking for clarification or other details. Simply being curious and using the most open-ended questioning style is invaluable. "What more can you tell me about that?," "How has that affected you?," or "What's been helpful to deal with that?" can gain discussion traction.

Showing those prone to this behavior that we're interested in what they have to say, or gradually exposing them to self-revelation and seeing it is not disastrous, can work wonders.

Clearly, if someone is not good at sharing themselves, a goal of therapy may have to be improving their ability to be more articulate and willing to share, so we can better understand and address the chief complaint.

Lastly, surely there will be purely oppositional silence, as with rebellious teenagers who see therapy as "stupid" and they feel they're forced to be there. No amount of cajoling is likely to make them participate, and it has nothing to do with being an unworthy therapist. Patients like this take significant rapport building, and supervision is often invaluable.

References

Cole, B.P., Petronzi, G.J. Singley, D.B., & Baglieri, M. (2018). Predictors of men's psychotherapy preferences. *Counselling and Psychotherapy Research, 19*(1), 45–56.

Good Reads (2023). *Thomas Carlyle quotes.* Goodreads.com.

Wendt, D. & Shafer, K. (2016). Gender and attitudes about mental health help seeking: Results from national data. *Health & Social Work, 41*(1), 20–28. https://doi.org/10.1093/hsw/hlv089

Chapter 10

Strive to Cultivate Substance in Each Session

When I interview people about their mental health care history it's not unusual to hear they've had several therapists. Two common answers as to why they've been changing providers indicate sessions had little substance.

The first complaint is, "They just asked me the same questions each session: 'What did you do this week?,' 'How are you feeling?,' 'Why did you feel that way?,' 'Have you felt like hurting yourself?'" The second gripe is, "I felt I did *all* the talking. I need feedback."

Indeed, it's not therapeutic to conduct each session as a kind of prolonged mental status evaluation. While therapists should of course evaluate patients' symptom picture and risk status, just talking about symptoms each week or "smiling and nodding," while well-intended, isn't what people come to therapy for. It's not difficult to see how this can feel impersonal.

Recalling my initiation to the field, consistently asking similar questions provided a semblance of clinical intervention, in an evaluative sense, when I wasn't sure how to focus in and guide a constructive session. One supervisee who had this experience confessed it seems like a way to learn about the patient, but rarely goes anywhere.

Another reason for such a focus on symptoms and risk evaluation is the fear some patients might harm themselves. Thus, the therapist dedicates a large part of each session seeking reassurance the patient is alright and providing safety planning. Ultimately, focusing on mental status and risk deprives both patient and therapist. There's little improvement for the former, which sustains the heightened awareness of the latter.

Regardless of the reason, it would of course behoove a therapist stuck in such patterns to review the matter in supervision and gain traction. I've found supervisees who have a tendency to follow this pattern are inquisitive by nature. If they can work on shifting the focus of their inquiry, they encounter much richer experiences and more productive therapy naturally unfolds. One way to do this is reviewing the initial visit and presenting complaint, like the experience of a supervisee named Theo.

DOI: 10.4324/9781032631400-12

Theo encountered a patient named Blaine, age 25, who entered therapy complaining, "My life is going nowhere." He was in the midst of a significant depression and having suicidal thoughts, but had never made an attempt and didn't think he would. Theo found himself spending the first few sessions focused on discussing Blaine's melancholy patterns and suicidal thinking. Theo offered, "I seem to revert to stuff like, 'When did it get worse?,' 'What seemed to cause that?,' and then I offer some ideas for coping skills or give psychoeducation about depression and work through his risk that week. Blaine gives me a lot of details, and I think I'm somehow helping him learn about himself. He's tried some things I suggested, but with little improvement. He seems frustrated."

"Theo, you've got the right idea," I began. "You're curious and want to help him learn about himself, to explore, right?"

"Yeah, it's just that I feel compelled to know all about his symptoms to tell him how to cope. If the symptoms get worse, he could consider suicide," said Theo.

I continued, "We'd be remiss if we didn't watch out for those things and provide some psychoeducation and tools, but I think you're discovering we need to look beyond the symptom picture. Let's consider that Blaine didn't complain so much about depression, but rather that he felt his life was going nowhere. How do you feel about exploring *that*?"

"Well, wouldn't he feel stagnant in life because he's depressed?" asked Theo.

"Possibly, but we won't know until you ask him to tell you what he means by 'going nowhere.' Applying the same questioning about symptoms to the presenting complaint might open some doors for a therapy material goldmine. There's a good chance he's depressed *because* he feels so stagnant. If we know about his stagnation, we can work to help him gain momentum, which just might alter that depression," I finished.

During the subsequent supervision, Theo was happy to report that Blaine revealed he is disappointed with himself for not pursuing the things he wants because he is unsure of himself. It turned out Blaine suffered from anxiety, and his depression worsened as he aged and watched life go by because he worried about everything ending in a worst-case scenario. Having established this, Theo's confidence rose as he understood what needed to be surmounted for Blaine's depression to improve.

Equally disheartening to many a patient is, as one researcher put it, a "passive, vague, and silent" therapist (Curran et al., 2019). Having attempted psychotherapy with two providers who "interacted" this way, I understand the frustration. One therapist, for each of three sessions I attended, only offered "Such as?" or "Tell me more" in between nodding. It felt like a weak interrogation. Another was a psychologist of fewer words, whose responses were occasional little smiles of acknowledgment. The two sessions I attended were nothing more than listening to myself give details in exchange for a few extremely open-ended questions.

One can easily see how it's hard for therapy goals to be reached under such circumstances, and the pressure a patient must feel to do all the talking. People seeking help are looking to *interact*. Whether it's feedback, education, reassurance, learning a skill, or a cathartic discussion, therapists delivering these experiences are likely to have more constructive sessions.

Some students struggling with little to say, spurring the patient to provide most of the material, have confided they're not sure how to gain footing and hope the patient says something that will spur them to explore. For those grappling with similar situations, a calculated action plan can engender dialogue and encourage direction.

To accomplish this, it's helpful to set the tone in the first session by asking how the therapist can be helpful. This, of course, might dictate the patient consumes much of that session sharing. Therapists can make this more interactive and show interest in helping them navigate their concern with a couple of easy activities. These are simply asking clarifying questions or for more details as they deliver, and occasionally offering understanding by paraphrasing. Making notes along the way of material the therapist might like to revisit can be helpful to pick up where they left off last session, and continuing the dialogue. Consider the case of Betty.

Betty entered therapy because she had had enough of her husband, Colin, being ambivalent and yielding. "Whether it's what to have for dinner, where to go, or if we should have another child, all I get is 'I don't know,' or 'It's up to you,'" she explained. Attempts to talk to Colin about it led to him saying he doesn't care so long as she's happy, or guilt-tripping her by saying he's sorry to disappoint her. Life with such a passive partner seemed like she was taking care of another child. "He can't see how frustrating this is. I feel like I just constantly strike an attitude with him! I know it's not the solution, but it just happens!" Betty finished.

Seeing an opportunity, I offered, "Betty, we've only got about 10 minutes left already. I want to make sure I'm hearing you right, and suggest something that could be helpful between now and the next session." I continued, "Correct me if I'm wrong, but by working with me, you're hoping to more effectively communicate with Colin about how his indecisiveness impacts the family, and for yourself to not get so worked up. To learn to be more responsive than reactive?" After Betty affirmed with a nod, I continued, "From what you've described, it seems Colin's idea of how to satisfy you chronically backfires and he is not getting it. If that's what's going on, it would be unusual if you didn't feel irritated!"

"If you're a reader," I finished, "I'd like to recommend a couple items to read about constructive communication in relationships. Next time, we can talk about applying some of the ideas specifically to your marriage, and exploring how to be less reactive."

There is a lot going on at the end of the first session that lets Betty leave knowing therapy will be a two-way street. First, she knows her concerns were heard and she affirmed what we would be focusing on. Then, Betty was offered something to *do* towards resolving the matter. Suggesting reading material is an effective supplement to therapy sessions (Pehrsson & McMillen, 2007). Patients can read at their leisure, refer back to useful items, and the therapist can help them apply the material to their own situation.

Readers are invited to place themselves in the patient's position. Would they feel more confident in returning to therapy where smiling/nodding and revolving questions occur, or with the understanding they are being attended to and partnered with, like Betty?

References

Curran, J., Parry, G.D., Hardy. G.E., Darling. J., Mason. A.M., & Chambers, E. (2019). How does therapy harm? A model of adverse process using task analysis in the meta-synthesis of service users' experience. *Frontiers in Psychology, 10.* doi:10.3389/fpsyg.2019.00347

Pehrsson, D.E. & McMillen, P. (2007). Bibliotherapy: Overview and implications for counselors. *Professional Counseling Digest, ACAPCD-02.* https://www.counseling.org/resources/library/ACA%20Digests/ACAPCD-02.pdf

Chapter 11

Ask About Meaning

"How does that make you feel?" has its place in the psychotherapist's arsenal, but it's not the sharpest tool. If therapists want to cut deeper, asking "What does that mean to you?" or "What's that like for you?" can engender more robust revelations and therapeutic exchanges.

It's been my experience that asking about feeling can be a perfunctory activity leading to a dead-end answer. Great, the therapist knows the patient is anxious, depressed, or feeling betrayed, but then what? There might be a great leap from "How does that make you feel?" to offering depression or anxiety management skills. Perhaps the therapist attempts to reason with the patient that they have a right to feel betrayed. There is then a comment that the patient doesn't deserve that, rendering the therapist a cheerleader. Then what?

Although well-meaning, these responses miss a major point of therapy. That is, the necessity to explore the patient's experience. Whether analytic, cognitive, or person-centered-based approaches, patients must get to know themselves if they are going to change. Thus, feelings are not always the most lucrative quarry.

Therapists need to be able to mine for, and work with, substantive data for clinical gains. Thankfully, a little curiosity can go a long way. For instance, talking to someone grieving a close relative or friend, their feelings of sorrow and emptiness are often palpable. Asking what the loss *means* to them, however, can open new therapeutic doors. The emotional turmoil is often not only the effect of the deceased's absence, but the death causes reflections that instigate anxieties about their own mortality or unresolved conflicts.

One patient with this experience offered that, since her parents died, it was as if there was nothing between her and the grave now and there is so much more she wanted to do. This revelation made it clear that the loss, though more than a year prior, stirred her own existential angst. Exploration of her life satisfaction and how to achieve goals to feel she had "lived more" followed. Another individual, in therapy after losing a long-term, close friend, lamented that the friend's absence meant they could never

DOI: 10.4324/9781032631400-13

better resolve a conflict that lurked in the shadows. Clinical focus turned towards self-redemption for his role in the conflict.

In another example, Jackson, a 16-year-old teen, while working through his parents' divorce, discovered his girlfriend had cheated on him. "She said she was only sticking around because she felt bad for me," lamented Jackson, tearing up. "What's it been like for you the past week since it happened?" I asked. "So angry my head spun. I'm drained. I've got no energy to be angry anymore. I want to scream, but I don't have the energy."

"Sounds like insult to injury," I offered. "You were already dealing with so much." He nodded.

"Jackson," I continued, "what does all this *mean* to you?"

"It means I'm on my own. I can't trust anyone. My parents are too wrapped up in their mess to care about the mess they made for me, and, I guess, I just suck. I give my heart to someone for the first time, and without warning, it doesn't matter."

Asking Jackson about the meaning of his experience led him to put words to his internal landscape. This inside-out synopsis provided more than focusing on feelings could provide. His description created an opportunity to examine the maladaptive beliefs that germinated from the problematic experiences, which only served to compound his bad moods. Navigating these beliefs became part of the plan to relieve Jackson of depression.

Therapists working with trauma may also find it a therapy-accelerating question to help understand how trauma affected someone. Therapists can ask about symptoms and provide coping skills and guidance for achieving goals, but wouldn't it also be helpful to know how a patient is shaped by the meaning they assigned to their experience? Having a patient share that their traumatic experience made them feel "forever broken," for example, is more fertile ground than an inventory of symptoms to assign coping skills to for a treatment plan.

Asking this "forever broken" patient, "What exactly do you mean by 'forever broken?'" was crucial to our work. They described an overidentification with the role of victim, perpetuating the other symptoms. Hypervigilance soared, nightmares involved reaching for goals, only to be sabotaged. Understanding this schema helped treatment in that the focus centered on empowerment and cultivating and magnifying other components of her life that negated the role of victim.

A last example involves asking about meaning behind substance use. So often the juveniles I interview for court are enmeshed in daily marijuana use, binge drinking, or vaping nicotine. Problems follow like infractions for marijuana possession in school, perhaps public drunkenness, or getting caught stealing vaping paraphernalia. During the assessments I ask not only about their use history and how it affects them, but what sort of meaning do they assign to the substance use?

I've been given answers that it is how they identify with their family or that they can control how they feel and when. In the cases involving drug dealing, while the money is a motivator, drug culture guarantees excitement in an otherwise dull existence.

In each instance, asking about meaning yielded more potent information than "why" or "how" was likely to. Inquiring about meaning encourages an answer that captures more of the experience. This includes revealing deeper causal factors than self-medication or boredom, or at least factors that encourage the sustained use under the circumstances.

Chapter 12

Be Attentive to Your Intuition

My colleague, Joseph Shannon, a psychologist specializing in personality, once told me that "listening with the third ear" is a top skill to hone as a therapist. According to author Lee Wallas (1985), the term was first used by the existentialist Friedrich Nietzsche in his 1886 book, *Beyond Good and Evil* (Wallas, 1985). Given my lack of familiarity with the term I was intrigued, but quickly discovered it's simply an elaboration of something most people are familiar with: intuition.

While this clinical skill might sound unusual, if you have ever sensed there is more than meets the eye to what the patient is relaying, you've experienced it. Clinically, the third ear quietly deciphers indirect communication, helping the therapist read between the lines. Just as Spiderman heeds his tingling "Spidey sense" that something is awry and someone needs help, it's important for clinicians to heed *their* "Spidey sense."

Sometimes supervisees confess to encountering situations where they feel their patient is indirectly trying to say something. However, they wonder if it's too speculative or confrontational to heed the tingling and "go there." Usually, they fear they may be off the mark, in which case they would be deemed incompetent and push the patient away. Some have justified their defensive unwillingness to consider their intuition by commenting, "When the patient is ready, they'll tell me."

Or not. Not regarding the intuition could inadvertently prolong misery and unnecessarily perpetuate treatment.

Is it not part of the therapist's duty, part of the therapeutic process, to explore and help patients learn about themselves so they may advance? Is it not poor practice to potentially be encouraging internalization of things that need saying; to not help patients discover it's OK to point out, and deal with, emerging elephants in the room?

It's not unusual for patients to be on the couch due to some such ineffectual coping strategy such as internalization or denial. Thus, the very thing the therapist might be apprehensive of doing is just what they need, and perhaps are even carefully, consciously asking for. Would you be surprised

DOI:10.4324/9781032631400-14

to learn that sometimes patients (consciously or unconsciously) guide us to make the observation so they don't have to say it? Something that requires purging may be too painful or embarrassing to mouth, and it's easier to acknowledge than to explain in order to get it out there. Consider the case of Rob, a successful 34-year-old, who entered therapy because he was "feeling emptier with age" (Smith, 2020).

As we explored his life, Rob disclosed an early history of social anxiety that he overcame with therapy. He confessed he was a late bloomer for dating given his teenage angst, but had managed a few, year-long relationships as he emerged from his shell in his twenties. "As a kid, all I wanted was a nice girlfriend, but I didn't get that young adult dating experience. The older I get, the harder it is meeting eligible ladies," Rob lamented. Not about to let it sink him, he accepted singlehood as best he could, travelling abroad and exploring locally on his own.

Rob occasionally traveled with friends, but the ones he had traveled with began to have children and were no longer available for adventures. "My friends had to go have kids," he'd joke, "They don't know what they're missing!" Despite this, he regularly spoke of being "Uncle Rob" and beamed when talking about his friends' toddlers. Other times Rob said, "I do love kids, I just like to give them back. Kids aren't for me," noting they'd be hang-ups for his ostensible free spirit.

Soon, my Spidey sense tickled that Rob's emptiness may well stem from being childless, and I had enough evidence to justify exploration. In a subsequent session, I said, "Rob, we've met a few times now, and I'd like to review a bit deeper. Given your history of social anxiety, it's impressive you've become so social and had some successful romantic relationships. It's got to be disappointing to have progressed exponentially with social comfort, just to encounter the frustration of not securing the relationship you always wanted. While talking about your frustrations with the romantic void, though, you've also made some curious comments about kids that I feel deserve exploration. On the one hand, you depict how kids cramp your style. On the other, your happiness is palpable when you bring up kids that are in your life. Correct me if I'm wrong, but I can't help wondering if there's an internal conflict regarding kids of your own contributing to that complaint of increasing emptiness."

Rob eventually confessed, "It's much easier to say you don't want kids than to admit you can't pull it together enough to make it happen." What followed was an unfolding of Rob's fear he'd be like his father, plus he feared his own children could be tormented with anxiety as he was. Being in denial allowed him to save face about imperfections. As Rob reflected, he realized that while he enjoyed the women he was with, when talk of longevity and family surfaced, he invariably sabotaged the relationship. He was capable of getting what he wanted, but subconscious security guards only let romance go so far.

Rob isn't unusual in that patients may be avoiding the truth as ego damage control when they aren't procuring what they want. As we explored over time, it came to light that the more Rob could not find someone, the more he traveled solo to prove he did not need anyone and to convince himself of his rationalization defense that kids just complicate things. He needed an excuse not only for himself, but as deflection for appearing defective to others.

Imagine if I had not shared what was on my mind about Rob's material? Clearly, selective hearing for the third ear could have grave consequences for patients. Further, it is important to note that, unlike therapists we might see on the screen, it's not about trying to shake sense into someone, saying, "Listen to yourself! You're not finding a relationship because you're in denial about wanting kids."

Framed in a disarming way that makes patients see it's to their benefit if your hunch is explored will likely make them interested in examining the idea and weighing its merit. Even if it's off the mark, that's not synonymous with therapist incompetence. It demonstrates the need for curiosity about the self, urges willingness to explore, and shows the therapist wants to get to know and understand them, which only strengthens the therapeutic foundation.

Suggested Resources

There are precious few books about psychotherapist intuition. Of these, *Intuition in Psychotherapy: From Research to Practice* by Marilyn Stickle and Margaret Arnd-Caddigan (2019, Routledge) provides perhaps the most comprehensive, easily digestible account of intuition from historical, academic, and clinical standpoints. For readers wanting a more applied course on intuition, Janice Cohen's in *The Intuitive Therapist* (2016, Balboa Press) guides therapists in honing and applying this sixth sense for improved clinical outcomes.

References

Smith, A.D. (2020, December 18). The listening skill you never heard of: Honing the "3rd" ear helps therapists cultivate their intuition. *Psychology Today*. https://www.psychologytoday.com/us/blog/and-running/202012/the-listening-skill-you-never-heard

Wallas, L. (1985). *Stories for the third ear: Using hypnotic fables in psychotherapy*. Norton.

Chapter 13

Don't Rely on Psychological Archaeology

While reading research on the questioning process, I was struck by one group's observation that therapists, especially those in training, might not be aware of the quality and power of the questions they ask (James, Morse & Howarth, 2009).

I remember feeling I needed to know everything about someone's background in order to be helpful. After all, taking a history is important, and it's portrayed in the movies as such for a reason, right? Asking questions makes therapists seem interested in the patient, and, ostensibly, the more information, the better, yes?

Upon closer examination, there is quite a difference between a thorough bio-psycho-social or diagnostic history, and sifting the sands of time. While peeking under every rock is well-intended, I learned the results are similar to an archaeologist hoping to unearth something important by arbitrary excavation.

Regarding psychotherapy, this kind of prospecting can hinder momentum. Going down rabbit holes by unearthing detail after detail does nothing more than waste precious time that could be spent remedying the issue at hand. Patients come seeking relief, not to divulge their genealogy.

Such excavation, however, provided me with a sense of somehow having evolved with the patient, in turn magically imbuing me with the answers. Despite experiencing successful therapy in my teens and young adulthood that in no manner modeled this activity, it somehow seemed like the natural thing to do. This phenomenon was echoed by a 1980's researcher who noted therapists can be consumed "with more concern with the etiology of the problem and its transformation through insight" (Llewelyn, 1988). When I began teaching, I discovered that the activity remained popular.

When someone is new to the field and perhaps not sure how to work with a patient, it's easy to fall back on the stereotypical therapist command, "Tell me about your childhood." When being afraid of not having something to say, or being unsure of how to work with a patient, this activity gives a never-ending reason to talk, and, at first, is ostensibly therapeutic.

DOI: 10.4324/9781032631400-15

Not unusually, students begin asking about the patient's family, only for the session to be overtaken by squeezing out minutia about relationships or events that have nothing to do with the complaint. While it may be interesting information to have, it likely will not contribute anything to the solution.

Though gaining information, it's hard not to notice waning progress in therapy. Sure, it helped establish patient willingness to share. It can be reasoned that if someone learned how their history influenced their current concern that insight, coupled with some basic cognitive exercise like thought replacement, might be enough. This, however, can be akin to a cardiologist explaining that years of untreated hypertension influenced the development of a patient's pulmonary edema, and leaving it at that. Change takes a more intensive dynamic.

As will be detailed in upcoming chapters, there are many ways to engage with patients, and it is not necessary for a therapist to do the majority of the talking. The focus is on the patient, not the therapist.

Along with the preceding material, it's important to remember that it's most ethical to only seek information on a need-to-know basis. Being human, a therapist might find themselves inquiring out of personal fascination. It would be easy for interest to pique when a patient mentions an unusual sexual fixation, or is consumed by a bizarre delusion. Indeed, it can be helpful to understand the evolution and impact of the matter, but seeking details unnecessary to treatment could be considered intrusive. Patients are perceptive. Imagine what it must feel like to go from patient to spectacle.

Developing a habit of consulting with yourself and asking, "Is what I'm about to ask relevant?" can help avoid such obstacles and remain on track to solve the problem at hand.

References

James, I.A., Morse, R., & Howarth, A. (2009). The science and art of asking questions in cognitive therapy. *Behavioural and Cognitive Psychotherapy, 38*(1), 89–93.

Llewelyn, S.P. (1988). Psychological therapy as viewed by clients and therapists. *British Journal of Clinical Psychology, 27*(3), 223–237.

Section II

Things Therapists Shouldn't Say

Chapter 14

The Big Three

"The road to hell is paved with good intentions" is an ancient phrase. One interpretation is that sometimes trying to do a good thing can have unintended bad consequences. Sometimes, this road meanders through the therapy office.

Most of us have experienced or witnessed precisely how to say the wrong thing, or perhaps the right thing in the wrong way. Embarrassing blunders tend to have a way of ensuring we don't make the same mistake twice, but not all unconstructive exchanges generate obvious signals that we need to make a change.

Regrettably, therapists are prone to some utterances that seem relevant and supportive, but are more therapy-undermining than meets the eye. While well-intended, the following three phrases can generate feelings of being minimized or misunderstood, could suggest the patient is incorrigible, and even raise doubt about the practitioner's ability (Smith, 2021).

"I Understand"

This reflexive comment always seems like the right thing to say because it shows therapists are paying attention and/or empathizing, right? This, however, is a specious perception. Have you ever noticed that sometimes that phrase has earned you a snappy reaction?

Early on, I worked in acute settings where people were frequently in crisis. More than once, I thought I was nicely applying my attending skills as the patient or their family explained how disastrous an event was occurring. "OK, I understand," I sometimes mindlessly replied. And more than once, I was met with some derivative of, "Do you? Then get me/us out of this!"

My comment was taken as if I had had a similar experience and thus somehow knew how to rapidly resolve the matter. When it was clear I had no silver bullet, the moment was pierced by another dose of irritation aimed my way. I brushed it off that they were in a bad space and it therefore had little to do with me. Upon reflection, however, they were having the worst

DOI: 10.4324/9781032631400-17

time of their life, and it was as if I offered false hope of relief. Why wouldn't they become more irritated?

On another note, bear in mind that many people entering therapy feel entirely misunderstood by those around them and may not even understand themselves. Is it not premature and perhaps even patronizing, in a canned response sort of way, for a therapist, someone they have just met, to offer, "I understand"?

Considering these possible outcomes, I urge supervisees to take great care in how "understand" is used. Perhaps the one situation in which "I understand" is safe to say is in prefacing self-disclosure that could strengthen the therapeutic alliance, a topic covered in Chapter 34. Otherwise, for use as an attending skill statement, it's essential that "understand" be qualified with "that," such as, "I understand that it's a painful situation for you."

To avoid potential ricochets, even better, perhaps, is for therapists to generally avoid "I understand" and replace it with "I recognize …," "I can see that …," or "I hear you" to show they are following along and being empathic.

"There's not Much We Can Do About That"

A patient who struggled with tinnitus, or ringing in the ears, once complained that their neurologist's reply was, "There's not much we can do about that." Indeed, there are no known cures for tinnitus. Unfortunately, many things cannot be reversed, including people's painful histories that bring them to treatment. This, of course, does not mean the effects cannot be managed.

In therapy, this comment could seem like an appropriate way to ground a patient in reality and lead them to learn to accept the situation. Ironically, even if the intention is to ground them in reality and bring them to acceptance, is that not "doing something about it"?

Imagine being so desperate for relief that you decide to attend therapy or otherwise seek treatment for an ailment and being on the receiving end of "There's not much we can do about that." It implies the very thing you want help with cannot be dealt with. Period. Not surprisingly, my patient described increased anxiety. Tinnitus is itself anxiety-provoking (Kehrle et al., 2016; Abbas et al., 2019) which was then compounded by hopelessness.

Funny enough, the neurologist's response was inadvertently helpful in this case. Anxiety and stress are believed to exacerbate tinnitus (Guitton, 2006; Moon et al., 2018). We, therefore, capitalized on this opportunity, and the patient learned they had control over the tinnitus by revisiting the things from earlier in treatment that were most powerful in assuaging anxiety. As the anxiety decreased, the acuity of the tinnitus diminished, and they felt empowered.

Reflecting on my own early experiences and discussions with supervisees, "There's not much we can do about that" may be more a case of "I'm not sure how to help you with this." Naturally, this lends itself to a supervision topic.

In the meantime, however, it can be helpful to take a cue from solution-oriented psychotherapy and investigate times when the problem isn't as bad, or is even absent. What allowed for the exceptions? How might the therapist help the patient get more of that? When someone realizes something is not *always* unbearable or difficult, or sees they have had periods of control over it, that is empowering and therapeutic in itself.

"You *Just* Have to…"

"You *just* have to…" often precedes "try harder," "accept the situation," or a host of other ostensibly encouraging commentary.

If you were ever told to "*just* relax" while really upset, you know a patient may receive this instruction poorly. The word "just" implies minimization of the problem, maybe even weakness, and understandably can elicit negativity towards the therapist. Such trite commentary can also signal to a more astute patient, "This therapist has nothing to offer." Obviously, this might jeopardize faith in the provider, in turn diminishing the therapeutic alliance, which is well-documented as one of the most important components of treatment (Ardito & Rabellino, 2011; Flückiger et al., 2018).

Not being sure how to navigate certain situations is part of the learning curve and should be seen as an opportunity to refine one's skills. If a therapist finds themself thinking, "There's not much we can do about that" or "They *just* need to…" it's likely best to withhold commentary and seek supervision on the situation. Patients are struggling to find a solution and know they can't hit rewind. They're in therapy precisely because they couldn't *just* do this or that and are hoping for alternative resolutions.

Suggested Resources

Readers unfamiliar with solution-oriented psychotherapy can learn more about the skill mentioned above by reading *In Search of Solutions*, by Bill O'Hanlon and Michele Weiner-Davis (2003, Norton), or *Interviewing for Solutions* by Peter DeJong and Insoo Kim Berg (1998, Brooks/Cole).

References

Abbas, J., Aqeel, M., Jaffar, A., & Nurunnabi, M. (2019). Tinnitus perception mediates the relationship between physiological and psychological problems among patients. *Journal of Experimental Psychopathology,10*(3). https://doi.org/10.1177/2043808719858559

Ardito, R.B. & Rabellino, D. (2011). Therapeutic alliance and outcome of psychotherapy: Historical excursus, measurements, and prospects for research. *Frontiers in Psychology, 2*(270). https://doi.org/10.3389%2Ffpsyg.2011.00270

Flückiger, C., Del Re, A.C., Wampold, B.E., & Horvath, A.O. (2018). The alliance in adult psychotherapy: A meta-analytic synthesis. *Psychotherapy, 55*(4), 316–340. doi:10.1037/pst0000172

Guitton, M. (2006). Tinnitus and anxiety. More than meets the ear. *Current Psychiatry Reviews, 2*(3), 333–338.

Kehrle, H.M., Sampaio. A.L.L., Granjeiro. R.C., de Oliveira. T.S., & Oliveira, C.A.C.P. (2016). Tinnitus annoyance in normal-hearing individuals: Correlation with depression and anxiety. *Annals of Otology, Rhinology & Laryngology, 125*(3), 185–194.

Moon, K., Park, S., Jung, Y., Lee, A., & Lee, J. (2018). Effects of anxiety sensitivity and hearing loss on tinnitus symptom sensitivity. *Psychiatry Investigation, 15*(1), 34–40.

Smith, A. (2021, December 31). 3 things therapists shouldn't say: These responses can be harmful to the therapeutic relationship. *Psychology Today.* https://www.psychologytoday.com/us/blog/up-and-running/202112/3-things-therapists-shouldnt-say

Chapter 15

Beware of the "Suck-It-Up" Trap

Positing someone needs to "suck it up" might be invigorating coming from a sports coach or drill sergeant, but it has no place in constructive psychotherapy. It doesn't make sense that vulnerable people would experience well-being via harsh communication.

Therapy patients seek help because they have thus far been unable to deal with the obstacle at hand. To suggest the "treatment" for something so painful as to bring a person to therapy, regardless of how the therapist perceives it, is to simply imply they're weak and need to harden up, is dismissive and unempathic. Perhaps the patient does need some more backbone, but being put down by the therapist isn't going to grow it.

Further, should such a tough love, "talking to" stance be attempted as a therapeutic tactic, the patient may feel they are perceived poorly and the therapist is judgmental. This is certain to be menacing if one is trying to get the patient to share themself and be more open.

There could be even further ramifications if it happens while in therapy for the first time. This is because it might set a precedent that such interactions is what therapy is, and the patient may not seek needed treatment in the future. In fact, addictions researchers have noted that several decades of research behind the tough love approach in chemical dependency counseling have "failed to yield a single clinical trial showing efficacy of confrontational counseling, whereas a number have documented harmful effects, particularly for more vulnerable populations" (White & Miller, 2007).

Some years ago, while running a supervision group for practicum students, I wanted to illustrate that therapy is about more than categorical symptom reduction, so I presented a recent case from my practice. I was working with Marla, who struggled at work with her boss, Karen. Once she became Marla's superior, Karen's attitude changed and she bullied her former peer. She would ask Marla what she needed sick time for, chastise her for taking a moment to chat with colleagues, and heap work on her with unreasonable expectations. Meanwhile, Karen made personal calls and fixed her makeup.

DOI: 10.4324/9781032631400-18

Given Karen's position, Marla reasoned that going to human resources could fan the flames. Marla, who enjoyed her work helping students with career development interests, suddenly felt the bottom drop out of her world. Work became a grueling task and the stress of Karen consumed every thought throughout the day. Stress turned into panic and I could watch depression settle in as if Karen was pulling a shade down over her. Marla began to think about resigning, but that would mean losing her tuition remission benefits, and she was in the middle of a master's degree program.

Aside from working with Marla on how to manage her immediate anxiety and depressive symptoms, I was tasked with exploring with her how to navigate the predicament. Her mind was a tornado as she wondered if she should stay or go, attempt assistance from human resources, try and take a stand towards Karen, or hire a corporate attorney for more pointed guidance?

No sooner did I finish illustrating the case than a student, whom I saw shaking their head while I spoke, said, "Well, suck it up. She wants the job and the benefits, suck it up." The student next to them nodded in agreement.

"Is this the future of mental health care?" I thought. Realizing the students had little experience and perhaps felt Marla merely needed encouragement to stay strong, I engaged a discussion on the "suck-it-up" comment.

"How is telling them to suck it up helpful?" I inquired. "Someone needs to tell her to deal with it. Life isn't fair," the student sternly retorted. The like-minded peer offered a similar sentiment. Coming to understand my having given these students the benefit of the doubt was miscalculated, I asked, "So that's it? We just need to tell patients to suck it up? Therapists attend graduate school to flippantly tell patients to do what *they* might do?"

"What else are you going to do? She's not taking action and is just sitting there complaining to you!" finished the disapproving student.

This exchange opened the door to a healthy class discussion about patient needs, and particularly about not projecting what a therapist might personally do in a situation. Thankfully, another student recognized that Marla felt very isolated in her struggle and needed a stable support to help her wade through those turbulent waters. Marla was drowning in workplace misery because she was afraid to make a decision, the more practical-thinking student pointed out, because none of them, other than quitting, were a guaranteed solution. Even while quitting could rid her of Karen, Marla would lose enjoyable work and would have to accrue more educational debt if she were to finish her master's degree elsewhere. It was quite a crisis to maneuver around.

Believing or suggesting that a patient must "suck it up" signifies a blind spot about the therapeutic process. With supervision, the therapist might see not that the patient must toughen up, but there is a therapeutic gold mine at hand. Consider a man, Lincoln, who wants to end a romantic relationship

because his girlfriend is verbally abusive, but he seems to not have the fortitude. It's easy to think, "If it's *so* bad, just tell her it's over. What are you so
afraid of?" implying, "grow a pair."

But is it that simple? What *is* he afraid of? Should someone find themselves internally rolling their eyes at Lincoln, they are invited to objectively
consider the reaction. Just because they believe they would quickly terminate the relationship if in Lincoln's shoes, does not mean one size fits all.

Respect that there might be a bigger issue at hand. Perhaps, for instance,
it's been noticed that Lincoln could be yielding and quick to appease. Putting this observation together with an inability to break off his abusive relationship, it's quite possible the overarching issue is a long-standing inability
to stand up for himself. The girlfriend matter is the straw breaking Lincoln's
back and why he seeks therapy. The therapeutic discussion in such a situation would ideally focus on identifying and navigating the self-defeating behavior. Approaching Lincoln's complaint with tough love statements would
only serve to feed his pathology.

Therapists cannot make decisions for patients, but can wrestle with and
digest their problems with them to uncover solutions. It's this kind of supportive gesture, an emotional hand-holding while they allow themselves
to be vulnerable, navigate, and take risks, that may see a patient through.
Maybe they look up to the therapist, and feel more compelled to take a risk
because, if they fall, they know the therapist is available, like a good parent,
to provide a safe place to debrief and process the matter; the source of unconditional support.

As the psychiatrist Irvin Yalom (2002) told us, very often it is the therapeutic *act*, not the therapeutic word, that matters.

References

White, W.L. & Miller, W.R. (2007). The use of confrontation in addiction treat-
ment history, science, and time for change: A history of confrontational therapies.
Counselor, 8(4), 12–30.
Yalom, I. (2002). *The gift of therapy* (pp. 37–39). Harper Perennial.

Chapter 16

What Not to Say to Anxious Patients

Anxiety needs no introduction. Patients and therapists alike, at one time or another, have been in a nerve-wracking situation. Short-lived bouts of anxiety, like stage fright before an important speech, or loss of sleep from worrying about family dynamics, are common. For most people, afterwards, there is a return to the non-anxious state.

Imagine, however, being in a phobic or worried mind frame, or paralyzed by an obsessive-compulsive state, in perpetuity. Such baseline anxiety is severe enough to be significantly correlated to suicide (Nepon et al., 2010), especially when paired with depression (Zhang et al., 2019; American Psychiatric Association, 2022).

For the non-afflicted, it might be difficult to understand, and perhaps even irritating, why someone in an anxious state cannot compose themselves. Consequently, a therapist might say to a seismically nervous patient, "Let's try to calm you down and talk this through." Unfortunately, the therapist can almost count on the comment backfiring, as the offering suggests the therapist does not grasp what the patient is going through. In turn, the anxious person, seeking support, may feel alienated, engendering irritation/further angst, which does anything but cultivate wellness.

For those working with anxious patients who sometimes feel stumped over what to say during patients' acute anxiety, avoiding the following two phrases and replacing them with the suggested alternatives will likely yield more favorable results (Smith, 2022).

"Calm Down"

This suggestion to the anxiety-ridden always seems to pass advice-givers' lips as if the subject would never have thought of it on their own. Further, it is customarily delivered as a patronizing plea or authoritarian command. It's as if the observer cannot handle the anxious person's state, implying, "I can't deal with you." If the therapist is feeling riled by the person's angst, imagine

DOI: 10.4324/9781032631400-19

what the patient feels! Now, imagine being on the receiving end of "calm down" during a panic attack or trauma-related reaction.

Instead of asking the patient to calm down, a more effective response might be discovered with a simple, two-step approach, beginning by simply acknowledging the presence of high anxiety. For instance, the therapist could offer, "Jason, I can tell you're feeling pretty uneasy right now," setting a more empathic tone. The second part is showing willingness to assist and inquiring, "What would be helpful for you right now?" This engenders a constructive, problem-solving partnership atmosphere which will likely have an anxiety-dampening effect of its own (i.e., "someone is available to help me out").

While it could be tempting to try to immediately engage the person in a grounding exercise, the patient might wish to instead process their inner experience, a cathartic purge of the terrorizing experience. Others might feel the need to use the bathroom. Some could ask for guidance to quiet down and it is an opportunity for in vivo anxiety reduction skills management. Should someone seem in a helpless state, asking if they would like to do a calming exercise together might be appropriate.

Whichever manner the acute anxiety is managed in the moment, it's always useful to return to the event and digest the patient's internal experience. Insight can be gained into their thought processes, vulnerabilities, and triggers that can accelerate treatment.

"Just Don't Think About It"

It has long been known that pervasive anxiety is inextricably linked to thoughts (Ellis & Harper, 1997; Van Niekerk et al., 2016). In fact, for most psychological disorders, diagnostic criteria include pervasive thought processes. Regarding anxiety, phobias run on a thought loop of "this is dangerous," people with generalized anxiety disorder jump to worst-case scenario thinking, and traumatized individuals can inadvertently be reminded of the event, flooding them with intrusive, anxiety-provoking memories.

For those who have never experienced such things, think back to a song you don't like getting stuck in your head and tell yourself, "Just don't think about it." It doesn't work, does it? Now, consider that anxious thoughts are really perceptions of danger that feed the survival response of being on standby for fight/flight. With a biological response re-enforcing the thoughts, it is easy to see how it's even harder to try to ignore it. The result is incessant mental and physiological knocking.

Suggesting that someone "just not think about" whatever is gnawing at them can produce further irritation. This is because, similar to "calm down," if it was that simple, they would have done it. Further, employing the term "just" makes it seem as if it is easy and that they're flawed for not being able to do so. Consider the effect on a socially anxious person whose life revolves around the fear of scrutiny from others. Lastly, it's invalidating, in that it can imply that whatever is on their mind is not a big deal.

Rather than suggesting the person try not to think about it, when someone divulges a pesky thought attached to their anxiety, it's better to create a dialogue around the matter. Again, it is effective to partner with the individual to show support and constructively problem-solve to try to bring down the acuity. If Barbara, for example, is worried about flying, it's hard for her not to think about it when her mind is consumed with thoughts of airline crashes as she worriedly counts down the days until takeoff.

Responding with something more thoughtful can help a patient feel supported and empowered, assuaging their anxiety. So, for Barbara, one might say to her, "Barbara, I know you're not a fan of flying, but I can't help but recall you telling me about the times you flew and said you deplaned like nothing ever bothered you. How'd you keep it together so well on those flights?" She is reminded she has the ability to manage well, and, in this case, the therapist might consider a solution-oriented psychotherapy approach, helping Barbara cultivate more confidence by reviewing what she did that kept her stable on other flights.

In sessions after the flying, the therapist could settle into exploring Barbara's experience of the flight in more detail. Understanding her inner dialogue during the traveling, for example, would prove to be a goldmine for analytic, cognitive-behavioral, and existentialist therapists alike.

Thus, working with a patient experiencing acute anxiety may be best understood not as a crisis that involves a rescue, but an opportunity. Therapeutic allegiance can be strengthened, skills learned in-the-moment, and doors opened to examining and resolving the internal conflicts driving the symptoms that brought the person to therapy.

References

American Psychiatric Association. (2022). Depressive disorders. In *Diagnostic and statistical manual of mental disorders* (5th ed., text rev.).

Ellis, A. & Harper, R.A. (1997). *A guide to rational living*. Wilshire Book Co.

Nepon, J., Belik, S.L., Bolton, J., & Sareen, J. (2010). The relationship between anxiety disorders and suicide attempts: Findings from the National Epidemiologic Survey on Alcohol and Related Conditions. *Depression and Anxiety, 27*(9), 791–798. doi:10.1002/da.20674

Smith, A.D. (2022, November 28). 2 things not to say to an anxious person: Anxiety can't just be turned off, so don't suggest that it can. *Psychology Today*. https://www.psychologytoday.com/us/blog/and-running/202211/2-things-not-say-anxious-person

Van Niekerk, R.E., Klein, A.M., Allart-van Dam, E., Hudson, J.L., Rinck, M., Hut-schemaekers, G.J.M., & Becker, E.S. (2016). The role of cognitive factors in child-hood social anxiety: Social threat thoughts and social skills perception. *Cognitive Therapy Research, 41*, 489–497. https://doi.org/10.1007/s10608-016-9821-x

Zhang, J., Lou, X., & Fang, L. (2019). Combined effects of depression and anxiety on suicide: A case-control psychological autopsy study in rural China. *Psychiatry Research, 271*, 370–373.

Chapter 17

What Not to Say to Depressed Patients

In 2021, about 21 million adults and 5 million adolescents (NIMH, 2023) in the United States suffered at least one major depressive episode (MDE), not to mention those affected by other forms of depression. It's the top cause of disability worldwide (Friedrich, 2017), and the most common mental health complaint after anxiety (NAMI, 2023). Even if depression is not the reader's clinical interest, they are going to have to interact with depressed people.

Unfortunately, mental health professionals, despite working in the field, are not immune to harboring misconception, or even stigma, about certain disorders (Knaak et al., 2017; Thomason, 2022; Jauch et al., 2023). When teaching or supervising, I've noticed this seems rooted in popular culture ideas or beliefs that generated erroneous understandings about depression before the therapist gained field experience. It's no surprise that the faulty conception can then influence how the therapist approaches the diagnosis.

Consequently, like anxious people in the preceding chapter, depressed patients might encounter well-meaning but detrimental remarks from helpers. This can serve to distance the patient from the therapist because it suggests they do not understand what they're enduring. In turn, the depressed person feels further alienated, which does anything but bring about positive outcomes.

If one isn't familiar with working with depressed patients, avoiding asking, "What are you depressed about?" and replacing it with the suggested alternative below can improve the therapeutic alliance and accelerate clinical gains (Smith, 2022).

There's a popular culture misconception that being depressed is "about" something, that such a mood is always a reaction to some undesirable encounter. The truth is, while problematic circumstances can instigate pervasive depression, especially if there is genetic vulnerability, depression doesn't always need a reason to surface. This is especially true of melancholic depression, and the depressed phases of bipolar disorders which tend to be more spontaneous. These are observed as "endogenous" depressions, meaning

DOI: 10.4324/9781032631400-20

their manifestation requires no clear provocation and seems more influenced by genetic/neurobiological whims than unpleasant external events (Salvadore et al., 2010; Juruena et al., 2018).

Even if someone is depressed about a life event, asking what they have to be depressed about, which could be one's attempt to show one is trying to understand the situation or "put things in perspective," such as pointing out all the things going well in their life, can be perceived as invalidating and dismissive. It might be experienced by the patient as an implication they were foolish to let themselves get depressed. Chances are, it's more complicated than that.

There might be a problematic core schema ingrained since childhood that can encourage a depressed episode during a stressor (e.g., "No matter what I do, it won't turn out right, and this latest fumble is just another confirmation of my inadequacy"). There might also be simmering existential conflicts like a lack of purpose or feeling one does not belong.

Instead of asking what a patient is depressed about, consider just opening a conversation with an acknowledgment of the matter. A good example would be, "You mentioned feeling depressed. I know that's a different experience for different people. What can you tell me about what it's like for you?" Given depressed people tend to keep the experience to themselves for fear of stigma or other consequence (Knudsen & Silverstein, 2009; Silberner, 2009), having this arena to digest the experience with someone interested can become a bright spot.

Such a statement is also welcoming, acknowledging, and therefore inherently supportive and alliance forming. It's a reassurance they have a support network in the therapist. It also gives the therapist a picture of the symptoms.

While feeling supported and having a cathartic experience is not a depression eraser, it can amount to, as noted by military psychologist Dave Grossman (2009), "pain shared is pain divided."

This exploration of the depressive experience might be followed up with, "What's been helpful in managing the depression?" As taught in solution-oriented psychotherapy, getting someone to realize they're at least doing something to keep it from being worse than it has to be can feel empowering, as it provides a semblance of control over the situation.

Finally, pointing out any strengths is imperative, as depressed people can want to give up on treatment given the hopelessness factor of the mood, or frustration their gray skies aren't clearing fast enough. Pointing out small improvements or footholds can at least make it a brighter shade of gray, providing encouragement and "anticipation of getting well" as put by depression expert Francis Mondimore, MD (2006).

Finally, these conversations allow a therapist who is unfamiliar with working with depression to gather detailed data to bring to supervision for feedback on how to move forward.

References

Friedrich, M. (2017). Depression is the leading cause of disability around the world. *Journal of the American Medical Association, 317*(15), 1517. doi:10.1001/jama.2017.3826

Grossman, D. (2009). *On killing: The psychological cost of learning to kill in war.* Back Bay Books.

Jauch, M., Occhipinti, S., & O'Donovan, A. (2023). The stigmatization of mental illness by mental health professionals: Scoping review and bibliometric analysis. *PLoS One, 18*(1). https://doi.org/10.1371%2Fjournal.pone.0280739

Juruena, M.F., Bocharova, M., Augustini, B., & Young, A.H. (2018). Atypical depression and non-atypical depression: Is HPA axis function a biomarker? A systematic review. *Journal of Affective Disorders, 233,* 45–67.

Knaak, S., Mantler, E., & Szeto, A. (2017). Mental illness-related stigma in healthcare: Barriers to access and care and evidence-based solutions. *Healthcare Management Forum, 30*(2), 111–116. doi:10.1177/0840470416679413

Knudsen-Martin, C. & Silverstein, R. (2009). Suffering in silence: A qualitative meta-data analysis of postpartum depression. *Journal of Marital and Family Therapy, 35*(2), 145–158.

Mondimore, F. (2006). *Depression, the mood disease* (3rd ed.). Johns Hopkins University Press.

National Alliance on Mental Illness (NAMI) (2023, April). *Mental health by the numbers.* https://www.nami.org/mhstats

National Institute of Mental Health (NIMH) (2023, July). *Major depression.* https://www.nimh.nih.gov/health/statistics/major-depression

Salvadore, G., Quiroz, J.A., Machado-Vieira R., Henter, I.D., Manji, H.K., & Zarate, C.A. Jr. (2010). The neurobiology of the switch process in bipolar disorder: A review. *Journal of Clinical Psychiatry, 71*(11), 1488–501. doi:10.4088/JCP.09r05259gre

Silberner, J. (2009, August 28). Depression and families' fear of being labeled. Shots: *Health News from NPR.* https://www.npr.org/sections/health-shots/2009/08/depression_and_family_fear.html

Smith, A.D. (2022, September 5). 2 things not to say to someone who's depressed: It's not easy to just cheer up, so don't suggest that it is. *Psychology Today.* https://www.psychologytoday.com/us/blog/and-running/202209/2-things-not-say-someone-whos-depressed

Thomason, L. (2022). Understanding the clinician's subjective experience of hallucinations and delusions in their work [Doctoral dissertation, Aurora University]. ProQuest Dissertation and Theses Global. https://www.proquest.com/openview/15d8b7df68273807549ca8777f5cf8e7/1?pq-origsite=gscholar&cbl=18750&diss=y

Chapter 18

What Not to Say to People Who Hear Voices

Hearing voices is the most common and persistent type of hallucination (Ohayon, 2000; Waters, 2010). Remember, when someone is hallucinating, it is an internally generated sensory experience; there is no external input contributing to the thing(s) a person is sensing. While it may be a bizarre concept to the uninitiated, therapists find that it is not an uncommon presentation in mental health care settings.

Though most often associated with schizophrenia, auditory hallucinations are present in a variety of psychological disorders and organic medical conditions. Each year in the US alone, 100,000 people aged 15–25 experience first episode psychosis of a schizophrenia nature (Ziedonis & Small, 2017), let alone due to other conditions. Chances are, even if a therapist doesn't specialize in schizophrenia-spectrum illnesses, they will eventually encounter someone displaying hallucinatory activity.

Many students and supervisees have confessed to feeling stuck when encountering voice-hearers. They become perplexed as to why their well-intentioned efforts to learn about the voices sometimes engender frustration from patients. While many can appreciate mood or anxiety discomfort, hallucinations are generally such a foreign experience to therapists that they struggle to comprehend the voice-hearer's experience (Thomason, 2022), which obviously can create treatment barriers. No doubt, working with voice-hearers is an acquired specialty skill.

My professional experience began in a jail, and jails are full of severe mental illnesses. Many of the incarcerated mentally ill population would have historically required state hospitalization (Dvoskin et al., 2020). Thus, I was immediately exposed to people with a spectrum of hallucinatory presentations. From homeless, severely mentally ill people who forewent care, to substance withdrawal, stress reactions, and medical complications, it was a symptom realm that demanded my attention.

Over the years, I have often marveled how I got used to having a presence in the room I couldn't see, like when working with Jessie. Jessie's "girlfriend" often made an appearance. He lost eye contact with me, and,

DOI: 10.4324/9781032631400-21

cracking a smile, spoke to the invisible third party in the room. "I heard you," he sometimes replied to thin air. Once, he giggled while giving a dismissive wave of his hand. "She thought it would be a good idea to tell you a joke, but it's kind of dirty," Jessie explained.

When encountering people who hear voices, mental health professionals would be remiss not to collect certain information, especially in crisis situations. The following three questions may seem like straightforward ways of collecting that data, but could prove to be anything but productive (Smith, 2022).

"Are the Voices Real?"

This may seem like an innocuous "reality check" question to assess the person's level of impairment. Some patients retain enough clarity to know they're losing touch. Others may be in an entirely different reality and truly be confused by the way someone is speaking to them but they can't see them. Knowing where a patient falls on this continuum can be particularly important in crisis settings when considering an inpatient level of care.

Asking if the voices are real could backfire because it could seem as if one is discounting the person's experience, which can ruin rapport or therapeutic alliance. People who disclose they are hearing voices often share the information with angst. I've been told more than once, "It's been happening for a while. It's embarrassing telling someone you hear voices. Others think you're nuts or dangerous."

In short, the sufferer realizes it's a confession that can raise eyebrows, but they are desperate for a remedy and need to reveal it to improve. If that's met with, "Are the voices real?" it's not only discounting their experience, there could be further damage if it is perceived as the therapist saying, "I'm not so sure about that," as if the patient is a liar. I learned the hard way early on.

An inmate increasingly complained of voices the longer he was in solitary confinement. I asked if he believed the voices were real. He shot back, "What's that mean?" I reasoned, "Well, there's nobody in the cell with you, but you said it sounds like someone talking right in your ear when it occurs." He finished, "It doesn't matter if I'm alone or not. I don't know where it comes from. Yes, it's real. I'm listening to a voice from *somewhere*!"

An alternative approach to this question will be addressed in the following section, as the two items can be joined.

"What Are They Saying?"

When giving a training, I ask what people think is important to know about the voices someone is hearing. Almost immediately, a participant says, "Are they commands to hurt themselves or others?" Upon further discussion, this is a seemingly reactive inquiry. It's well-intended, not only for patient well-being, but to cover the professional legally.

Though that content is indeed a concern, if a professional's initial reaction to someone sharing that they're hearing voices is so direct, it can seem they are just checking boxes and aren't interested in the person's experience. It may also seem invasive. The voice-hearer has just mustered the strength to confess to the experience; the content may be embarrassing or shameful and the person needs time to develop trust before sharing.

Remember, too, that many people who hear voices are paranoid and the hallucinatory content follows suit. More than once I've been talking to someone clearly responding to voices and, trying to guide them back, offered, "You seemed distracted for a minute, are you OK?" This was met with a derivative of, "They're saying not to talk to you," or, "They don't trust you."

In acute situations, I've witnessed actively hallucinating patients become more tormented, crying, and getting agitated in interviews, explaining, "I can't talk about it anymore. They said to shut up, it's getting louder." It's easy to see how asking about content can quickly stoke the flames of paranoia if the person is prone, and shut down a discussion from the start.

The material that is being sought in the preceding two questions is important and shouldn't be ignored. Given the pitfalls of those lines of inquiry, though, interviewers need alternative routes to the same material.

Instead of asking the first two questions, it can be more effective to get the same material by adopting an experience-based approach. This may sound like an overwhelming shift in tactics, but simply being conversational rather than interrogative is the key. To illustrate, the following example supposes a more productive interview with the inmate mentioned in the first scenario:

Clinician: "I heard you've been having a hard time and wanted me to check in with you. What's going on?"

Inmate: Oh man! Stress! I've been in solitary for three weeks and I can't take it anymore! Locked in an 8 x 10 cell for 23 hours without contact except for meal delivery. My head is messing with me. People are talking but it's not through the vents and there's no one else in my cell!

Clinician: No wonder you're stressed if that's what going on. Fill me in about hearing these people that aren't there.

Inmate: It's one, sometimes two people it sounds like; in my ear, just like a phone call!

Clinician: And we know there's no phones in cells.

Inmate: Exactly.

Clinician: It's clear hearing these things from thin air is a nerve-wracking experience for you. I'm curious, how has what they're talking about been affecting you?

Inmate: It's nonsense, confusing. Sinister laughter, comments like 'What do you think!?' or 'Through that wall.' It can just sound like a crowded room, too, and I can't hear things clearly."

Clinician: Anything else, like comments that you should do things?

Inmate: No, just those random phrases and sounds.

Clinician: Clearly this isn't getting easier for you; being in solitary, now hearing those things. I know you've never been to solitary before, but have you experienced the voices before?

Inmate: No, that's what so scary about this.

Through this more conversational approach, we were able to learn about his perception of the voices – he was still rooted in reality (i.e., "my head is messing with me!") – and learn about the contents without the risky questions.

"Did You Take Your Medications?"

I've always felt this question is akin to a cross-examination, implying, "If you took your medications, you wouldn't be having this problem." There's an accusatory feel to it, and it ignores the complexity of the voice-hearer's experience. While we know that neuroleptic medication can be very helpful to voice-hearers, as in mood and anxiety disorders, stabilization is more complicated than medication compliance. Even if they are helpful, there are psychosocial contributions, side effects to contend with, medications may not be affordable, or paranoia about being poisoned or controlled can halt medication compliance.

To be responsible providers, we must, of course, ask about medication compliance. However, again, being curious rather than didactic is likely going to get a better response. "Did you take your medication?" will yield a "yes/no," "why/why not?" exchange.

Instead, if it's known someone has prescriptions, asking, "If I recall, you were taking some medications to help with the voices. What's the verdict on those?" This helps open a dialogue about their experience with the medications. If they do not mention noncompliance or missing doses, the therapist can respond, "Have you ever missed any doses?" or "Have you missed any doses lately?" This sounds much less interrogative and threatening than, "Have you been taking the medications?" which they know answering "No" to could lead to a scolding.

Talking to people who regularly hear voices, or have other hallucinatory experiences, can be an art in itself, and the above suggestions can help develop constructive conversations around the phenomena.

For readers interested in furthering their skills or who plan to work regularly with such populations, Hearing Voices Network (HVN) can be an invaluable resource. HVN began as a peer-based non-profit organization for people who hear voices to have a place to identify with others having similar experiences and share what helps. It expanded to offer trainings to professionals and caregivers interested in learning how to help people make sense of, and live with, hearing voices, which includes how to have productive discussions about the experiences.

In a similar vein, there is Open Dialogue, which focuses on deep listening, understanding, and the meaning of the experiences of those with psychosis rather than symptoms to be managed or eliminated. This practice can assist in the therapeutic alliance, and nicely adjunct cognitive behavioral or other approaches.

Suggested Resources

Students often ask what books I'd recommend for learning to effectively interact with people who hear voices. If one plans to work with this population, my first suggestion for gaining skills to discuss psychosis experiences is to get involved with the aforementioned Hearing Voices Network (hearing-voices.org) and Open Dialogue (dialogicpractice.net).

References

Dvoskin, J., Knoll, J., & Silva, M. (2020). A brief history of the criminalization of mental illness. *CNS Spectrums, 25*(5), 638–650.

Ohayon, M (2000). Prevalence of hallucinations and their pathological associations in the general population. *Psychiatry Research, 97*(2–3), 153–164. https://doi.org/10.1016/S0165-1781(00)00227-4

Smith, A.D. (2022, March 19). How to talk to someone who is hearing voices: Avoiding 3, forthright questions may improve your interactions. *Psychology Today.* https://www.psychologytoday.com/us/blog/and-running/202203/how-talk-someone-who-is-hearing-voices

Thomason, L. (2022). Understanding the clinician's subjective experience of hallucinations and delusions in their work [Doctoral dissertation, Aurora University]. ProQuest Dissertation and Theses Global. https://www.proquest.com/openview/15d8b7df68273807549ca8777f5cf8e7/1?pq-origsite=gscholar&cbl=18750&diss=y

Waters, F. (2010, March). Auditory hallucinations in psychiatric illness. *Psychiatric Times, 27*(3). https://www.psychiatrictimes.com/view/auditory-hallucinations-psychiatric-illness

Ziedonis, D.M. & Small, E. (2017, April 12). *Open dialogue and dialogic practice: Opportunities for improving outcomes in first-episode psychosis and acute psychiatric crisis* [PowerPoint slides]. University of Massachusetts Medical School Early Psychosis Professional Education Event.

Section III

Demystifying Diagnosis

Chapter 19

Ignore Popular Culture Portrayals of Mental Illnesses

It's no secret that mental illness is stigmatized, and stigma is rooted in misunderstanding (American Psychiatric Association, 2020). Unfortunately, popular culture regularly contributes to the problem with caricatures and misrepresentations of many diagnoses in entertainment. People with mental illness diagnoses also tend to be shown as unpredictable and dangerous (University of South Carolina Annenberg, 2023), or as exceedingly weak and vulnerable (Huetter, 2019). Other times, a diagnosis might inundate the news, and some chief symptom, like social awkwardness in autism, erroneously becomes synonymous with a disorder (Frances, 2013).

It would be unfair not to acknowledge that some diagnoses are presented accurately in Hollywood. Robert DeNiro's character, Travis Bickel, for example, in the 1976 movie *Taxi Driver,* was generally, other than the "heroic aggression" at the end of the movie, a meticulous representation of schizotypal personality. Though with comedic intention, Woody Allen's character, Mickey, in the 1986 movie *Hannah and Her Sisters* is not unlike the experiences of patients with hypochondriasis, otherwise known as illness anxiety. Jason Alexander's character of George Costanza on *Seinfeld* is an infallible imitation of someone with a dependent personality, right down to the passive-aggressive tendencies. None of these roles were overexaggerated or intentionally depicted as crazy and dangerous.

The same may not be said of many other diagnoses and characters. In particular, schizophrenia, bipolar disorder, dissociative identity disorder (DID), and obsessive compulsive disorder (OCD) tend to be distorted (Owen, 2012; Fawcett, 2015). In 2015, *US News and World Report* highlighted that researchers were discovering that portrayals of mental illnesses were indeed "stereotypical, negative, or flat-out wrong." On a slightly more positive note, one researcher shared that while misrepresentations continue, with the growing interest in mental illnesses, in online news media there are stories of intervention and recovery, prompting more positive public attitudes (Parrott, 2020).

DOI: 10.4324/9781032631400-23

Of all the mis-portrayed mental illnesses, DID is perhaps the most adulterated and a good example of the potential for diagnostic error. DID characters throughout film history exhibit dramatic, sometimes psychopathic, Jekyll-and-Hyde characteristics, sending the wrong message to nonprofessionals and professionals alike. Unless someone works at a trauma clinic, it is a rare day one may encounter a DID patient, thus it is easy to rely on the only reference point available.

In talking with even seasoned professionals over the years and asking if they have noticed signs of DID in severely traumatized patients I was evaluating, I've heard, "They always seem to be themselves" or quips such as, "They don't seem like Sybil." In the few cases of DID I've witnessed it is never as dramatic as in the movies where there is a spin of the head and a new person pops out. While this dramatic feature is thought of as the hallmark symptom, undoubtedly based in popular culture portrayal, alteration is usually subtle (APA, 2022). People with DID do not usually seek therapy complaining of a cast of characters they can't manage. In fact, many don't know they dissociate, only that they are losing track of time or are not sure of how they got somewhere or did something.

Unfortunately, even psychology students and mental health professionals are not immune to the power of popular culture, especially if they have little experience in the field. It's hard not to notice that sometimes conditions are described as if the diagnostic criteria were based on colloquialisms, which surely come from the media. Reviewing a bipolar disorder diagnosis, for example, I might hear how the patient is impulsively angry, thus "moody," and is therefore bipolar. As readers will discover in upcoming chapters in this section, symptoms need to be contextualized and diagnoses should never be made based on one representative symptom. There are many other diagnoses that harbor "moody" traits, but people naturally rely on what they have been exposed to the most.

In a special-topics course I teach called "Behind the Diagnosis," which focuses on understanding misrepresented diagnoses and developing empathy for the sufferers, I ask students to write about what their understanding is of each disorder before we thoroughly investigate them. Despite abnormal psychology being a prerequisite for the course, it isn't unusual for their descriptions to fit popular culture molds. For example, regarding OCD, students may still write that it means cleaning all the time and keeping things overly organized. It is the classic, simplified, erroneous, pop culture representation that stuck.

I have read more than one evaluation whereby a child was diagnosed with OCD because the parents reported the child had an "obsession" with something and becomes dysregulated if they cannot have access to it. Upon interview, there is no evidence of obsessions as defined in OCD criteria.

This would be intrusive thoughts/images/impulses that are anathema to the person's normal way of thinking, are anxiety provoking, and the person can't suppress them. Nor are ritualized behaviors usually present in said kids.

Clearly, non-professionals' perceptions, based in popular culture ideas, can color clinicians' lenses. The effects of the entertainment industry and news providers can reach farther than meets the eye. Students and new therapists are encouraged to use media portrayals of diagnoses as a critical thinking learning opportunity by comparing the character to diagnostic criteria and biographical accounts.

Suggested Resources

To instill a more accurate understanding of diagnoses commonly misportrayed in popular culture, my students' required reading includes the following autobiographical/biographical accounts. This not only helps clarify accuracy, but the inside-out view of the illness experience encourages empathy and conceptualization of patients as more than a collection of symptoms.

- Bipolar disorder: Kay Redfield Jamison's *An Unquiet Mind* (1995, Vintage) is a classic memoir about the evolution, endurance, and recovery from bipolar disorder type 1. Jamison, an affective disorder researcher, provides a compelling case that bipolar disorders are much more complicated than the simplified popular idea of "up and down moods."
- Borderline personality: Kiera van Gelder's *The Buddha and the Borderline* (2010, New Harbinger) is a poignant, but entertaining, narrative that assembles the vexing behaviors of the disorder into an understandable experience.
- DID: In *All of Me* (2012, Chicago Review Press), Kim Noble dispels the notion that DID is a dangerous "Jekyll and Hyde syndrome." Her biography recounts a vulnerable history of living with lost blocks of time and learning she juggled identities, usually hidden in plain sight.
- OCD: In *Life in Rewind* (2010, Harper), Terry Weibel Murphy provides a graphic account of a young man crippled by obsessions and compulsions, complete with an understanding of the intrusive thoughts and the function of the compulsions. It quickly becomes clear OCD is not just anxiety about being clean and organized.
- Schizophrenia spectrum: In *The Quiet Room*, by Lori Schiller and Amanda Bennett (2011, Grand Central Publishing), readers enter Schiller's years of altered realities, superimposed manic episodes, and eventual recovery. This story and the stories of Esmé Weijun Wang in *The Collected Schizophrenias* (2019, Gray Wolf Press) sharply illustrate the complexity of these illnesses.

References

American Psychiatric Association (APA). (2020, August). *Stigma, prejudice and discrimination against people with mental illness.* https://www.psychiatry.org/patients-families/stigma-and-discrimination

American Psychiatric Association (APA). (2022). Trauma and other stressor-related disorders. In *Diagnostic and statistical manual of mental disorders* (5th ed., text rev.).

Frances, A. (2013). *Saving normal: An insider's revolt against out-of-control psychiatric diagnosis, DSM-5, big pharma, and the medicalization of ordinary life.* Mariner Books.

Fawcett, K. (2015, April 16). How mental illness is misrepresented in the media: Insidious portrayal on TV shape perceptions about real-life people with psychological disorders. *U.S. News and World Report.* https://health.usnews.com/health-news/health-wellness/articles/2015/04/16/how-mental-illness-is-misrepresented-in-the-media

Huetter, A.E. (2019). *The representation of mental illness in the media: The use of the nature documentary* [Master's degree dissertation, University of Montana]. https://scholarworks.montana.edu

Owen, P.R. (2012). Portrayals of schizophrenia by entertainment media: A content analysis of contemporary movies. *Psychiatric Services, 63*(7). https://doi.org/10.1176/appi.ps.201100371

Parrott, S (2020). Media stereotypes about mental illness: The role of the media in nurturing and mitigating stigma. In A. Billings & S. Parrott (Eds.), *Media stereotypes: From ageism to xenophobia* (pp. 239–255). Peter Lang Publishing.

University of South Carolina Annenberg (2023, July 6). Distorted depictions: Popular movies misrepresent the reality of mental health conditions. https://annenberg.usc.edu/news/research-and-impact/distorted-depictions-popular-movies-misrepresent-reality-mental-health

Chapter 20

In Defense of Diagnosis (Part 1)

Diagnosis can be a contentious topic in mental health care. At one end of the spectrum, it's argued that diagnosis is just a harmful label; at the other, some practitioners may become hyper-focused on the diagnostic process. Therapists are likely to find that what is most practical falls in the middle. On the one hand, diagnosis is important largely because diagnoses can share symptoms, but that does not mean they are necessarily treated alike. On the other hand, symptoms need not perfectly conform to *Diagnostic and Statistical Manual of Mental Disorders* or *International Classification of Diseases* (*DSM*) criteria for treatment to commence.

When I was in graduate school, my internship was at a jail in which I eventually worked. My tasks involved crisis evaluations, diagnostic assessments, and brief therapy interventions for inmates. Because screening for services was a large part of our work, which involved assessing if mental illness was present, my supervisor suggested I become intimately familiar with the array of psychiatric diagnoses. I not only reviewed my assessments with him to gage my accuracy, but compared my assessments to the seasoned psychiatrists' diagnostic opinions.

One inmate I worked with, Eugene, presented with significant anxiety. He complained of fear that he would do something stupid and get made fun of if he came out of his cell and interacted with others. "I feel paranoid," is how he summed it up. While I was new in the field, I realized this was not paranoia. Usually, paranoia is of a more persecutory nature. People with true paranoia don't realize they are paranoid, and other symptoms, like hallucinations, often co-occur.

Eugene did not appear to have lost touch with reality and denied any mental health care history. Rather, he described a background of being an anxious kid and usually shy, though he wanted to socialize. He increasingly fought to manage the anxiety and shyness as he aged. Being someone who suffered considerably from social anxiety disorder when I was younger, I could see that Eugene struggled with social anxiety himself, and my diagnosis reflected the evidence.

DOI: 10.4324/9781032631400-24

Excited, for I was sure of my clinical work and that it would parallel the psychiatrist's evaluation, impressing my supervisor, I eagerly peeled to their note after Eugene met with them. Scanning through the doctor's diagnostic summary, my brow furrowed: "paranoid schizophrenia." The prescription was Risperdal, an antipsychotic medication. Thinking I had missed something, I re-read the doctor's diagnostic note. Their justification for a paranoid schizophrenia diagnosis was that Eugene complained of "paranoia" and feared leaving his cell because others might be watching him. No context was provided.

It didn't take long for Eugene to develop akathisia, a Parkinson's disease-like shakiness, a common side effect, and he asked to discontinue the Risperdal. He refused to meet with a prescriber again, even if I advocated that he was mistakenly diagnosed and would more likely benefit from medication to help him with anxiety. I couldn't help but wonder where I would be if such had been my experience when I sought help as a teen.

Unfortunately, this is but one example. Misdiagnosis in mental health care is rampant. In 2021, it was reported that 39.16 percent of 309 psychiatric patients in a specialty clinic had been misdiagnosed (Ayano et al., 2021). It was noted that three contributors to this were providers' diagnostic inexperience, that symptoms of disorders can overlap, and that evaluators did not routinely review diagnostic criteria while making the initial diagnosis.

While the preceding is one route to misdiagnosis, some patients are intentionally misdiagnosed. This seems most correlated to a therapist's fear that managed care might not cover a particular diagnosis (Lake, 2023). This could be considered fraudulent.

Consider, for instance, someone who suffers from borderline intellectual functioning. This is a neurodevelopmental condition whereby the person's intelligence quotient (IQ) is between 70 and 85 (Wieland & Zitman, 2016). They can struggle with low frustration tolerance, communication, and socializing, especially in that they may be taken advantage of. Intervention may be more of a supportive psychotherapy, and perhaps some family work.

Borderline intellectual functioning is recorded with a "V" code, and these are not necessarily billable as they are not considered "disorders." Although the patient does not fit the autism mold, the therapist, who happens to have a background working with autism, construes the presenting struggles as mild autism to justify the treatment and obtain reimbursement.

In time, the therapist leaves the practice and no one else has autism experience to treat this apparently autistic individual. There are wait lists for autism specialty providers and this individual who relied on the services they obtained, which generalist therapists could provide, is left unsupported.

In addition, sometimes therapists will deny an obvious diagnosis, especially personality disorders in youth (Kingsley, 2022), to ostensibly spare them stigmatization, which they pay for later given they may not be provided with the disorder-specific care required to maintain stability. This is covered in more detail in Chapter 41.

Another contributor to misdiagnosis is that the anti-diagnosis crowd argues that diagnoses should be avoided due to their stigmatizing nature, and therapists treat symptoms, not disorders, anyhow. This is a dangerous and unethical practice. Is it not more important to acknowledge that many conditions have symptom overlap but require entirely different interventions than to ignore this and provide a misguided intervention attempt all in the name of "not labeling someone"?

It's hard to take seriously the idea that so long as a therapist is focusing on someone's moodiness the diagnosis does not matter. Consider that the moodiness could be bipolar disorder, borderline personality, or from the low frustration tolerance in ADHD. Further, it could be caused by a general medical condition or a substance. The moodiness springs from different wells and thus requires different interventions.

Critical thinkers will wonder why diagnosis is so acceptable in other areas of medicine but criticized in mental health care. It is not the diagnosis that is stigmatizing, it is the psychological or behavioral concern associated with the diagnosis. Even if diagnoses were reduced to such vagaries as "they have emotional concerns," or "they're victims of trauma," these are psychological in nature, and given the general stigma of mental health, would still lead to stigma.

If the argument is that the person reduces themselves to a label and just keep living up to it, such as "I'm bipolar," if instead they were identified as having an "emotional complication," could this not also be taken on as their identity? The next step leaves therapists with not acknowledging the presenting problem at all. How will providers know what they're working on resolving if it isn't identified? Diagnoses help therapists identify a set of experiences and allow these behaviors to be studied, through which practitioners learn about treatment and prognosis.

Imagine a couple arriving for counseling with complaints of infidelity. Would it not be important to identify that one of the patients exhibits symptoms of a histrionic personality, versus another couple where the infidelity may stem from one of them experiencing lack of sexual response due to a medical condition and their partner feels the need to satisfy themselves elsewhere? The diagnosis dictates the route to be taken for treatment, what the therapist can likely expect, and a prognosis.

Those with histrionic personalities are very attention-seeking, flirtatious, and sexual, and might not see the problem with it. A therapist will need to realize they may have to alter treatment to 1:1 work with the "victim" partner, helping them cope with being with such a person if they choose to continue the relationship. Someone with sexual unresponsiveness where true love still exists and there is remorse on the part of cheater, will more likely work out another solution.

And another thought – medical conditions like diabetes can't become role-forming? How many people refer to themselves as "a diabetic," "a cancer survivor," or "an amputee?" Perhaps the argument that using terms like "someone with an amputation" or "someone with schizophrenia" is better because it is not an outright label or it doesn't reduce the person to the diagnosis, but the diagnosis still stands.

In the end, if diagnoses are so damaging, then why do many say they experience relief at discovering there is a name for what they are experiencing (NAMI, n.d.; O'Connor et al., 2022)? This may have even happened to you or someone close. If so, readers are invited to revisit that experience and recall what it was like prior to diagnosis.

I can't help but think of myself and my family when, as a 14-year-old I developed spontaneous, intrusive thoughts about harming myself and had sexually grotesque images flashing in my mind. It was discovered that I was experiencing OCD, and I learned the intrusive thoughts didn't mean that I actually wanted to engage in the ego-dystonic activities. I didn't feel so weird and alone anymore, and felt hopeful because if doctors understood it, it was treatable. One only has to read the biographies of mental illness sufferers, such as *The Collected Schizophrenias* (Wang, 2019), to hear tales of relief upon diagnosis.

References

Ayano, G., Demelash, S., Yohannes, Z., Haile, K., Tulu, M., Assefa, D., Tesfaye, A., Haile, K., Solomon, M., Chaka, A., & Tsegay, L. (2021). Misdiagnosis, detection rate, and associated factors of severe psychiatric disorders in specialized psychiatry centers in Ethiopia. *Annals of General Psychiatry, 20*(10). https://doi.org/10.1186/s12991-021-00333-7

Kingsley, D. (2022). Debate: Child and adolescent mental health professionals have a responsibility to diagnose Personality Disorder. *The Association for Child and Adolescent Mental Health, 27*(2), 196–198. https://doi.org/10.1111/camh.12557

Lake, E. (2023). *Intentional misdiagnosis and ethical considerations of mental health counselors working with managed care* [Doctoral dissertation, University of South Dakota]. https://www.proquest.com/docview/2816677482?pq-origsite=gscholar&fromopenview=true

National Alliance on Mental Illness (NAMI). (n.d.). *Understanding your diagnosis.* https://www.nami.org/Your-Journey/Individuals-with-Mental-Illness/Understanding-Your-Diagnosis

O'Connor, C., Seery, C., & Young, C. (2022). How does it feel to have one's psychiatric diagnosis altered? Exploring lived experiences of diagnostic shifts in adult mental healthcare. *Frontiers in Psychiatry, 13.* doi:10.3389/fpsyt.2022.820162

Wang, E.W. (2019). *The collected schizophrenias: Essays* (pp. 5–6). Graywolf Press.

Wieland, J. & Zitman, F.G. (2016). It is time to bring borderline intellectual functioning back into the main fold of classification systems. *BJPsych Bulletin, 40*(4), 204–206. doi:10.1192/pb.bp.115.051490

Chapter 21

In Defense of Diagnosis (Part 2)

Subscribers to the idea that accurate diagnosis isn't necessary because "we treat symptoms, not diagnoses," should consider the potential for it being a source of iatrogenic illness. It encourages haphazard diagnosing, some of the problems of which are discussed below and in later chapters.

One could argue that at times therapists don't seem to be treating a diagnosis per se. Examples may include marital problems like communication or infidelity. Perhaps someone is struggling with a spiritual problem, or there are parent-child relationship concerns. However, providers should be attuned to the idea that these presenting topics could be the tip of the iceberg.

It's well-documented, for example, that depression or other neuroses are present in couples counseling (Gorman & Blow, 2008; Rokach & Chan, 2023), whether as an etiological factor of, or end result to, infidelity. Consider the man who struggles to show affection, whose partner finds themselves in an emotional affair. A male's inability to show affection is probably more complicated than "it's just the way males are" given that, for example, attachment trauma or depression can engender emotional flatness.

It is true that a 100 percent accurate diagnosis is not required to begin working with a patient. Regardless, "we don't treat diagnoses, we treat symptoms" is still a specious observation. If the whole is greater than the sum of its parts, symptoms are parts that can only really be understood in the context of a specific disorder/disorder category, (e.g., "the whole").

Consider that while many symptoms are similar and therefore could ostensibly be treated similarly, the diagnosis conceptualizes the *nature* of the similar symptoms/what is driving them, and therefore how to treat them. For example, social anxiety disorder and avoidant personality are very similar in their prominent symptom of social avoidance, but each requires different interventions.

Social anxiety is a more phobic malady, and can be readily approached with exposure therapy, social skills training, and psychiatric medication like selective serotonin reuptake inhibitors (Bandelow, 2020). The avoidance pattern of those with avoidant personalities, on the other hand, is more of

DOI: 10.4324/9781032631400-25

an inter-relational issue, based in the person's core schema revolving around fears of rejection because they feel grossly under-par to others. A careful, relational approach will likely be required to establish the trust of these timid individuals (Sperry & Casteliero, 2022) before any meaningful sharing will occur that is necessary for analysis, cognitive, or behavioral intervention to restructure the deeply ingrained deconstructive core schema that led to the social inhibitions.

Another common example involves latency-aged children who are restless, don't sleep well, and cannot pay attention. The child's symptoms are evaluated to be reflective of ADHD and they're prescribed a stimulant. After a month of the medication and talk therapy to learn grounding techniques for combatting the inattention, symptoms are noticeably more intense. The medication is changed to a different stimulant but the symptoms persist, and maybe worsen yet again. They are indeed being targeted, but nothing improves.

Rightfully so, the parent decides a second opinion is warranted. The new evaluator does not conclude ADHD, and is more thoughtful around a differential diagnosis. They consider age of symptom onset and more closely examine the child's thought process and inner dialogue. It comes to light that this child is internalizing a lot of worry. People who worry exhibit restlessness, which is a physical expression of the restlessness of the mind. They have a hard time focusing as a result of thinking too much, and it is also hard to sleep when the worry does not subside. This is all indicative of generalized anxiety disorder (GAD). Thus, the child's restlessness and inattention are driven by anxiety, not stimulation seeking as in ADHD.

The child is therefore taken off of stimulants, which were likely the culprit of worsening the anxiety, and talk therapy focuses on examining the worry and learning mindfulness and relaxation. Thus, reducing matters to "treating the symptoms" produced poor results. If "treating symptoms" and disregarding the diagnosis was an effective philosophy, would the child not have improved regardless?

Indifference about diagnosing is an ethical matter. It is as problematic to be treating patients for what they do not have as it is to not be treating what they do have.

It's of course possible that some therapists' diagnostic indifference philosophy is influenced by un-honed diagnostic skills or unfamiliarity with the range of diagnoses or differential diagnostic practice. Thankfully, there is a wide spectrum of continuing education and books that can help providers in this position improve their competency in this arena. Further, it can be helpful for any new practitioner to get a current abnormal psychology book and review material that may not have been studied for a couple of years. The easily-digestible refresher will at least provide re-exposure and critical thinking about the different diagnoses as they enter the field.

According to the World Health Organization (Fernández et al., 2021), mental health care dropout rates range between 30 and 45 percent. Given the high rates of mental health misdiagnoses (Stahnke, 2021; Hall, 2022; McIntyre et al., 2022) it's hard not to consider that one contributor is being treated for the wrong diagnosis, rendering patient dissatisfaction leading to dropout, and ongoing suffering.

Anyone feeling laissez faire towards accurate mental health diagnosis is invited to consider if it were themselves or a loved one, would that lens on diagnostic accuracy remain?

References

Bandelow, B. (2020). Current and novel psychopharmacological drugs for anxiety disorders [Abstract]. In Y.K. Kim (Ed.) *Anxiety disorders: Advances in experimental medicine and biology*, Springer. https://doi.org/10.1007/978-981-32-9705-0_19

Fernández, D., Vigo, D., Sampson, N., Hwang, I., Aguilar-Gaxiola, S., Al-Hamzawi, A.O, Alonso, J., Andrade, L.H., Bromet, E.J., de Girolamo, G., de Jonge, P., Florescu, S., Gureje, O., Hinkov, H., Hu, C., Karam, E.G., Karam, G., Kwakami, N., Kiejna, A., & Haro, J. (2021). Patterns of care and dropout rates from outpatient mental healthcare in low-, middle- and high-income countries from the World Health Organization's World Mental Health Survey Initiative. *Psychological Medicine, 51*(12), 2104–2116.

Gorman, L. & Blow, A. (2008). Concurrent depression and infidelity. *Journal of Couple & Relationship Therapy, 7*(1), 39–58. doi:10.1080/15332690802129705

Hall, H. (2022) Dissociation and misdiagnosis of schizophrenia in populations experiencing chronic discrimination and social defeat [Abstract]. *Journal of Trauma & Dissociation, 25*(3), 334–348. doi:10.1080/15299732.2022.2120154

McIntyre, R.S., LaLiberte, F., Germaine, G., MacKnight, S.D., Gillard, P., & Harrington, A. (2022). The real-world health resource use and costs of misdiagnosing bipolar 1 disorder. *Journal of Affective Disorders, 316*, 26–33.

Rokach, A. & Chan, S.H. (2023). Love and infidelity: Causes and consequences. *International Journal of Environmental Research and Public Health, 20*(5). https://doi.org/10.3390/ijerph20053904

Sperry, L. & Casteliero, G. (2022). Avoidant personality disorder (p. 553). In R.E. Feinstein (Ed.) *Primer on personality disorders.* Oxford University Press.

Stahnke, B. (2021). A systematic review of misdiagnosis in those with obsessive-compulsive disorder. *Journal of Affective Disorders Reports, 6.* https://doi.org/10.1016/j.jadr.2021.100231

Chapter 22

Post-Diagnosis Considerations

As outlined in the previous chapters, arriving at an accurate diagnosis takes a lot of consideration. Paying attention to the following three observations *after* arriving at a diagnosis can help therapists remain ethical and accurate.

Diagnosis is a Tool, not an Identifier

A diagnosis summarizes a clinical presentation, but it should not reduce patients to their collection of symptoms. If therapists reflexively think, "Jane is a schizophrenic" or "Bob is a narcissist" there's a possibility that, at least subconsciously, they will always be seeking diagnostic identity affirmation in an action called confirmation bias. In other words, the therapist might rely on seeing the patient as X collection of symptoms, given that's how they are identified. This is troubling because, while therapists would be remiss if they didn't pay attention to symptoms, seeking symptoms to confirm a diagnosis/identity can come at the expense of noticing symptom reduction.

Consider the case of Shelley, a patient with borderline personality disorder (BPD) who called me after hours one evening. "Sorry for calling outside the normal hours, but I wanted to let you know I can't make tomorrow's appointment. Can we reschedule for next week?" she asked. Shelley explained that work and car trouble took up her day and would continue for part of the following day. I realized that she had not called me after hours in many months, and this call was out of courtesy to me. Despite an exhausting day, Shelley had found time to let me know about what had happened and asked to reschedule, showing continued investment in her treatment. Further, Shelley hadn't tried to engage me in a "phone session" or extra attention as she once did. I thanked her for honoring my policy of 24-hour notice if appointments needed changing, despite her chaotic day, and said I would call her the next day to reschedule.

If I had identified Shelley merely as "borderline," it would have been easy to conceptualize her late call as a return of the notorious BPD boundary-pushing and called her out on it in the next session, or even on the phone.

DOI: 10.4324/9781032631400-26

Such an accusation could have proved devastating to Shelley, who was otherwise making progress. Instead, in our next session, I offered praise and we focused on how she managed such a stressful day without resorting to her old habits of demanding my availability or self-destructive activity.

There Could Be More Than One Diagnosis

Arriving at a diagnosis can be a relief for both patient and therapist, but it should be considered that *multiple* diagnoses are possibly at play. A perusal of the *DSM*, for instance, shows therapists that there are almost always co-morbid conditions to every diagnosis. Depression and anxiety disorders, for example, generally have a 60 percent co-occurrence rate (Salcedo, 2018). Some are higher, as in people with social anxiety, who are up to 70 percent likely to also experience depression (Kalin, 2020).

This is an important factor in treatment because, while the person might present for depression, paying attention to, in this case, the social anxiety is just as important. Anyone working with socially anxious patients will likely discover they tend to get seriously depressed, and will express that at least part of his stems from feeling they're missing out on life. In effect, it is a matter of diagnoses influencing one another. Thus, while it's important to manage the depression, there must *also* be a focus on the social anxiety, for it is a major contributor to the depressive state.

The same might go for children with learning disabilities. Children suffering from specific learning disabilities or ADHD can also be depressed and anxious. As they age, learning takes on more autonomy. For example, as grades progress, instead of learning to read, there comes a point when they must read to learn, and they quickly fall behind. Not keeping up academically can lead to feeling like a misfit in the classroom and feeling stupid for not getting it. Self-esteem suffers, and depression and/or anxiety settles in, compounding the problems with motivation and focus.

Here, addressing the anxiety and depression will probably provide some relief, but without recognizing the role of the learning disability, there is little chance of fully stabilizing the corollary mental health struggles. Collaborating with learning disability interventionists will be an important part of treatment. If the child's ability to grasp learning improves, chances are, so will self-esteem, chipping away at depression, along with angst about not keeping up.

Finally, people presenting for trauma often come to present other diagnoses like depression, panic, psychosis, OCD, eating disorders, impulse control disorders, and substance abuse. It might be seen that these are the result of the trauma and can thus be subsumed by post-traumatic stress disorder (PTSD). Unfortunately, working on resolving the trauma won't always be sufficient to deconstruct these concerns because they have taken on a life of their own and matured into a separate diagnosis. A good rule to be mindful of is that if something becomes a consistent focus of separate clinical attention, it warrants its own diagnosis. This makes sure this pillar of the clinical presentation stays in focus as a point of treatment.

A Diagnosis Might Need to Be Changed

It's possible that, as a therapist gets to know the patient, clues emerge that indicate what initially seemed accurate must be reconsidered. Therapists need to be flexible in their diagnostic conceptualization because, for example, they could be seeing someone during emerging pathology. Consider that a young adult presenting for major depressive disorder (MDD) might develop a manic episode. The diagnosis would change *from* MDD *to* a bipolar disorder, as the latter includes major depressive episodes.

I experienced the importance of diagnostic flexibility over the course of a year with a patient, Claudia. Claudia never missed a session, and even chided me for having to cancel the day a tornado went through the area. She was a mystery from the start. For being such a stickler about coming, she also seemed only passively interested in being there. When I asked what she liked about coming in, Claudia shrugged and said, "It's good to get stuff off my chest." Her material was usually frustration about her lazy husband and that his laziness made her anxious. Initially she did complain of panic, but any focus on learning to resolve it, or have a better relationship with her husband, would be deflected. She eventually began appearing depressed, but remained working and took care of her children. I attempted to intervene to little effect, even in just trying to explore her emotional landscape.

Once, during this depressive spell, Claudia confessed she had been cutting and burning herself, something she denied a history of when we first met. Soon, she offered that she had phases of drinking with her girlfriends, sometimes used cocaine, and was engaging in an affair with a married man at work. From panic to depression to what appeared to be the characteristics of a personality disorder, or perhaps bursts of manic activity, were presentations that unfolded in short order.

About six months after sessions began, I started noticing she could become distracted in conversation, but would reign back in. "I lost you there for a minute, what happened?" I would ask. Claudia appeared to be responding to internal stimuli, hearing voices or seeing things I could not. She answered that she sometimes heard voices, but claimed that she did not understand them.

The next session, Claudia slipped and named one of the voices. She continued to explain the two others and "who they were." In one of my last sessions with her, I was introduced to one of "them." After asking her what it was like sharing details about hearing voices in the previous sessions,

Claudia's expression altered, a masculine voice appeared, and she breathed heavily, making threats. As Claudia became more verbally aggressive and physically agitated, I exited the office. After several minutes she came out in tears, looking for me. She asked why I left her alone in the office. There was no recollection of the encounter.

Claudia suffered from dissociative identity disorder (DID), hence the plethora of different presentations and lack of treatment progress. She said she was kept from fully engaging all this time by one personality trying to stop her from revealing too much. That day, he had had enough.

It would have been easy to see Claudia's behaviors as indicative of depression with anxious distress, a bipolar spectrum illness with psychotic features, or perhaps view her as suffering more from a personality disorder. However, being flexible to the idea that there were various possibilities kept me vigilant during the nebulous situation. Thus, I was able to eventually conceptualize that Claudia's collective symptom picture was indicative of DID and not an assortment of comorbid diagnoses I might have attempted to fruitlessly chisel away at. Given DID is the result of severe early trauma, she was referred to trauma specialists.

References

Kalin, N.H. (2020). The critical relationship between depression and anxiety. *American Journal of Psychiatry 177*(5), 365–367. https://doi.org/10.1176/appi.ajp.2020.20030305

Salcedo, B. (2018, January 19). The comorbidity of anxiety and depression. National Alliance on Mental Illness blog. https://www.nami.org/Blogs/NAMI-Blog/January-2018/The-Comorbidity-of-Anxiety-and-Depression

Chapter 23

Never Diagnose Based on One Chief Symptom

Diagnosis is the springboard from which therapists leap, but there is little preparatory training in many programs other than a one-semester survey of the *Diagnostic and Statistical Manual* (*DSM*). Thus, new practitioners are reliant upon what may have been retained from a class that was possibly two years before they began practicing. Couple this with supervision deficits, and it's easy to see how therapists could struggle with accurate diagnosing.

Of course, it could be argued that all one has to do is reference the *DSM* criteria. However, as noted in the "Use of This Manual" portion of *DSM-5* and *DSM-5 TR* (American Psychiatric Association, 2013, 2022), accurate diagnosis takes much more into account than checking off symptoms. Symptoms must be looked at from many angles. Are they pervasive and enduring? Are the apparent symptoms actually acceptable in the person's culture? What pattern are they a part of? Can the pattern be subsumed by another diagnosis? For instance, the criteria for oppositional defiant disorder (ODD) includes many items that can be present during depression. Hence, it is noted in the *DSM* that ODD should not be diagnosed if symptoms occur in the context of a depressive episode.

Depressed children are often irritable and touchy, especially if they have insomnia and decreased appetite. This irritability can be viewed as disrespectful by adults, and arguments ensue, ostensibly making the child oppositional or defiant. Therefore, a therapist must carefully investigate the history and quality of the symptoms. Otherwise, if a child is indeed depressed, but they are viewed as "ODD," it's likely their unwanted behaviors will be the chief focus. This is not likely to be productive, given the depressive foundation. Chances are, resolving the depression could contribute to dissolving the unwanted behavior.

With this example in mind, readers are cautioned not to assume a diagnosis based on an apparent key feature. Remembering the three insights below (Smith, 2021) can help stave off the tendency to use a chief symptom as justification for a diagnosis. Readers are also invited to refer to the review

DOI: 10.4324/9781032631400-27

guide provided at the end of the chapter that covers thorough considerations for five diagnoses prone to application based on one key element.

A Symptom Must Be Contextualized

It's natural to pick up on a chief complaint or observable symptom, but that item requires contextualization. While the edicts of psychiatry past are often forgotten, we can still take a cue from Emil Kraepelin, the father of modern psychiatric disease classification. Kraepelin (Spitzer et al., 2002, p. 487) told us, "A single symptom, however characteristic it may be, never justifies a diagnosis by itself ..."

This is because, as alluded to in the ODD example, categorically different diagnoses can have similar symptoms. Thus, a symptom must be put into perspective. For example, if a clinician perceives obsessional thinking, it must be considered if it is:

- The actual OCD criteria definition of "obsession" meaning intrusive thoughts/images/urges.
- A colloquial definition of someone that cannot let things go, like a tendency to dwell on arguments or someone doing them wrong, as in many personality disorders.
- An intensely focused interest, as in autism spectrum conditions.
- Intrusive memories like in trauma.
- Ruminations on negative self-perceptions/guilt as in depression.
- Persistent worries about life in general observed in generalized anxiety disorder (GAD).
- Preoccupation about possibly having a disease, as in illness anxiety (hypochondria).

Clearly, obsession is not obsession; therefore, "obsession" does not equal OCD.

At first glance, it may seem overwhelming to consider how to tease that all apart, but again, simple questioning will assist:

- If the patient uses the word obsession to describe their experience, saying, "Tell me more about what you mean by obsessed," and asking for examples of "obsession" can help clarify.
- If the therapist thinks to themselves, "This person is obsessed," considering the nature of the "obsession" (worry, rumination, intrusive thoughts/images, perseverative fixation like in delusions) can guide further questioning that will lead to a diagnosis. If, for instance, the therapist feels a patient is obsessed because they perseverate on how the neighbor put up

cameras, that is a tip-off they may be paranoid. The attentive therapist will explore if this accusation is true or if the patient is delusional. If the patient keeps talking about an unpleasant image flashing in their mind that they can't get rid of, that's indicative of OCD obsessions, and investigating a possible OCD diagnosis would occur.

Diagnostic Conclusions Can Take Time

It's alright to not be 100 percent sure of a diagnosis, and even seasoned practitioners take time to know for sure. In fact, some researchers on diagnostic accuracy have recently shown that the most-sound diagnostic outcomes are associated with practitioners who take their time (Brechbiel & Keely, 2019).

Instead of rushing to a conclusion in the first session, therapists are instead encouraged to digest the information, perhaps in supervision if new to the field, and prepare follow-up questions to see what pattern the chief symptom is part of. For example, if the patient reports being obsessed with everything going wrong, that indicates worry, and we know that worry is indicative of GAD. In the next session the therapist can follow up:

> "Last time we met you described having what you called 'obsessions.' You explained how that meant often thinking the worst-case scenario is about to happen. I'm curious to know what else happens when those thoughts set in, like how it affects your mood, sleep, ability to focus, things like that."

If the rest of the symptoms align with GAD, there's the answer. If not, such as if the worry is only in particular situations, like relationship-related matters, it's important to keep learning about the pattern. It could be a personality disorder or separation anxiety. This is the important process of differential diagnosis.

If, while the therapist is still clarifying a diagnosis, one must formally be applied, such as for billing purposes, the *DSM-5* and *DSM-5 TR* provide "Other" and "Unspecified" categories (formerly collectively referred to as "Not Otherwise Specified" (NOS in earlier *DSM* editions).

"Other" is frequently used when a patient has some pervasive symptoms of a particular disorder but somehow does not meet full criteria. It might be applied if a therapist is leaning towards a particular diagnosis but is still getting to know the patient and not sure.

"Unspecified" can be applied in a couple of situations. The first is when it is not clear if a patient's symptoms are purely psychological, caused by an underlying medical condition, or a substance related matter. This is common in fast-paced triage situations like psychiatric crisis settings. Second, it is applied when a therapist deems someone's presentation is not something listed in the *DSM*. Examples include shared psychotic disorder, self-defeating personality, or a culture-bound diagnosis, like Ataque de Nervios in Latino populations.

A Sure Diagnosis Is Not Required for Treatment to Commence

Even if a therapist isn't entirely sure of the clinical picture, treatment can begin by establishing therapeutic alliance. The therapist could also begin implementing stress management, and exploring strengths-based interventions such as cultivating things the patient has found helpful in managing the distress. Keep in mind, however, that despite seeing some gains in treatment without fully knowing the diagnostic picture, this does not mean practitioners can forget about accuracy.

Remember, disorders can share symptoms but that does not mean they are treated alike. Therefore, when there is no sure diagnosis, treatment should include re-assessing the diagnostic picture, especially by observing for patterns.

For instance, a patient presented for moodiness and seemed to have a rapid-cycling bipolar spectrum illness at first. Since coping skills, lifestyle adjustment suggestions, and medications provided some relief, this became the focus of sessions. The frequent suicidal thinking and self-injury that occurred was considered a natural part of having a major affective disorder.

Frustrated at the lack of sustained stability, the patient eventually sought another therapist. This provider was curious why, despite adherence to treatment, no prolonged stability occurred. Understanding the importance of symptom context, this therapist wanted to know more about the nature of the moods. They discovered that the mood instability was reactive, correlated to relationship complications. Coupling this with the patient's penchant for chronic self-injury, they realized the moods were more likely due to a personality disorder. Treatment shifted to the more sustaining work of managing the fears of abandonment that drove the moodiness.

Earlier providers, seeing some gains under the bipolar diagnosis treatment plan, applied a revolving door of coping mechanisms whenever the patient seemed moody. Intervention was merely a game of symptom "Whac-a-Mole" and the patient did not reach sustained stabilization.

There was no further vigilance to the pattern, which, coupled with the lack of stability, despite treatment adherence, should have raised flags another diagnosis may be at hand.

Suggested Resources

It's suggested that students and new therapists regularly study criteria in the *DSM* or *International Classification of Diseases* (*ICD*) for any diagnosis they provide. In addition, studying *DSM* casebooks, such as psychiatrist John Barnhill's *DSM-5 Clinical Cases* (2014, American Psychiatric Publishing) can provide good exercises in differential diagnosis. These books provide case vignettes with detailed digestion of the differential diagnosis process. Further, some supervisees have found it helpful to obtain an up-to-date abnormal psychology textbook to periodically refresh their memory. This can be helpful because textbooks tend to condense the latest research with diagnostic criteria and case studies.

References

American Psychiatric Association. (2013). *Diagnostic and statistical manual of mental disorders* (5th ed.).

American Psychiatric Association. (2022). Diagnostic and statistical manual of mental disorders (5th ed., text rev.).

Brechbiel, J.K. & Keely, J.W. (2019). Pathways linking clinician demographics to mental health diagnostic accuracy: An international perspective. *Journal of Clinical Psychology, 75*(9), 1715–1729.

Smith, A.D. (2021, May 17). Tips for accurate diagnosing: A symptom is part of a pattern –a single symptom is not proof of a diagnosis. *Psychology Today.* https://www.psychologytoday.com/us/blog/and-running/202105/tips-accurate-diagnosing-symptom-is-part-pattern

Spitzer, R.L., Gibbon, M., Skodol, A.E., Williams, J.B.W., & First, M.B. (Eds.). 2002. *DSM-IV-TR casebook: A learning companion to the diagnostic and statistical manual of mental disorders* (4th ed., text rev.). American Psychiatric Publishing, Inc.

Diagnosis Accuracy Review for Five Commonly Misdiagnosed Disorders

The disorders listed are among the most over-diagnosed/misdiagnosed because of popular culture misportrayals or a stand-out feature that could lead to diagnosing based on one chief symptom. The following contains review material for each to guide therapists through considerations for more accurate differential diagnosis.

Readers are reminded that for each of the following, it is assumed general medical or substance-related causes of the presentation have been ruled out. Lastly, readers are encouraged to also carefully review the more expansive diagnostic criteria and differential diagnosis discussions in the *DSM* or *ICD* for each of the following.

AUTISM SPECTRUM

The Problem

Some therapists might begin thinking "autism" when they perceive social awkwardness and/or sensory peculiarities. Autism is much more than this, however.

Pay Careful Attention

- Autistic social awkwardness is not mere quirkiness. It includes:
  - Deficits in social reciprocation (e.g., give and take conversation, sharing).
  - Restrained affect (including hand gestures and voice intonation) while interacting.
  - Inability to grasp that other's ideas, emotions, beliefs, etc. might differ from one's own (i.e., lacking "theory of mind").

- Autistic sensory peculiarities are more intense than not liking a certain kind of clothing or preferring a certain food (both common amongst children in general). Rather, autistic individuals' sensory uniquities include items such as:
  - Feeling weight upon them is required for soothing.
  - Hyperacute hearing/misophonia (certain noises create rage), very sensitive to light.
  - Indifference to pain or extreme temperatures.
  - Gravitate only towards foods of a particular texture/taste/smell.

- Therapists should evaluate if the following other autism symptoms are present:
  - Developmental delays.
  - Strict adherence to routine (e.g., sequences of events, timing) to maintain equilibrium.
  - Intense preoccupations (e.g., activities, hobbies pieces/parts of things, collecting).
  - Mood dysregulation if frustrated, especially if deprived of routine or preoccupations.
  - Repetitious motions (e.g., rocking, tapping, constant hand wringing and pacing).
  - Cognitive impairments, often evidenced in IQ, but also in processing and/or executive function ability.
  - Catatonia.

Other Details Associated with Autism

- It can run in families.
- Gestational risk factors (e.g., substance use, pre-eclampsia, gestational diabetes).

Differential Diagnosis Considerations

- If the "social awkwardness" seems to meet the social deficit criteria but other symptoms are lacking, consider reviewing social-pragmatic disorder. If the central symptom is stereotyped behaviors and other symptoms are lacking, visiting stereotyped movement disorder is recommended.
- If there is cognitive impairment, consider reviewing global developmental delay, borderline intellectual functioning, or intellectual disability.

If the patient fits into any one of these categories, it is a good idea to refer for neuropsychological testing to seal the diagnosis with a formal evaluation. This can aid in verification of diagnosis and extent of impairment in case the individual requires special education, government-assisted services, or other accommodations.

ATTENTION DEFICIT HYPERACTIVITY DISORDER (ADHD)

The Problem

ADHD is a quick assumption for children/teens with restlessness, inattentiveness, and impulsivity. Many diagnoses can present these symptoms, rendering the necessity to carefully contextualize them. Even if a child scores high on ADHD standard measures, the evaluator must consider that this only shows the symptom profile and further interviewing will be required to contextualize this.

Pay Careful Attention

- Did symptoms appear before or during elementary school? If symptoms arose after this timeframe, the therapist should carefully review differential diagnosis possibilities.
- Attention deficits are *not* only an inability to remain focused. The attention deficit can also be an inability to transition focus (called hyperfocus).
- Therapists should also evaluate if other symptoms co-occur with the hallmark restlessness, inattentiveness, and impulsivity, including:

  - Low frustration tolerance.
  - Flights of ideas/inability to remain on topic.
  - Irritability.
  - A sense of urgency – finishing things quickly to get to the next task.
  - Executive functioning impairment (e.g., difficulty with planning and follow-through).
  - Stimulation-seeking, often involving risky activity (e.g., fighting, substance abuse, daredevilry).

Other Details Associated with ADHD

- It can run in families.
- Gestational risk factors (e.g., smoking, substance abuse, pre-eclampsia, gestational diabetes).

Differential Diagnosis Considerations

Anxiety, depression, and trauma can masquerade as ADHD, as can early onset psychosis. It's therefore essential to evaluate the individual's thought process for anxious, depressive, trauma, or psychosis-related material to help with differential diagnosis. During the diagnostic process, therapists might consider:

- Generalized anxiety presents restlessness, inability to focus due to worry, irritability, and inability to sleep.
- Depression can include slowed cognition/inability to focus, agitation, irritability.

- Trauma sequelae includes restlessness from feeling on edge, inability to focus due to intrusive thoughts and dissociation (which can render one appearing "daydreamy" and unfocused), irritability, heightened reactivity that could be viewed as poor impulse control, and self-destructive activity that might be viewed as stimulation-seeking.
- Prodromal psychosis can include internal preoccupation that looks like disinterest/daydreaming, scattered thoughts/flights of ideas, and gradual decline in executive functioning (like ability to plan and then carry out activities).

If any of the above are present and the "ADHD" symptoms coincide with the onset of them, especially if developed after elementary school age, then an ADHD diagnosis might be considered dubious. Of course, ADHD can be comorbid with any of the above. This can be evaluated by considering if there is a preceding history of ADHD symptoms, especially with presence of family history of ADHD and gestational risk factors. It is not unusual for ADHD to co-occur with depression and anxiety which evolve corollary to ADHD because sufferers feel they are falling behind, or perhaps not feeling good enough or even "bad" for always being told to behave. Depression and anxiety can exacerbate the underlying ADHD symptoms of restlessness and inability to concentrate and ideally will be tackled with similar clinical zeal. Otherwise, the conditions will feed one another, stalling progress.

BIPOLAR DISORDER

The Problem

Any mention of "mood swings" seems to conjure ideas of bipolar disorder. However, many conditions include significant moodiness, and the nature of mood alterations must therefore be carefully contextualized.

Pay Careful Attention

- Bipolar disorder is *not* someone's proclivity for spontaneous moody reactions to someone or something in their environment.
- In bipolar disorder, the depressive and manic/hypomanic/mixed episodes often build over days, sometimes weeks, and tend to be sustained for days, weeks, or months.
- Therapists should also evaluate that symptoms other than "moodiness" are present. In manic/hypomanic/mixed episodes, there is also:

  - Heightened energy/restlessness/decreased need for sleep (e.g., not appear tired after only three hours of sleep per night).

- Pressured thoughts and speech (they can't speak fast enough to get the thoughts out).
- Speaking in circles, derailed and otherwise disorganized thoughts.
- Grandiosity/inflated self-esteem (which can even reach delusional proportions, like being convinced they have superpowers or are a deity).
- Increased creativity or goal-oriented activity (e.g., exercising, cleaning, school/work projects).
- Increase in pleasurable or stimulation-seeking activity (e.g., gambling, shopping, substance abuse, sex, theft, fighting).
- Hallucinations and catatonia are not unusual in severe cases.

Other Details Associated with Bipolar Disorders

- It can run in families.
- Some patients experience numerous full mood episodes per year ("rapid cycling"), while others may experience one or less mood events annually, especially if treated.
- Bipolar 1 tends to be more mania/hypomania/mixed episodes than depression. Bipolar 2 tends to have more depressive episodes, and the depressive episodes are often long-lasting and severe.
- People seem to present for intervention more often during depressive phases, as hypomania is not usually impairing, and, unless severely impaired and needing hospitalization, fully manic people may be enjoying their energy and charisma. Therefore, it is a good idea to always screen for a history of manic/hypomanic/mixed episodes whenever someone presents for depression.

Differential Diagnosis Considerations

- If mood symptoms are not severe, but are palpably different every few days, reviewing cyclothymia is suggested.
- In the absence of *true* manic/hypomanic/mixed episodes, moods that are in reaction to the environment or others should be investigated as significant of antisocial, borderline, histrionic, or narcissistic personality disorders.
- In juveniles, disruptive mood dysregulation disorder, a depressive condition, might be reviewed as a possibility. These children tend to be depressed at baseline with regular, superimposed episodes of severe reactivity.
- If the person, during *and* in between mood episodes, exhibits psychotic symptoms, schizoaffective disorder, bipolar type, is likely.

OBSESSIVE-COMPULSIVE DISORDER (OCD)

The Problem

The nuance of obsession as defined in OCD is not always understood and any preoccupations or fixations might be considered "obsessive." Further, particularly neat people or germophobic patients might be quickly assumed to have OCD because of popular culture portrayals of the need for order and cleanliness.

Pay Careful Attention

- "Obsession" as defined for OCD is an intrusive thought, image, or impulse that heightens anxiety, is hard to suppress, and in contrast to how the person normally thinks (e.g., someone with intrusive thoughts of killing their family is actually very loving and gentle, thus the severe anxiety about the thoughts). It is *not* an inability to quit perseverating on a topic or an attachment to an activity like video gaming.
- More often than not, there is compulsive behavior (an action in attempt to neutralize the anxiety/somehow feel in control). This is usually a ritualized activity such as doing something so many times, cleaning, or performing a seemingly arbitrary activity upon an intrusive thought (e.g., an image of an airplane overhead crashing into a neighborhood is managed by tapping the steering wheel in a certain fashion). There is no logical connection between the obsession and the compulsion. Rituals can also be thought processes like rethinking something a certain number of times for reassurance that something bad will not happen.

Other Details Associated with OCD

- It can run in families.
- Often co-occurs with tic disorders and ADHD.
- Tends to evolve by teenage years, but might happen much later in life.

Differential Diagnosis Considerations

- If an obsession is with pieces and parts of things, collections, or certain actions, consider reviewing the autism spectrum.
- Should the fixation be on worrisome thoughts, and there is an absence of ritualized behaviors, the presentation is likely in the realm of generalized anxiety. There is also an absence of the ritualized behaviors. If the preoccupation is limited to the idea that one has serious illnesses, and the compulsive activity is seeking doctor evaluations, the therapist can consider illness anxiety disorder (hypochondriasis).
- Depressed people often "obsess" on their failures and how unworthy they are. There is also an absence of the ritualized behaviors.

- If an obsession is related to bodily blemishes/disproportions or the need to retain otherwise useless items or arbitrarily obtained animals, body dysmorphic disorder, or hoarding disorder should be considered.
- If the "obsessions" are restricted to rules, details, schedules, and routines and the need to interpersonally control others, consider reviewing obsessive-compulsive (perfectionistic/anankastic) personality disorder.

SCHIZOPHRENIA

The Problem

Perhaps the most common hallmarks of schizophrenia are hallucinations and delusions, especially paranoid thinking. Both symptoms are common in numerous other conditions including mood and personality disorders and PTSD.

Pay Careful Attention

- People with schizophrenia usually don't all of a sudden develop the hallmark symptoms. They are usually preceded by a prodromal phase where the person becomes increasingly isolative, loses expression, develops odd ways of thinking (such as clairvoyance) or perhaps begins seeming suspicious, not quite fully paranoid.
- Schizophrenia can manifest in a primarily disorganized manner, meaning the person's actions and verbalizations are nonsensical and bizarre, perhaps with little to no hallucinatory or delusional material.
- Those with schizophrenia might also become periodically or indefinitely catatonic after exhibiting hallucinations, delusions, or disorganized behavior.

Other Details Associated with Schizophrenia

- It can run in families, but it is not the general rule.
- There is a history of traumatic events (not all trauma sequelae end in PTSD).
- Schizophrenia generally manifests in the late teens to early 20s for males, while females often experience initial symptoms in their mid-20s to early 30s.

Differential Diagnosis Considerations

- If psychotic symptoms occur *only* during a mood episode, be sure to review major depressive or bipolar disorder with psychotic features.

- If symptoms are baseline and there are frequent superimposed depressive and/or bipolar presentations, consider schizoaffective disorder.
- Should symptoms be limited to years (beginning by early adulthood) of odd/eccentric activity, suspiciousness, slightly disorganized actions, and fleeting hallucinations/delusions, schizotypal personality disorder might be the most accurate diagnosis.

Chapter 24

Re-Evaluate Historical Diagnoses

Just because a patient tells you they have X disorder, a previous therapist provides a particular diagnosis, or a certain condition is documented in records, *do your own careful diagnostic evaluation*.

I am often called upon to review diagnostic and treatment histories for the juvenile courts and offer second opinions. In so doing, I've discovered unbroken chains of misdiagnosis, many originating in nothing more than a pediatrician's diagnostic suggestion or from a therapist who knew the person only briefly.

After interviews and record reviews, "ADHD" is discovered to be generalized anxiety or depression, "ODD" is social anxiety, "bipolar disorder" is borderline personality, and "intermittent explosive disorder" is PTSD. Years of misdiagnosis gave way to unhelpful treatment approaches, allowing the true diagnosis to fester, the symptoms of which are often correlated to problematic behaviors landing the juvenile in front of a court.

Accepting historical diagnoses might seem convenient in that it takes the leg work out assessing, and the therapist can jump to treatment more quickly. However, it can make matters less convenient in the long run when the patient is not improving.

Therapists should consider that historical providers could have made snap diagnoses based on brief interviews, or had a tendency to diagnose most of their patients with the same condition (Frances, 2013). Others could have been influenced by fad diagnoses (Jesus et al., 2022) and still others could have intentionally misdiagnosed to ensure insurance coverage (Lake, 2023). Knowing this, coupled with the awareness of the havoc that misdiagnosis can wreak, there is an airtight case for why a therapist should conduct their own assessment. Accurate diagnosis *is* intervention.

To impress the point, imagine your car is sputtering and you bring it to a mechanic. They tell you they've checked the sparkplugs and the vacuum for leaks, both common causes of sputtering, but all seems well. Meanwhile the sputtering increases. You go to another mechanic and tell them the

DOI: 10.4324/9781032631400-28

first one thought it was sparkplugs or a possible vacuum leak. The second mechanic only considers what the first one had to say, checks the sparkplugs and vacuum for leaks and concludes they can't find anything wrong, either. Clearly, if the common or obvious is not fixing it, should they not be evaluating other possibilities and do their own diagnostic assessment if they are to get your car running properly again?

Given the above, it's clearly wise to harbor some level of skepticism about previous diagnoses. Such informed skepticism serves us well in our diagnostic evaluations but might not always be heeded, especially early on when confidence is lower. I recall, as a starting practitioner, reflexively concurring with others' assessments simply because they were more seasoned or well-respected, so figured they must know better.

Eventually, though, reading diagnostic assessments, I noticed some patients received diagnoses with little evidence for it, or without investigation of the context of symptoms. It was then that a graduate school professor's words of wisdom came echoing back. She said that when we inherit a patient with a diagnosis, we should see if there is evidence against it rather than acquiesce. In other words, investigate its accuracy.

It did not resonate much with me when I was in school, but as I practiced and became acutely aware of misdiagnosis being blindly passed along, misinforming treatment, this became an integral part of my process. It was especially helpful learning to be wary of "popular" diagnoses like bipolar disorder, autism, ADHD, and PTSD. These seemed more liberally applied probably from popular culture attention. Further, popular diagnoses tend to be ones portrayed in media and entertainment, and media is known to misrepresent mental illness by, for example, exaggerating symptoms (Srivastava et al., 2018) or practicing gender bias in certain disorders (Smith et al., 2019).

Unfortunately, uninformed or new therapists may fall back on what they know from any source, including media. Remember, most therapists starting out have had a mere semester of studying psychopathology and are not yet honed, so may simply use what they know, however they know it.

Considering the remarkable misdiagnosis rates in mental health care (Glazier at al., 2015; Rakofsky & Dunlap, 2015; Fresson et al., 2018; Beatson et al., 2019), taking the time to carefully review diagnosis is never a waste of time. When inheriting a patient with a previous diagnosis, even if it is from someone whose opinion the therapist trusts, it can't hurt to review the diagnosis and see for themself. Check the math and be particularly careful especially if any of the following five items apply (Smith, 2021):

1. The patient has a long history of the same diagnosis, yet despite being invested in their psychotherapy/medications, they have shown little to no improvement.

2. It's a popular diagnosis such as ADHD, autism, or bipolar disorder, especially in the absence of specialized evaluations for autism spectrum conditions.
3. The diagnosis is from a non-mental health professional, such as their primary care provider.
4. Historical documentation does not include a thoughtful diagnostic formulation and is missing information like symptom context, duration, and only focuses on a symptom or two.
5. The patient diagnosed themselves. With online diagnostic checklists, media portrayals, and pharmaceutical commercials, it is easy for a patient to quickly conform to what they assume are accurate depictions of particular mental illnesses. Desperately wanting to identify the problem so they can obtain treatment, they may convince themselves, and thus try to convince providers, "This is me (or my kid/spouse, etc.)!" While they may ostensibly appear to have symptoms of X or Y, patients do not understand that a diagnosis isn't a mere checklist of symptoms. Remember, as detailed in Chapter 23, diagnoses are much more complicated than checklists of symptoms.

Thinking of your encounter as a second opinion can lead to a world of improvement for the patient. Consider Jacques, a 12-year-old boy involved with the court due to threatening a teacher. It was documented in the referral for evaluation that, for about a year, he had been experiencing increasing trouble focusing, struggled with irritability, was often restless, impulsive, and easily distracted. Sometimes Jacques appeared to be daydreaming. During that time, Jacques began treatment for what his pediatrician believed to be ADHD and was on his second therapist in eight months. The court requested a diagnostic evaluation to better understand the youth and to see if he was receiving proper care.

After interviewing the family, I collected collateral data. This included contacting Jacques' then-therapist, Anna, a long-standing member of a particular therapy practice. I asked what diagnosis and symptoms they were working on. "ADHD," said Anna. "I've seen that in other documents and the family reports it, too," I replied, furthering, "What evidence of the condition have you observed? What specifically are you addressing in the sessions?" Anna explained, "That's the diagnosis he arrived with." I pressed, "I know it's in his history, but do you think it's accurate?" "That's the diagnosis he came to us with," Anna repeated, adding, "I'm working on helping him focus." Knowing there was a parental separation happening, I asked if there was any discussion about family dynamics. "Yeah, the stress has definitely made the ADHD worse," she finished.

I sometimes joke that my job is to disprove all court-involved youth have ADHD. It seems the bulk of the population we evaluate have this diagnosis in their charts. Not infrequently, ADHD turns out to be inaccurate. Sometimes there is indeed ADHD, along with other conditions, the symptoms of which were historically assumed to be accounted for by the ADHD.

Numerous other conditions can masquerade as, or overlap with, ADHD. These include trauma, dissociative disorders, generalized anxiety, and depression, each requiring a different and/or additional treatment approach. ADHD is a "popular" diagnosis and even a cursory look at the literature reveals concerns of over-diagnosis (Bruchmüller et al., 2012; Schwarz, 2016). Unfortunately, if it is an inattentive, restless boy, the knee-jerk response tends to be ADHD, and it sticks.

As I checked the math, the variables just were not adding up:

- Jacques had no early developmental history typical of ADHD, such as the surfacing of inattentiveness and hyperactivity by kindergarten or thereabouts.
- There was no family history of the condition.
- Jacques' mother had no prenatal concerns correlated to ADHD, like smoking, alcohol use, preeclampsia, or gestational diabetes.
- Jacques had a clean bill of physical health and did not take any prescriptions that might encourage ADHD-like symptoms.
- Jacques had no history of mental health concerns until middle school, and it would be extremely unusual for someone with ADHD to spontaneously burgeon at that point.
- Jacques also did not have a history of educational difficulties up until 6th grade.

What occurred was that when Jacques was 10, his parents began having marital complications, which they thought they kept quiet. By the time Jacques was 11, in 6th grade, his parents were living in separate parts of the house and often fighting after he went to bed. Now, when Jacques was 12, his father was preparing to move out. It was no coincidence that Jacques' difficulties skyrocketed at this time.

Indeed, when I asked Jacques how the family situation had been for him, he admitted he was very angry at both parents and worried about what life was going to be like. Picking at his cuticles and bouncing his leg, Jacques' anxiety was palpable as he explained how his parents hated each other. His ultimate fear was that his mother was going to keep him from seeing his father.

It seemed as if, were Jacques' historical diagnosis a math problem, a sum was somehow calculated with only one variable, and no one ever checked the math. Some minor detective work went a long way. While Jacques indeed was inattentive, irritable, and restless, the symptoms developed as his parents' relationship deteriorated in front of him. A more appropriate diagnosis was adjustment disorder with mixed disturbance of emotions and conduct.

No matter how hard a therapist might try to get Jacques to calm down and focus with interventions for ADHD, nothing was going to change until he digested the separation and, ideally, family therapy also took place.

Another illustration regards schizoaffective disorder, a rare psychotic condition. About 20 years ago, it became an in-vogue diagnosis where I worked. It seemed that any patient presenting mood and psychotic symptoms received the diagnosis. From what I recalled of psychopathology class, schizoaffective disorder was less common than schizophrenia. How did so many cases end up in my work location?

Not only is schizoaffective disorder uncommon, but I knew it caused significant, frequently chronic, impairment. It made no sense that people who had been out of treatment for the past year or more, and often living on the street, were not showing any significant symptoms. My then-supervisor noted my increasing questioning of some of our patients' diagnoses, and confirmed my suspicion that patients are often ascribed a convenient, arbitrary diagnosis. In the case of schizoaffective disorder, it was simply an easy way for the practitioner to quickly account for any disorder that could have mood and psychotic symptoms. This is a good example of "we treat symptoms, not diagnoses," which, as illustrated in earlier chapters, is not sound practice because, while some disorders share symptoms, it does not mean they are treated similarly.

Keeping in Check

Clearly, diagnosing is a weighty matter and comes with a lot of responsibility. Scrutinizing historical diagnoses might therefore seem like a daunting task, but it is largely a matter of becoming familiar with differential diagnoses. This involves not only learning diagnostic criteria, but studying case conceptualizations that illustrate the differential diagnosis process and how diagnoses are more than the sum or their parts. It will also be important to hone one's interviewing skills. While both topics are much too expansive to be contained in a chapter of this volume, there are numerous publications, provided below, from which students and supervisees have learned a great deal in short order.

Suggested Resources

Regularly studying diagnostic criteria in the *DSM* or *ICD* provides a foundation for diagnostic accuracy. Those wishing to witness differential diagnosis and case formulation in action are referred to *DSM* casebooks, such as psychiatrist John Barnhill's *DSM-5 Clinical Cases* (2014, American Psychiatric Publishing). While written for a psychoanalytic audience, psychologist Nancy McWilliams' *Psychoanalytic Case Formulation* (1999, Guilford) provides easy-to-follow guidance on interviewing for categorical assessment domains (e.g., developmental complications, thought processes, relational patterns, defenses) and digesting it into a clear clinical picture.

References

Barnhill, J.W. (2014). *DSM-5 clinical cases*. American Psychiatric Publishing.
Beatson, J.A., Broadbear, J.H., Duncan, C., Bourton, D., & Rao, S. (2019). Avoiding misdiagnosis when auditory verbal hallucinations are present in borderline personality disorder [Abstract]. *Journal of Nervous and Mental Disease, 207*(12), 1048–1055. doi:10.1097/NMD.0000000000001073
Bruchmüller, K., Margraf, J., & Schneider, S. (2012). Is ADHD diagnosed in accord with diagnostic criteria? Overdiagnosis and influence of client gender on diagnosis [Abstract]. *Journal of Consulting Clinical Psychology, 80*(1), 128–138. doi:10.1037/a0026582
Frances, A. (2013). *Saving normal. An insider's revolt against out-of-control psychiatric diagnosis, DSM-5, big pharma, and the medicalization of ordinary life*. Morrow.
Fresson, M., Meulemans, T., Dardenne, B., & Geurten, M. (2018). Overdiagnosis of ADHD in boys: Stereotype impact on neuropsychological assessment. *Applied Neuropsychology Child, 8*(3), 1–15.
Glazier, K., Swing, M., & McGinn, L.K. (2015). Half of obsessive-compulsive cases misdiagnosed: Vignette-based survey of primary care physicians. *Journal of Clinical Psychiatry,76*(6), 761–767.
Jesus S., Costa, A., Simões, G., Alcafache, J., & Garrido, P. (2022). Falling for fads? Diagnostic and therapeutic fads in psychiatry. *European Psychiatry, 65*(S1), S882. doi:10.1192/j.eurpsy.2022.2290
Lake, E. (2023). *Intentional misdiagnosis and ethical considerations of mental health counselors working with managed care* [Doctoral dissertation, University of South Dakota]. https://www.proquest.com/docview/2816677482?pq-origsite=gscholar&fromopenview=true
McWilliams, N. (1999). *Psychoanalytic case formulation*. Guildford Press.
Rakofsky, J.J. & Dunlap, B.W. (2015). The over-under on the misdiagnosis of bipolar disorder: A systematic review [Abstract]. *Current Psychiatry Reviews, 7*(4), 222–234.
Schwarz, A. (2016). *ADHD nation: The disorder, the drugs, the inside story*. Little, Brown.
Smith, A.D. (2021, June 13). 5 signs that a previous psychiatric diagnosis may be inaccurate. *Psychology Today*. https://www.psychologytoday.com/us/blog/and-running/202106/5-signs-previous-psychiatric-diagnosis-could-be-inaccurate
Smith, S.L., Choueiti, M., Choi, A., Pieper, K., & Moutier, C. (2019, May). Mental health conditions in film and TV: Portrayals that dehumanize and trivialize characters. https://assets.uscannenberg.org/docs/aii-study-mental-health-media_052019.pdf
Srivastava, K., Chaudhury, S., Bhat, P.S., & Mujawar, S. (2018). Media and mental health. *Industrial Psychiatry Journal, 27*(1), 1–5. doi:10.4103/ipj.ipj_73_18

Chapter 25

Five Quick Tips for More Thorough Assessments

Although it might seem that one is covering all the bases, especially with the extensive initial evaluation forms clinics use, there is a good chance there's still room for improvement.

This is not only a matter of clinical thoroughness, but of managing liability. For instance, while one may cover all of the bases and ask lots of questions, *how* questions are asked, such as if one "leads the witness," or makes assumptions because a patient did not report certain things, can make all the difference.

Don't "Lead the Witness"

Leading the witness is legal speak for a method of questioning by which the interviewee is expected to answer in a certain manner. The nature of the query suggests to them how it is to be answered. Therapists and providers probably are not intentionally employing this semantic dynamic for particular outcomes as one might in a court room. However, it is nonetheless a dirty habit that must be altered, for one is not truly *evaluating* the patient if this is how one sometimes "questions."

It has been my experience that interviewers seem to do this most when they perceive a problem is not there, but nonetheless want to cover the topic. Consider a patient that does not look depressed, nor are they presenting for suicidal thinking. The therapist might therefore conclude suicide probably is not an issue, but nonetheless it must be asked about.

Thus influenced, they may say, "You haven't had any suicidal thoughts, have you?" during a mental status evaluation. Perhaps the patient *has had* suicidal thoughts that are important to know about. Maybe the patient thinks the therapist means at the time of questioning, and affirms their pre-negated inquiry, but earlier in the month they did have those kinds of thoughts.

DOI: 10.4324/9781032631400-29

Cover the Current and the Past

Inquiring about both current and past suicidal thinking, symptoms, substance use, domestic violence, etc. is essential. Keeping with the above example, it is more responsible to say, "Do you have any history of thinking about suicide, or have you ever attempted it?" This ideally is followed up with, "Have you had any thoughts about hurting yourself today?"

Another example I see with supervisees regards asking about patients' drug use. The patient may admit to smoking marijuana, for instance, and the therapist's follow-up is, "Nothing else?" This might *seem* like this patient is being asked to divulge any other substance abuse history. However, it is much more thorough to deliberately question, "OK, marijuana. Have you been using any other substances (for which it is a good idea to include nicotine, inhalants, caffeine, and anabolic steroids), or do you have a history of using substances other than marijuana?" Following such a deliberate line of questioning will help avoid missing important information.

Get Descriptions

If someone complains of depression, a therapist might run down a list of depressive symptoms to which the patient can answer "yes/no". As noted in earlier chapters, diagnosis is not a process of checking off symptoms.

While reviewing a list of diagnostic criteria with a patient, or using a standardized symptom checklist could seem an airtight approach to diagnosis, it must be taken into account that symptoms aren't necessarily contextualized. An ADHD checklist measure, for instance, might indicate a child possesses clinically significant restlessness, is easily distracted, has low frustration tolerance, and can be irritable. While this package is indicative of ADHD, it's also telltale of generalized anxiety disorder, trauma, and even depression. Thus, symptoms require descriptive discussions for contextualization and differential diagnosis. Asking for details allows the therapist to get a sense of the quality of the symptom(s).

Further, if someone has an agenda, as in forensic populations, and wants to make themselves look as impaired as possible, an action called malingering, they'll answer "yes" to everything. Conversely, some, like in hospital settings, if they want to be discharged, might answer "no" to everything to try to make themselves seem stable.

To gain a more accurate clinical picture, therapists might consider a more curious approach to asking about presenting symptoms/complaints. A therapist could begin, "Depression is a different experience for different people. What's it like for you?" Sometimes the patient has a hard time putting an experience into words. I often encounter this when interviewing people with anxiety. They initially say, "I don't know I just *feel* nervous a lot."

In these situations, it helps to ask, "If I was to watch you when you're nervous, what would I be noticing?" Or, perhaps, "I'd like you to give me an inside-out tour of anxiety. When that's happening, what are you feeling with your body? What's on your mind?" This kind of questioning can be tailored to any concern, from people complaining about cycling moods, to trauma reactions, to relationship complications.

Should follow-up inquiries be required, using the examples of depression or anxiety, which include sleep and appetite changes, if the patient didn't mention these, they can be asked, "What has your sleep and appetite been like?" and then asking for details as needed.

One can see how this line of symptom interviewing not only provides the therapist with a richer view of the patients' experience, but can also weed out malingering. This is because only someone who is truly experiencing a mental health disorder is likely to have answers congruent to diagnostic criteria.

Pay Attention to Pertinent Negatives

Therapists must not only inquire about what symptoms are present. It is just as important to be mindful of what *is not* present. A therapist's diagnostic work is more conclusive and credible if they show they considered differential diagnoses, through observing for pertinent negatives. This means looking for what can't immediately be seen in order to avoid a biased diagnosis. This practice shows the provider thoroughly investigated to rule out alternative and/or additional diagnoses (Siegel, 2020).

Early in a therapist's career, making sure one covers the basic diagnostic categories in an interview is a good starting point. Evaluating for anxiety, affective, psychotic, trauma-related, and psychosomatic disorders can help build a foundation on which to cultivate more sophisticated diagnostic skills, including considering personality disorders.

To illustrate, imagine a therapist meets with someone who complains of anxiety in the form of panic attacks. To gain a clear clinical picture, during their evaluation the therapist should not just ask about panic. Ideally, it should be assessed if the person has experienced other anxieties like phobias, chronic worry as in generalized anxiety disorder, or always wonders if they have an illness like in illness anxiety disorder.

Further, it needs to be investigated if mood problems, both depressive or bipolar in nature, or symptoms of psychosis are present. It is also helpful to inquire about psychosomatic symptoms such as sensory deficits, seizures, or pain for which doctors have been unable to any physical cause. Any of these could be the root of, or somehow be contributing to, the presenting panic. Someone might panic about hallucinatory activity, or being preoccupied with having a serious medical disease. Resolving these issues would be important in the treatment planning to ultimately resolve the panic attacks.

Another illustration is if someone clearly presents with depression, it's important to inquire about manic or hypomanic experiences. This is because the "up" phase of bipolar disorders, especially hypomania, often is not complained about because the person feels good. It's useful to ask, "Have you ever had the exact opposite experience of how you feel lately? Like days or weeks of feeling energized, didn't need to sleep much, were extra-talkative and social?" If so, asking them to describe the experience can assist in considering if it is part of bipolar mood cycling.

Treating bipolar disorder can be more complicated than unipolar depression, and it would inform treatment planning. Checking to see if mania/hypomania has ever been present is the pertinent negative investigation.

"None Reported" Doesn't Cut It

Another hazard is being content that something does not exist because the patient didn't report it. Clinical documentation is riddled with "none reported." It is a therapist's job as a diagnostic detective to ask *all* the relevant questions that could contribute to the current picture. If they do not, it could also open them up to liability.

To illustrate, imagine a patient arriving for help with depression. Given this is their chief complaint, and they didn't mention any hallucinatory activity, nor appear psychotic in their interview, in the documentation it is noted "no hallucinations reported." A couple of weeks later, the patient attempts suicide, acting on command hallucinations. In the hospital, they're asked how long the hallucinations have been occurring, and they say, "months." If the patient/family is litigious, and their attorney obtains the therapist's records, they could allege negligence after seeing "no hallucinations reported" in paperwork from two weeks earlier.

Upon questioning the attorney could inquire, "My client says their hallucinations began months ago. Two weeks ago, you documented that no hallucinations were reported. Did you ask?" The therapist's answer would confirm the lack of inquiry. Their attorney could then leverage, "Isn't it part of a basic mental status evaluation to ask about a wide range of symptoms, including hallucinations?" The attorney could then try to make a case that their client wouldn't have attempted suicide if that therapist had known about the hallucinations and intervened.

Though such a scenario is unlikely, it is possible, and doing anything to limit liability is good practice for therapist and patient. Limiting liability is addressed in detail in Chapter 45. If nothing else, asking directly about all clinically-relevant material and symptoms provides a better understanding of the patient's experience and shapes intervention.

Aside from not asking about symptoms, other areas prone to "none reported" are medical issues and medication side-effects. As will be seen in

Chapter 26, general medical conditions can figure significantly in psychological suffering, and therapists can be the first line of defense in recognizing side-effects that might prove detrimental.

Asking about all clinically-relevant material and documenting the patient's responses protects everyone involved.

Reference

Siegel, M.D. (2020, July 12). Notes on notes. Yale School of Medicine. https://medicine.yale.edu/news-article/notes-on-notes

Chapter 26

Always Consider Medical Mimicry

In the hundreds of diagnostic assessments I've read over the years, perhaps the most overlooked diagnostic consideration is that the patient's presentation is caused, or at least exacerbated by, a general medical condition. In fact, researchers (Gleason· 2015; McKee & Brahm, 2016; Welch & Carson, 2018) stress the necessity to consider whether a general medical condition is responsible for psychiatric symptoms.

This is so important that in the *DSM* many diagnoses have a criterion to remind practitioners to keep vigilant that: "The disturbance is not attributable to the effects of a substance... or another medical condition." Further, at the end of many diagnostic categories in the *DSM*, there is listed a diagnostic code reserved for just such occasions: "Due to Another Medical Condition."

How Medical Etiology Gets Overlooked

"Due to Another Medical Condition" is in acknowledgment of the fact that general medical/physiological complications can mimic mental health conditions. It is not that the person isn't psychologically suffering, but that the symptoms are physically driven and require physician intervention, not a therapist. This does not mean a therapist can't also be helpful, as the patient might be found to have a significant physical illness that holds meaning and conflicts that need emotional navigation.

Over the years, two reasons for this being overlooked have consistently surfaced (Smith, 2021). The first is, "I forgot about physical possibilities." This is understandable, especially for newer therapists, given mental health professionals are largely trained to see patients' problems through a psychogenic lens.

The second reason is that practitioners seem to feel they are overstepping a boundary if medical conditions enter the discussion. Despite this, I have yet to see a rule that says non-medical practitioners cannot address the possibility that a mental health diagnosis is caused, or exacerbated, by a general

DOI: 10.4324/9781032631400-30

medical condition. Therapists are not diagnosing or treating a physical problem. Those actions are, or course, forbidden, barring the appropriate medical degree. A therapist asking about medical complications is simply considering what might be contributing to the patient's psychological suffering. In fact, it would be unethical if therapists did not consider medical etiology. Trying to use talk therapy to manage something that needs a physician's intervention is neglectful.

To illustrate the second point, when patients complain of panic symptoms, I ask if they have diabetes or if the symptoms seem to occur around mealtimes. While not the norm, sometimes they have answered in the affirmative and I suggest they visit an endocrinologist. More than once, symptoms were deemed to be from insulin problems. If I tried to apply panic interventions for an insulin problem, the patient would be coming to sessions week after week without progress, all the while their medical condition likely worsening.

Some other illustrations of medical mimicry include hypothyroidism, low iron, and Lyme Disease causing depressive symptoms; hyperthyroidism causing bipolar-like symptoms; metabolic, autoimmune diseases, and infections causing psychosis; and respiratory or neurological illnesses leading to anxiety symptoms.

Perhaps some of the most interesting cases of medical conditions disguised as psychological problems are pediatric autoimmune neuropsychiatric disorders associated with streptococci (PANDAS), and anti-NMDA encephalitis due to a teratoma.

PANDAS occurs in children who have had frequent strep infections. Here, the strep infection does not just affect the throat, but may enter the brain. Antibodies rush in to fight it, not only destroying the bacteria, but also the brain tissue (Columbia, 2015). This is correlated with sudden onset of aggression and impulsivity, vocal or motor tics like in Tourette's Syndrome, and repetitious behaviors and obsessions as in OCD (Swedo et al., 2015; Thienemann et al., 2017). Thankfully, antibiotics often help, and some children's tonsils are removed as a long-term solution. In people with actual OCD or Tourette's Syndrome, strep infections may exacerbate them.

The second condition, believed to be quite rare, is inflammation of the brain related to a teratoma. Teratomas are unusual tumors, often found on an ovary, consisting of various tissues including bone, teeth, and hair. Initial symptoms can include seizures and other neurological problems, but psychotic and manic symptoms are usually prominent (Yen et al., 2012). Journalist Susana Cahalan's memoir, *Brain on Fire* (2012) details the vexing journey from evaluation to recovery from this bizarre condition. It also sheds light on the importance of quick medical evaluation in unusual psychiatric presentations, discussed further in Chapter 27.

References

Cahalan, S. (2012). *Brain on fire: My month of madness*. Simon & Schuster.
Columbia University. (2015, December 15). How recurrent strep A infection affects the brain: Newly discovered route by which immune cells reach the brain may underline an autoimmune neuropsychiatric disorder in children. https://www.cuimc.columbia.edu/news/how-recurrent-strep-infections-affect-brain
Gleason, O.C. (2015). Introduction: The connection between medical illness and psychiatric disorders. *Psychiatric Times, 32*(5). https://www.psychiatrictimes.com/view/introduction-connection-between-medical-illness-and-psychiatric-disorders
McKee, J. & Brahm, N. (2016). Medical mimics: Differential diagnostic considerations for psychiatric symptoms. *The Mental Health Clinician, 6*(6), 289–296. doi:10.9740/mhc.2016.11.289
Smith, A.D. (2021, May 22). Tips for diagnostic accuracy: Consider medical mimicry: Navigating medical conditions masquerading as primary psychopathology. *Psychology Today*. https://www.psychologytoday.com/us/blog/and-running/202105/tips-diagnostic-accuracy-rule-out-medical-etiology
Swedo, S.E., Seidlitz, J., Kovacevic, M., Latimer, M.E., Hommer, R., Lougee, L., & Grant, P. (2015). Clinical presentation of pediatric autoimmune neuropsychiatric disorders associated with streptococcal infections in research and community settings. *Journal of Child and Adolescent Psychopharmacology, 25*(1), 26–30. doi:10.1089/cap.2014.0073
Thienemann, M., Murphy, T., Leckman, J., Shaw, R., Williams, K., Kapphahn, C., Frankovich, J., Geller, D., Berstein, G., Chang, K., Elia, J., & Swedo, S. (2017). Clinical management of pediatric acute-onset neuropsychiatric syndrome: Part I – psychiatric and behavioral interventions. *Journal of Child and Adolescent Psychopharmacology, 27*(7), 566–573. http://doi.org/10/1089/cap.2016.0145
Yen, L.K., Hsing, F.T., Ming, C. L., Chien, H. L., & Yen, K. Y. (2012). Anti-NMDA receptor encephalitis with the initial presentation of psychotic mania. *Journal of Clinical Neuroscience, 19*(6), 896–898. https://doi.org/10.1016/j.jocn.2011.10.006
Welch, K.A. & Carson, A.J. (2018). When psychiatric symptoms reflect medical conditions. *Clinical Medicine (London), 18*(1), 80–87. doi:10.7861/clinmedicine.18-1-80

Chapter 27

How to Evaluate for Medical Mimicry

Many people are referred to psychotherapy by their primary care physician. They have a clean bill of physical health, but have anxiety, mood, or sleep issues, or other problems that are deemed psychological. Barring this "pre-evaluation," while therapists are not physicians, it is not difficult to ascertain if current psychological symptoms could be influenced by a physiological complication and need referral for medical assessment. Therapists will find it helpful to keep the following items in mind (Smith, 2021).

Are There Any Medical Complications Present?

Ask if the person has historical or current medical complications. If so, did their psychological/behavioral symptoms seem to coincide with the development of the medical problem? Consider the case of Penny.

Penny met with her therapist, Dr H, for an initial evaluation. She complained, "This may sound weird, but I've been feeling displaced from my body, and that everything isn't quite real even though I know it is." She said it had been happening for the past several months leading up to her appointment. Dr H knew that Penny was describing depersonalization, a form of dissociative disorder. Knowing that dissociation symptoms are usually associated with trauma or drug abuse, Dr H asked Penny about these matters, which she denied any history of.

While taking her medical history, Dr H discovered Penny had been experiencing significant headaches for two years, which had worsened over the past six months. She had not met with a physician because she was afraid that she would be instructed to take pain killers. Noting that Penny's depersonalization symptom onset coincided with the worsening headaches, Dr H referred Penny to a neurologist, who diagnosed her with migraines and confirmed her psychiatric symptoms were due to this.

It's not unusual for patients with neurological conditions like migraines and seizures to experience dissociation symptoms (Sengul et al., 2018; Saçmaci et al., 2020) and perceptual disturbances like hallucinations (Sacks, 2013).

DOI: 10.4324/9781032631400-31

Penny's diagnosis was recorded: unspecified dissociative disorder due to migraine with depersonalization features.

Note the "unspecified" that is necessary if diagnosing based on the *DSM-5 TR*. This is because, despite acknowledgment in criterion for depersonalization/derealization disorder that it must be ruled out that symptoms aren't caused by substances or general medical conditions, there is no dissociative disorder due to another medical condition category in the dissociative disorders section of the *DSM* (American Psychiatric Association, 2022).

Chances are, in a case like Penny's, care from a neurologist would be helpful in reducing the headaches and thus the depersonalization. Psychotherapy may indeed still be required to help Penny cope with living with migraines, and learning to lower stress in her life, given it is often correlated with migraines.

A History Devoid of Similar Symptoms or Likely Contributors

Is there a lack of personal or family history of psychological problems similar to the patient's complaints, and no recent psycho-social stressor that may have influenced the symptoms? Alex's case presents a good example.

Alex, a 20-year-old sophomore university student with no psychiatric history, presented for treatment of depression that settled in over a couple of weeks. He told his therapist, Annie, "Life is good, I don't get why I'm feeling this way." Reassuring Alex that it could be just a phase, Annie set to work providing Alex with coping skills and some therapy homework. When Alex returned the next week, Annie noticed an alarming increase in Alex's fatigue, irritability, loss of appetite, and concentration problems.

After reviewing the case with a supervisor, Annie encouraged Alex to visit the university health center, where a physician's assistant ordered blood work. Alex learned he was positive for Lyme Disease, not something likely to change with psychotherapy. After initiating antibiotics, Annie noticed that Alex's depressive fog began to lift, and he soon resumed his usual "life is good" demeanor.

Lyme Disease, a neuropsychiatric condition caused by tick bites, is a well-known culprit for mimicking depression (Fallon & Nields, 1994; Bransfield, 2018). Alex's mental health diagnosis would be documented: depressive disorder due to Lyme Disease, with major depressive disorder features.

Is the Symptom Presentation Very Unusual?

If the patient's symptom presentation includes the following bullet points, physical examination should be immediately suggested:

- Was there a very rapid/acute symptom onset, especially in the absence of any previous experience of the symptoms?

- Do symptoms inexplicably come and go?
- Was the age of onset unusual? It would be strange, for instance, for someone to develop symptoms of ADHD, bipolar disorder, or OCD in their 40s.
- Are the symptoms themselves exceptional? For example, is someone experiencing tactile, olfactory, or gustatory hallucinations? These are not so common in psychogenic psychosis (Birnie et al., 2018). These types of hallucinations, particularly in the absence of any verified history of psychosis-related diagnoses, can indicate an underlying medical cause, especially a tumor, infection, or head injury (Cleveland Clinic, 2022; Graff-Radford, 2022).

The case of Bess illustrates the importance of paying attention to the above clues. Bess, a 35-year-old, single, working mother, sought therapy because she noticed a new moodiness about herself. She had never required previous mental health care. Although she had some stress in her life, this was not like the irritability she usually felt when under pressure. All of a sudden, she found herself fluctuating daily between feeling a lethargic sadness that would randomly give way to feeling giddy and restless. She was never totally down, nor out of control, but complained of feeling like a rapidly undulating rollercoaster.

At first glance, Dr H, an experienced practitioner, thought Bess might have a bipolar spectrum disorder called cylcothymia. Though onset is usually much earlier, it's not unheard of to surface in someone's 30s. Dr H was concerned, however, at how fast Bess's symptoms arose and the rapidity with which they fluctuated. It was not typical of bipolar presentations, even cyclothymia, where symptoms chronically shift every few days.

At the end of their first session Dr H explained his observation to Bess, and asked if he could speak with her primary care physician to explain his concern. Upon medical examination, doctors discovered that Bess had a tumor on her pituitary gland, influencing her moods. Bess's diagnosis would be: bipolar disorder due to pituitary tumor, with features of cyclothymia.

For Bess, the tumor influenced a dysfunctional pattern of hormones, which are highly correlated with mood (Mondimore, 2014), to be released. The first line of treatment was surgery, not psychiatric medications and therapy.

Learning what medical conditions might mimic the diagnosis a therapist considers is another step towards strengthening their diagnostic capability. The therapist may not be a medical professional, but asking if the patient has medical conditions is not simply perfunctory information gathering. It can lead to their psychological relief and may even save a life.

References

American Psychiatric Association. (2022). Dissociative disorders. In *Diagnostic and statistical manual of mental disorders* (5th ed., text rev.).

Birnie, K.I., Stewart, R., & Kolliakou, A. (2018). Recorded atypical hallucinations in psychotic and affective disorders and associations with non-benzodiazepine hypnotic use: The South London and Maudsley Case Register. *British Journal of Medicine Open, 8*(9). https://bmjopen.bmj.com/content/8/9/e025216

Bransfield, R.C. (2018). Neuropsychiatric Lyme borreliosis: An overview with a focus on a specialty psychiatrist's clinical practice. *Healthcare, 6*(3). https://doi.org/10.3390/healthcare6030104

Cleveland Clinic. (2022, August 9). Formication. *Health Symptoms.* https://my.clevelandclinic.org/health/symptoms/23960-tactile-hallucinations-formication

Fallon, B.A. & Nields, J.A. (1994). Lyme disease: A neuropsychiatric illness [Abstract]. *American Journal of Psychiatry, 151*(11), 1571–1583. https://doi.org/10.1176/ajp.151.11.1571

Graff-Radford, J. (2022, June 21). Phantosmia: What causes olfactory hallucinations? https://www.mayoclinic.org/diseases-conditions/temporal-lobe-seizure/expert-answers/phantosmia/faq-20058131

Mondimore, F.M. (2014). *Bipolar Disorder: A guide for patients and families* (3rd ed.). Johns Hopkins University Press.

Sacks, O. (2013). *Hallucinations.* Vintage Books.

Saçmaci. H., Cengiz, G.F., & Aktürk, T. (2020). Impact of dissociative experiences in migraine and its close relationship with osmophobia [Abstract]. *Neurological Research, 42*(7), 529–536. doi:10.1080/01616412.2020.1753417

Sengul Y., Sengul H.S., & Tunç A. (2018). Psychoform and somatoform dissociative experiences in migraine: Relationship with pain perception and migraine related disability. *Ideggyogyaszati Szemle Journal, 71* (11–12), 385–392. English. doi:10.18071/isz.71.0385.

Smith, A.D. (2021, May 29). Tips for accurate mental health diagnosis: Four unusual clues to consider. *Psychology Today.* https://www.psychologytoday.com/us/blog/and-running/202105/tips-accurate-mental-health-diagnosis-four-unusual-clues-consider

Chapter 28

How to Discuss Diagnoses with Patients

Providing patients with their diagnosis is considered a critical part of treatment (Outram et al., 2014). In 2022, for instance, the organization Bipolar UK reported that 84 percent of bipolar disorder sufferers said that knowing their diagnosis was "helpful or very helpful" in taking control of their life.

It's easy to see how this seemingly simple action validates and explains symptoms and helps set the stage for treatment. Imagine, for example, someone with a problem they have never encountered and they feel they're losing their mind. Understanding that others have experienced it, too, and thus it is likely something treatable, would clearly be of benefit.

Providing the diagnosis helps sufferers not feel so isolated, along with learning about treatment, which can instill hope and investment in the therapy.

Further, knowing one's diagnosis can protect the patient's rights. In effect, as a consumer of mental health services, patients should be able to self-advocate and ascertain if they are receiving proper care for that condition, or ask for a second opinion. Others might be wrongly self-diagnosed or misdiagnosed. It's only ethical to explain to someone, who believes, for example, they have schizophrenia based on perceiving their hypervigilance as paranoia and flashbacks as hallucinations, that they are in fact experiencing PTSD.

Talking about diagnoses cannot be "by the way" commentary if therapists are to put patients at ease and foster curiosity about their mental health, which can accelerate treatment.

To be effective, therapists need to present a digestible understanding of diagnoses and what it means for patients' care. This means that practitioners must be well-versed in diagnoses, and not just the symptoms, but the dynamics of the condition. The following five examples (Smith, 2021) illustrate how to pull these components together for therapeutically-constructive dialogue about diagnoses.

DOI: 10.4324/9781032631400-32

Borderline Personality Disorder

Steve called for an appointment because of anxiety and irritation around his inability to maintain successful romantic relationships. After learning about his internal experiences in relationships, behavioral patterns, and long-standing relationship turmoil, it was clear Steve met criteria for borderline personality disorder (BPD).

I summarized, "This has been ongoing since middle school, and is getting more intense for you. Lately it seems you just have to have someone to be with, or you feel really empty, sometimes even becoming physically numb it's so bad. When relationships do happen, they're intense, short-lived scenarios ending in blow ups or people saying they feel smothered by you. Does that all sound accurate?"

Steve sheepishly looked up and nodded; "What's wrong with me!? Why does everyone give me a hard time in relationships!?" he exclaimed. I began, "If it's any comfort, Steve, you're not alone. It's called borderline personality disorder." Familiar with the movie *Fatal Attraction*, he stared at me and fumed, "I'm turning into that psychotic wacko woman who ruined that guy's life!?" "Not so fast," I reassured him; "That was more like a Hollywood caricature for entertainment. Hollywood usually embellishes psychological problems."

Making the diagnosis relevant to Steve, I informed him, "Essentially, what borderline personality means is you have a lot of anxiety about relationships, and it makes them difficult to manage. If you perceive anything uncomfortable in the relationship, especially if you think the person might not like you and leave, it's frustrating. That frustration turns to anger, which can be intense, pushing people away. It's like making a self-fulfilling prophecy that no one likes you when that's not true. It's tough for them and you to handle that level of emotion. Things aren't dealt with constructively."

Moving forward, I finished, "Thankfully, we know that working on learning to be responsive and not reactive, and changing the lens relationships are seen through, people with BPD can do well and work towards the stable relationships they're seeking. If that sounds like something you'd like to explore with me, I can help with that."

Depersonalization/Derealization Disorder

Robin called for an appointment complaining of anxiety; "I've been panicky and feel out of sorts," he said. At his appointment, I asked him to describe the anxiety in detail, and when it began. Robin noted he would get panicky during spells of feeling he was living in a dream. "It's scary. I'm able to function but I feel like I'm removed from everyone and everything," Robin finished.

Expanding on his answer, Robin detailed that a few months earlier he tried marijuana for the first time and ever since had bouts of this dream state. He feared the drug experimentation altered the course of his life for the worse. Outside of trauma/stressors and some personality disorders, cannabis is a common culprit for unlocking dissociative states. When it was clear Robin was experiencing depersonalization/derealization disorder, my first inclination was to put him at ease.

"Great job explaining that experience to me," I told him. "I can definitely see why you've been anxious about it. Rest assured, though, you're not the first person to describe it." This piqued Robin's attention, as it was so outlandish to him, he figured he was the only person experiencing such a thing.

I continued, "You're experiencing what's called depersonalization-derealization disorder. This is a fancy way of saying things can seem surreal or even like out-of-body experiences. It's not unusual to develop the symptoms after major stressors or sometimes after using marijuana if it doesn't agree with you. I know it's scary to you, but the good news is, I can help you learn to manage it, and chances are, as that gets better, the panic will also subside. It's often exacerbated by stress, so keeping stress down, and learning to ground yourself to feel more in touch when it happens are key things we'll explore to get you back on track."

Generalized Anxiety Disorder

Calvin's wife encouraged him to see a therapist when she heard him grinding his teeth in his sleep. He sat on the couch, wringing his hands as he recounted years of worried thoughts and sleepless nights. "Calvin," I began, "believe it or not, that teeth grinding in your sleep isn't too uncommon. I've seen a lot of people who have a tendency to worry and feel on edge, like you've described. It's like it's hard to relax even in your sleep. I can see why you wake up a lot."

Calvin looked up, explaining, "I wake up and my jaw hurts sometimes. I'll probably get dental problems now. There's another bill I don't want!" His penchant for worry was palpable. "Hopefully it won't come to that," I acknowledged. "I'm glad your wife suggested you come in, because what you describe is something I've helped a lot of people out with. It's a kind of anxiety called generalized anxiety disorder. Essentially, worrying makes it hard to relax, or even focus sometimes. Have you heard of this?"

"No, but that about sums it up," said Calvin.

"There's a lot of people who experience this kind of worry. In today's world with all of the conflicts and world events, it seems it might be getting more common," I offered. "Considering that, there's a lot of focus in the therapy world on helping people learn to control those gnawing worries and learn to relax. Getting a better night's sleep can work wonders in itself. If this sounds like something you'd like to explore with me, I'm happy to assist."

Major Depressive Disorder

Alexis complained, "I've been in these funks, each one lasting longer." Tearfully, she continued, "A couple of times a year I crawl under a rock and wait for it to pass. It's tough with a family." Alexis felt crushed, with an air of hopelessness about her ever feeling stable again. Her history and presentation in the office aligned with recurrent major depressive disorder.

"Thanks for being so thorough about your background and letting me in on how you're currently feeling," I began. I continued, "From what you described and what I'm seeing, that 'funk' sounds like depression. In particular, what is called major depressive disorder." Alexis chimed in, "So 'major,' like 'big problem'? A black hole I'll keep getting pulled into?"

"Well, clearly it's been problematic, but it doesn't have to remain so. A lot of people experience it, so we know a lot about treatment," I replied. "'Major depression' is psychology speak for 'way beyond feeling blue,' and the symptoms significantly take away from your quality of life," I explained.

"The positive thing here," I continued, "is that by exploring and cultivating your strengths, learning to undercut the thoughts that contribute to the bad mood, and making lifestyle changes like diet and exercise habits, we usually gain control over the depression. Also, if you're interested, antidepressant medications often accelerate progress, too." Finishing, I offered, "Once you're feeling better, we work on prevention and learning to recognize signs an episode may be surfacing, so we can cut it off at the pass."

Schizophrenia

Dalia arrived with her family for an appointment after being discharged from a psychiatric hospitalization. Dalia said, "I saw on the discharge paperwork that the psychiatrist diagnosed me with schizophrenia. What do you think?" She added that she wondered if schizophrenia is accurate, and if it was really as debilitating as she had read.

"Glad you asked," I replied. "From what you and your family have told me, it seems that over the past year, you've had periods of being distracted by hearing voices and sometimes seeing and smelling things you weren't sure were there. Your family also described that you didn't seem very expressive anymore, and often wanted to be left alone, which historically was unlike you. Does that all sound accurate?" The family all nodded in agreement.

"It does sound like you experience schizophrenia," I continued. "To answer your other question, Dalia, schizophrenia is not always as dramatic as in the movies. Also, descriptions are often just a list of symptoms and don't necessarily give a good idea of what it all means."

Dalia asked, "So will that keep happening? I mean, I feel back to my old self for the most part now." "Schizophrenia is like other illnesses in that symptoms are more or less severe in some people and can come and go more or less often," I furthered. "It's not unusual for it to go into remission with treatment and people to resume a good quality of life. That doesn't mean the symptoms can't return, though."

"Well, what do we do about it?" followed up Dalia. I explained, "First, I'd like to say that it's a real positive that you received intensive intervention during the initial episode. That's correlated with better long-term outcomes. Part of what we do in therapy is help you and your family to be vigilant for *any* signs that symptoms might be returning. That way, we can get a handle on things faster and hopefully not require the hospital again. I've found that patients often like to begin by digesting the experience of schizophrenia and how it has affected them, and developing goals to fully reintegrate themselves in relationships, school, and work.

"What about if symptoms do start coming back?" Dalia asked. "Along the way, we'll definitely talk about managing the symptoms if they start to occur, and also address stress management, as we know prolonged stress can influence a return of symptoms. Lastly, outside of our work, you'll continue to meet with your psychiatrist, as we know medication is pretty helpful to keep symptoms from resurfacing."

Tips for Reviewing Diagnoses with Patients

1. For a constructive experience, discussing a diagnosis must be more than a comment (i.e., "I think your discomfort is major depression. Now, let's set up our next appointment...").
2. Being prepared to answer questions for the patient goes a long way in helping them understand their diagnosis and feel more hopeful about improving.
3. Become intimately familiar with more common diagnoses, and/or ones you may encounter in specialty settings. Then practice how you might convey the material in a compassionate and informative manner.
4. Don't just provide an explanation of a diagnosis. People will want to know what that means for treatment. Therapists ideally will convey information about treatability and what interventions might entail.
5. If the therapist isn't sure of what the diagnosis is yet, and the patient hasn't inquired, it's best to wait until details are clearer. Otherwise, they may become confused when it changes, especially if there are a few things to rule out. Perhaps worse, someone could go researching them all and create undue anxiety.

6. If the patient does inquire, but the diagnosis isn't yet clear, it's OK for the therapist to say it's not yet certain, as they are just getting to know them. Providing some observations would be appropriate, such as, "You and your child described they can have significant, sometimes destructive, reactions to seemingly minor frustrations, and they feel pretty bad about it afterwards. I'd like to get to know them more before saying for sure, but it can be indicative of an impulse control disorder. Believe it or not, it could also be a form of depression called disruptive mood dysregulation disorder."
7. For newer therapists still learning about differential diagnosis, it's always a good idea to review patients' diagnoses in supervision before disclosing them.

Discussing a diagnosis may be anxiety-provoking for therapist and patient alike. Framed in the ways discussed above, diagnostic disclosure doesn't have to be complicated. It can be a foundational, rapport-building discussion that provides not only relief in putting a name to the patient's struggle, but generate hope about managing it.

References

Bipolar UK, (2022, March). *Hidden in plain sight: A lived experience report by Bipolar UK* (p. 10). https://eprints.soton.ac.uk/457022/1/bpuk_lived_experience_report_march2022_final.pdf

Outram, S., Harris, G., Kelly, B., Cohen, M., Sandhu, H., Vamos, M., Levin, T.T., Landa, Y., Bylund-Lincoln, C.L., & Loughland, C. (2014). Communicating a schizophrenia diagnosis to patients and families: A qualitative study of mental health clinicians. *Psychiatric Services, 65*(4), 551–554. https://doi.org/10.1176/appi.ps.201300202

Smith, A.D. (2021, January 18). How to effectively discuss diagnosis with patients: Talking about diagnoses doesn't have to be an anxiety-provoking experience. *Psychology Today.* https://www.psychologytoday.com/us/blog/and-running/202101/how-effectively-discuss-diagnosis-patients

Suggested Steps to Formulate a Diagnostic Explanation for a Patient

The following questions will help the therapist collect the material required to formulate a user-friendly, respectful description:

What is the diagnosis I want to explain? _____

What are the diagnostic criteria?

_____

_____

How does this patient exhibit the above criteria, especially the defining characteristic (examples of their personal symptoms)?

_____

_____

_____

How would I describe this diagnosis in layperson's terms (thorough, but to the point)?*

_____

_____

_____

How does the diagnosis affect someone's functioning (using specific patient examples)?

_____

_____

_____

What can I explain about the prevalence of the diagnosis and how it is treated/my approach?

_____

_____

_____

Order of Operations for Explaining a Diagnosis

- <u>Diagnosis name:</u> "What you've described seems to be what is known as …"
- <u>Thumbnail sketch:</u> "Basically, what this means is …"
- <u>How it effects</u>: "People who experience this can struggle to/encounter hardships in …"
- <u>Check if they're following</u>: "Does this all make sense?"
- <u>Establishing treatability/How it's treated:</u> "What we know about treating X is that it can respond well to (e.g., treatment modalities, medications) … If you'd like to explore that with me, I can help."

*An idea of a condensed description for a diagnosis can be found in the introduction of the *DSM* chapter in which the diagnosis is included.

Section IV

Special Topics

Chapter 29

Interview, Don't Interrogate

Therapists spend a lot of time interviewing to gather information and provide feedback. Thus, one of a therapist's biggest assets is the ability to effectively relate and communicate. The term "interview" might bring to mind a formal, clearly delineated question-and-answer session. While this is not erroneous, it's not necessarily the most user-friendly conceptualization for therapist or patient. Ideally, the interview is more of a flowing conversational process; a discussion.

Sometimes, particularly during initial assessments and diagnostic interviews, feeling they'll forget what to ask, a therapist might seek reassurance from a question template, pointedly asking each question and moving on. Other times, the information gathering might be practiced as a routine round of questioning, rendering the patient feeling as if they are on an assembly line. This is a particular hazard in today's computerized, drop-down menu style assessment approach.

Interactions like these can lead to a rather dry and otherwise ineffective exchange, resulting in the patient, who already feels vulnerable, possibly thinking they are being cross-examined, raising their defenses. Cut and dry, yes/no answers could ensue. The conversation can also feel impersonal, not boding well for the therapeutic relationship. As noted in Chapter 25, descriptions are desirable!

If templates or questionnaires must be used, using them as a conversation guide, and not a checklist, can help facilitate more fruitful interactions. Create a new conversation for each patient.

To see the difference in the two manners of information gathering, imagine the scenario below.

An inmate at a correctional facility, placed on special observation for hallucinating, being depressed, and reporting suicidal thinking, was interviewed by a clinician. The following transpired:

Clinician: "Hi, I'm Tom and I'm meeting with you because you are on suicide watch."

DOI: 10.4324/9781032631400-34

Patient:	Nods.
Clinician:	I read in the officer's observation log that you were saying you heard voices behind the walls last night.
Patient:	*Stares.*
Clinician:	"Are you hearing voices today?"
Patient:	"Not right now."
Clinician:	"Do you think they're real when you hear them? What do they say?"
Patient:	"Of course they're real, I'm hearing them! It's like people stuck behind the wall trying to get out."
Clinician:	"Do they tell you to hurt yourself or others?"
Patient:	"I just told you what they sound like!"
Clinician:	"I need you to tell me if they say to hurt yourself or others."
Patient:	"What are you talking to me for!?"
Clinician:	"I need to assess how you are to see if you need to stay on suicide watch. I need you to answer some questions for me to do this."
Patient:	"Fine, if it'll get me out of here!"
Clinician:	"How do you sleep?"
Patient:	"I can't because of the voices in the wall."
Clinician:	"Are you eating normally?"
Patient:	"I didn't eat dinner or breakfast."
Clinician:	"Do you feel depressed, angry, bitter, anxious, manic, or hypomanic?"
Patient:	"I'm angry, I don't know. It's stressful."
Clinician:	"Are you delusional?
Patient:	"No."
Clinician:	"Do you hear any voices?"
Patient:	"I already told you about that."
Clinician:	"Are you disorganized?
Patient:	"I can organize myself."
Clinician:	"Do you feel like harming yourself or someone else right now?"
Patient:	"No. Last night I did because of the talking behind the walls, I couldn't sleep!"
Clinician:	"OK, you can go back to your cell."

While a fabricated example, it actually reflects some exchanges I witnessed when supervising co-workers struggling with clinical effectiveness. The hypothetical patient, already in a bad space, was not at all comfortable with the interaction, and, being defensive, provided little information. It was especially troubling that mental status questions were read verbatim from a form, particularly about things that should have been learned from observation. For example, a delusional person doesn't know they're delusional; the delusion is their reality.

Now, let's reflect on how the interview could be different if it was more conversational.

Clinician:	"Hi, I don't think we've met before. I'm Tom from mental health services. I wanted to check in on you. The officer said you were having a hard time last night. What's been happening?"
Patient:	"Ugh, this is so stressful! I don't know what was going on, I told them I was hearing voices and it was making me nuts! Then they put me on suicide watch."
Clinician:	"That does sound stressful if that's what's happening. That's all you said and they put you on suicide watch?"
Patient:	"I said I wanted to die. I was awake for four nights. Last night I finally felt I was safe enough to get some rest, then the people behind the wall started yelling."
Clinician:	"Four nights is a long time to go without rest. I couldn't help noticing you said you finally felt safe enough to be able to rest. What did you mean by 'safe enough?'"
Patient:	"They moved my cell and I was away from the big window, so the satellites wouldn't be able to get me in their view while I slept."
Clinician:	"Satellites? What about them?"
Patient:	"Since I've been here, my accuser's lawyer has been trying to send messages to me that will infiltrate my ability to think in the courtroom and make statements in their favor."
Clinician:	"No wonder you're stressed. Do those voices in the wall have anything to do with it?"
Patient:	"No. I don't think so, it just sounds like a crowded room with people yelling. I can only make out a word here and there."
Clinician:	"Did the voices ever say to do anything? Like tell you to hurt yourself, or tell you to harm anyone else?"
Patient:	"No. I've been so stressed! I'm so down. I couldn't care less about living at this point if this is how it is going to be!"

By not treating the interaction as a checklist, the exchange in this illustration was much more informative and consequently a more solid view of the patient's dilemma was gained.

Clearly, conversational interviewing uses a lot more of the attending skills discussed earlier, which are conducive to a patient being more forthcoming. In the second example, although the patient was experiencing a break with reality, the clinician understood it was real to them, and validated the patient's experiences instead of acting skeptical. This led to the patient being willing to share more, and the clinician could better gage how ill the patient was, which enables more accurate care.

Chapter 30

Try Not to be Alarmist

Therapists can spend a lot of time helping patients learn to be responsive and not so reactive, but may fall into the reaction trap themselves (Smith, 2021a). There are numerous scenarios that could give rise to feeling alarmed, but the following few examples illustrate the unintended effects of some well-intended, but potentially damaging, excitement.

A common anxiety-provoking situation for therapists is when patients report suicidal thinking (Michaud et al., 2021; Barzilay et al., 2020). Along with this, it isn't uncommon that a therapist over-reacts to a patients' report of suicidal thoughts (Hom et al., 2021; Knapp, 2022). If they call 911 in an "abundance of caution," it could be premature. This is because suicidal thoughts don't always lead to suicidal actions, there are often protective factors, and the patient agrees to safety planning. Calling 911 could unduly land them in a hospital, which may quickly discharge them after their own evaluation with a big bill and destroy the therapeutic relationship. What sort of trust could be maintained if such conclusions were jumped to? Perhaps the patient finally trusted the therapist enough to share such vulnerability and explore the matter, but were essentially punished for it.

Next, take a patient who has confessed to committing a serious crime they were never investigated for, or perhaps alerted the therapist that they were a suspect in an ongoing investigation. Even for people used to working in forensic environments, this could engender goose bumps if provided in a psychotherapy setting. Questions race through the mind of the therapist: "This isn't the person I thought they were. Are they a psychopath? Am I in danger?" "What do I say?" "Do I report this?"

A colleague once shared that a co-worker encountered such a scenario. In a state of near-panic, they pulled aside the others in the group practice, providing all the details except the patient's name, wondering what to do. While an alarming situation that required consultation, a co-worker could somehow be connected to victims, engendering conflict for them knowing the person came to their office. Further, it might raise concern about the patient proving dangerous at some time in the setting, making co-workers

DOI: 10.4324/9781032631400-35

more anxious, unsettled in their offices. Lastly, believe it or not, confessions of crimes have confidentiality parameters. It's advisable to consult with one's professional organization or consulting attorney supplied by the therapist's liability insurance provider in these situations.

Lastly, I once attended a conference on evaluating and treating juveniles with problematic sexual behaviors. One presenter, now an adult, discussed his history of seeking help for pedophilia when he was a teen. Pedophilia does not always equate to criminal, as many people with the problem realize it's not appropriate, don't want to hurt anyone, and want professional assistance (Smith, 2021b). However, pedophilia is so stigmatized that sufferers often avoid asking for help for fear of judgment or accusation. Thus, they suffer in silence, hoping they don't ever give in to their impulses.

As one might imagine, it must take a lot of fortitude to reveal such an issue to anyone. The presenter recounted his experience as a juvenile seeking assistance. They recalled feeling increasingly guilt-ridden and frustrated while sexually maturing, and wanted to try and resolve the strife to have healthy, satisfying romantic and sexual relationships. Believing therapists were supposed to be non-judgmental and create safe places for people to work out their troubles, he asked his mother to make an appointment because he was feeling anxious.

His mother began to bring him to the therapist's office and would wait in the lobby. After several sessions of getting comfortable with the therapist, he worked up the courage to explain that his anxiety related to trying to deal with his attraction to young children. The therapist's face, he recalled, took on a look of fear and disgust. A chasm expanded between the two as her warm demeanor subsided. The presenter recalled feeling like a worse person than he already berated himself for. Though it was only a few seconds, it seemed like days of discomfort with the therapist in that moment. When the therapist spoke, it wasn't regarding his experience and how they might be of help. Rather, they said, "I think I need to go get your mother."

Clearly, this therapist was not prepared to encounter such a situation and became alarmed. She did not listen to the patient's concern and only heard the pedophilic statement, losing sight of the fact that he was desperate for assistance. Even a brief exploration of the matter might have produced a more responsive interaction.

The alarm, however, created embarrassment and shame for the patient, and a ripple effect. His mother entered the room and the therapist explained the exchange to her. Parents worry about their children. The patient's mother was already concerned about her son reporting heightening anxiety, and now she learns he is "one of *those* people".

Finally, the therapist placed herself in perilous waters. The patient had good insight, had not harmed any children, did not want to, and wanted to keep it that way. No imminent risk was at hand. Not only codes of ethics, but state laws, dictate that parents are not globally privileged to their children's material. While it is standard practice for therapists to discuss the child's progress, for example, it is not standard practice to divulge their innermost secrets unless there is a risk to themselves or others.

Invariably, therapists will encounter situations that make them uncomfortable, sometimes alarmingly so. Regardless of the material, it is a therapist's duty to work to remain composed and responsive in order to be effective. While it would be impossible to predict everything that might encourage reactivity, knowing one's triggers or the situations in which there is anticipation of apprehension can help.

Clearly, one wouldn't focus on a population, such as those most prone to self-injury/suicide, if the topic is too unsettling. Despite this, surprising incidents can arise, as illustrated in the pedophilic concern example.

Given the not-uncommon occurrence of therapist anxiety and emotional reactivity in the office, enhancing therapists' mindfulness has been a topic of research (Shamoon et al., 2017; Macdonald & Muran, 2021). In what is perhaps just an alternative lens on countertransference, the idea of the "self-as-the-therapist" (Durtschi & McClellan,2010), sometimes termed "person-of-the-therapist" (Aponte & Kissel, 2017), has brought a renewed interest in therapist experiences in the session, which readers might find helpful to research.

If therapists feel prone to any session anxiety or reactivity that can't be addressed in supervision, or they're seeking heightened self-awareness to enhance sessions, training on the topic is available. Also, studying basic countertransference can be a good starting point to learn to monitor the self in sessions for more productive therapeutic outcomes.

Resources

Readers wishing to better understand how to explore personal concerns that may arise and influence therapy sessions are invited to read Nancy McWilliams' *Psychoanalytic Psychotherapy* (2004, Guilford). While the book is aimed at analytical therapists, McWilliams' exploration of transference and countertransference is applicable to most practitioners.

References

Aponte, H.J. & Kissil, K. (2017). The person of the therapist training model. In Lebow, A. Chambers & D.C. Breunlin (Eds), *Encyclopedia of Couple and Family Therapy* (pp.1--8). https://www.researchgate.net/publication/313850576_The_Person_of_the_Therapist_Training_Model

Barzilay, S., Schuck, A., Bloch-Elkouby, S., Yaseen, Z.S., Haws, M., Rosenfield, P., Foster, A., & Galynker, I. (2020). Associations between clinicians' emotional responses, therapeutic alliance, and patient suicidal ideation [Abstract]. *Depression and Anxiety*, *37*, 214–223. https://doi.org/10.1002/da.22973

Durtschi, J. A., & McClellan, M. K. (2010). The self of the therapist. In L. Hecker (Ed.), *Ethics and professional issues in couple and family therapy* (pp. 155–169). Routledge/Taylor & Francis Group.

Hom, M.A., Bauer, B.W., Stanley, I.H., Boffa, J.W., Stage, D.L., Capron, D.W., Schmidt, N.B., & Joiner, T.E. (2021). Suicide attempt survivors' recommendations for improving mental health treatment for attempt survivors. *Psychological Services*, *18*(3), 365–376. doi:10.1037/ser0000415

Knapp, S. (2022). Helping psychotherapists adopt productive responses to suicidal patients. *Psychotherapy Bulletin*, *57*(2), 6–10.

Macdonald, J, & Muran, C.J. (2021). The reactive therapist: The problem of interpersonal reactivity in psychological therapy and the potential for a mindfulness-based program focused on "mindfulness-in-relationship" skills for therapists [Abstract]. *Journal of Psychotherapy Integration*, *31*(4), 452–467. https://doi.org/10.1037/int0000200

Michaud, L., Greenway, K.T., Corbeil, S., Bourquin, C., & Richard-Devantoy, S. (2021). Countertransference towards suicidal patients: A systematic review. *Current Psychology*, *42*, 416–430. https://link.springer.com/article/10.1007/s12144-021-01424-0

Shamoon, Z.A., Lappan, S., & Blow, A. (2017). Managing anxiety: A therapist common factor. *Contemporary Family Therapy*, *39*, 43–53. https://doi.org/10.1007/s10591-016-9399-1

Smith, A.D. (2021a, July 7). The unrecognized side of pedophilia: Those seeking help may nonetheless be tarred and feathered. *Psychology Today*. https://www.psychologytoday.com/us/blog/and-running/202107/the-unrecognized-side-pedophilia

Smith, A.D. (2021b, August 11). In therapy: Listen better by mastering your presence – effective listening requires some physical etiquette. *Psychology Today*. https://www.psychologytoday.com/us/blog/and-running/202108/in-therapy-listen-better-mastering-your-presence

Chapter 31

Be Familiar with the Defenses

If there is one topic that I wish I had learned more about in my training, it's the psychological defenses.

Aside from the ubiquitous *denial* and *repression*, I had no idea of the expanse, and relevance, of the palette of psychological defense mechanisms. Occasionally hearing terms like "compartmentalization" or "omnipotent control," I figured they were just anachronistic, Victorian analytic jargon that seeped in.

Little did I know that these, and other common terms like "splitting" and "acting out," usually conveyed as nothing more than behavioral descriptors, were defensive maneuvers that, if paid attention to, have much to do with understanding patients' struggles and how to intervene. Realizing that these vexing dynamics were patients' subconscious mitigators of psychic distress (Vaillant, 2011) helped me cultivate further patience, empathy, and curiosity that served me well in years to come.

As I matured in the field and my interest in personality, where defenses are discussed at length, evolved, I discovered the role of subconscious defense mechanisms was inseparable from how people experienced life and must be studied. Defense plays such a significant role in relating, and personality pathology is, at its core, disturbance of effective relating. This is not to say that psychological defenses are always somehow pathological. Unfortunately, as noted by the pre-eminent psychoanalyst Nancy McWilliams (2011), hearing that someone is defensive seems universally understood as a criticism. Rather, like most things, it is where the defensiveness falls on a continuum of severity and pervasiveness.

Denial, for instance, can be an adaptive defense to maintain integrity and persist in the face of difficulty. Consider the sleep-deprived mother of a toddler and newborn, whose husband, normally a partner in duties, is away on business. The mother is so sleep-deprived, she might literally forget what day it is, but insists she is fine. If she heeded the summons for extended rest, the children might not be sufficiently attended to and the household fall

DOI: 10.4324/9781032631400-36

into a dysfunctional state. Thus, the denial is a short-term, adaptive defense against the overwhelming anxiety of assuming all the responsibilities.

Denial becomes maladaptive when someone consistently refuses to acknowledge a problem despite its fallout. A classic example of pervasive denial is someone with an addiction who, in an attempt to "defend against painful aspects of external reality" (Paulhus et al., 1997), insists they function well and do not need rehabilitation.

Without understanding this as defense against fragility, it can be easy to see the person as simply not wanting to quit abusing the substance and thus, perhaps, "treatment resistant." However, a therapist who realizes the denial is not a conscious action, as true defenses are not (Shahrokh & Hales, 2003), might work with the person in a manner that will not further raise the defense, but rather guide them to insight and change contemplation. Therapists often blame patients for lack of progress (Frances & Goldfried, 2023), but, stepping back, it is easy to see how the therapist could be at fault in such a situation and, in their own defensive maneuver, blame the patient.

Delving more into the world of defenses it became clear to me just how pervasive they can be and the role they play in many diagnoses. My sense of empathy for people with difficult characteristics grew as I understood they acted out of a dire need for self-protection based on how, given early suffering, they learned to relate to the world. This is no better illustrated than with the defense of splitting in borderline personality disorder (BPD).

Those suffering from BPD more often than not encountered an early sense of abandonment/rejection. Branded by the pain of this experience, they find themselves desperately seeking attachment and gestures indicating that they matter or are acceptable. Upon forming a relationship, for instance, they are prone to place extensive value on the other party, as if they're a savior. However, so heightened is the rejection sensitivity of those with BPD that almost anything can be misconstrued as a sign of pending dismissal. Upon sensing this alarm, those with BPD are prone to sabotage the relationship by then casting the savior as a villain, extensively devaluing them. The pendulum of splitting swings with seismic force, for those with BPD have a penchant to experience things as all good or all bad (Mondimore & Kelly, 2011).

On the surface, this may seem ironic and vexing, provided they are impulsively repelling that which they seek. However, understood as a defense, this act of splitting is a pre-eminent strike. In the view of the person with BPD, they beat the other party to the punch; "You didn't abandon *me*, it was *I* who abandoned you," thus assuaging the ego. Despite the damage it accrues, it remains a favorite tactic for its potency in reducing anxiety and maintaining self-esteem in the face of threats to self-image (McWilliams, 2011).

Readers may be more familiar with another form of splitting, that is, as an act of interpersonal triangulation. Think of a child whose mother does not satisfy their desire for something, who in turn attempts to appeal to the father. They might vilify the mother in the process to get the father's sympathy and a favorable result. Perhaps they ask the father for what they want, who agrees, and the child returns to the mother saying, "Daddy said it's OK."

Anyone who has worked on inpatient psychiatric units or in institutions is probably familiar with how adults initiate this dynamic, too. This process might seem simply a method of achieving something tangible. However, what's more valuable to the patient, subconsciously, is the sense of acceptance they manufacture by generating a situation whereby one party, who perhaps disappointed them, is complained about to another in a manner that breeds sympathy and maybe even confrontation between the two. This is a satisfying display when one so craves the feeling of being rescued.

Another defense readers might be familiar with is "acting out." Acting out is a way of managing inner conflicts in a way that gets a lot of attention, as the disruptive behavior cannot be missed. Having worked in adult correctional institutions and juvenile courts for the past 20 years, whenever the term "acting out" is applied, it is seemingly with a derisive tone. I cannot help but feel that when I hear "S/he is acting out again," it's implied they are just being a difficult person who can control themselves *if they want to*. Be sure, however, acting out should not be reduced to a synonym for "bad behavior" (DiGiuseppe & Perry, 2021).

To continue, some people consciously cause a disturbance to get a need met, like an inmate looking to get moved to protective custody, or a kid wanting to get kicked out of class to avoid taking an exam. For others, it's more complex. I frequently meet with juveniles who are accused of acting out. They are described as easily dysregulated, argumentative, and destructive. More often than not these youth carry diagnoses of oppositional-defiant disorder (ODD) or disruptive mood dysregulation disorder (DMDD).

Upon evaluation, it's clear these children are depressed and anxious, perhaps traumatized. Their emotional landscape is complicated and painful, harboring significant emotional turmoil. Emotions can be difficult for adults to navigate, never mind children whose verbal capabilities are still evolving. Given the emotions require expressing, if verbalization is not possible, they must be acted out.

An acquaintance once explained to me that, while growing up, they, almost nightly, literally beat themselves. Upon reflection as a rehabilitated adult, they realized their self-hatred began much earlier than they could have imagined. They didn't understand why they did it at the time, adding to the already poor self-image, engendering the need to further punish themselves. Other examples of acting out include the hair-trigger, unsavory actions of people who "don't get their way," who get managed with limit setting and punitive measures by parents, school, or institutional staff. While individuals must be held accountable, encountering them in a "firm but fair" manner is likely to be more effective than finger-wagging. It may help therapists to conceptualize such referred patients as people whose descriptive ability handicap leads to a situation where actions literally speak louder than words.

Limit setting and punishment alone are akin to high-volume distortion creating immediate "Turn it down!" reactions, when, if only the person could learn to communicate at a tolerable volume, others would hear them more clearly. With that in mind, therapists might find that focusing on the patient learning to identify conflicts and emotions and put into words what has been unspeakable is akin to volume control.

A final example of defenses that newer therapists might have heard of is "projection," which is the externalization of an inner conflict. Readers might be familiar with one variety of projection common in depression. Oftentimes depressed patients socially isolate. In therapy, it's revealed that the patient believes their friends just see them as disappointing, so why bother coming around? Upon exploration, they discover they are projecting their propensity for self-devaluation onto others, assuming others perceive them as they perceive themselves. It sometimes looks as if they say, "Others can't handle me," displacing the conflict onto others. In other words, "The problem is them, not me," once again assuaging the ego. Unfortunately, this can create a self-fulfilling prophecy in that, after enough refusals of social invites, friends stop contacting the person, making them really feel that nobody likes them, adding to a negative self-image and more depression.

Projection is also known to play a role in paranoia, from everyday experiences to psychotic delusions.

The word "paranoia" is derived from the Greek *para*, meaning "beyond" or "outside" and *noos,* meaning "the mind." Literally translated, we arrive at "outside the mind" (Smith, 2023). While various thought processes, like depressive rumination or intrusive thoughts of OCD are distracting, what differentiates paranoia, as noted by McWilliams (2011), is that "Paranoia intrinsically involves experiencing what is *inside* as if it were *outside* the self" [emphasis added]. Hence, the ancient Greeks may well have understood projection, for *true* paranoia means externalizing an internal conflict; "outside the mind."

For example, a patient, Cyrus, returned to the gym. He said he was glad to be back, but saw a local man there, Gary, whom he loathed. Gary was known to use the main street as a drag strip, and his property was an eyesore to neighbors. Despite never having had a personal exchange, Cyrus felt very defensive seeing Gary at the gym. Cyrus described, "I just *know* he's got an attitude! I can *feel* him looking my way." Analyzing Cyrus more closely, his negative thoughts about his neighbor included covertly glaring at Gary and fantasizing about confronting him. Cyrus came to realize he had projected his festering negativity towards Gary onto him, justifying his distaste.

On a psychotic level, there is the well-formed paranoid delusion as in the case of Greta, who initially presented for anxiety treatment. It quickly became clear that her angst was rooted in intense paranoia. At age 32, she had lived at home since finishing college, due to a seizure condition that challenged her independence. Greta was convinced her parents were going broke, despite their upper-class status, and would abandon her. This scared her because of her dependence on them. She had frequent arguments with them about "not being honest" with her and would place tape recorders under their bed to spy on private conversations. Further, she harbored elaborate delusions regarding her mother persecuting her. Unfortunately, Greta became so impaired she was hospitalized indefinitely.

In speaking with her parents, they recalled that, on moving back home, Greta expressed feeling burdensome to the family's financial and emotional well-being. It can be safely surmised that Greta's delusions were a product of projecting her self-persecution regarding her guilt of being burdensome; "I'm not the problem, they are."

Clearly, patients' vexing behaviors are not necessarily nefariously-calculated actions that require confrontational responses from therapists. Rather, understanding when a defense is at play and what purpose it serves can assist in more productive therapeutic processes regardless of one's theoretical orientation.

Suggested Resources

Readers interested in expanding their understanding of psychological defenses are encouraged to read psychologist Nancy McWilliams' *Psychoanalytic Diagnosis* (2011, Guilford). Dr McWilliams not only presents detailed, easily-digestible definitions and examples of 26 different defenses, but discusses their architecture and how they affect patients.

References

DiGiuseppe, M. & Perry, J.C. (2021). The hierarchy of defense mechanisms: Assessing defensive functioning with the defense mechanisms rating scales Q-Sort. *Frontiers in Psychology, 12.* https://doi.org/10.3389/fpsyg.2021.718440

Frances, A. & Goldfried, M. (2023, April 3). Don't blame the patient. *Talking Therapy Podcast: An Ongoing Conversation Between Two Psychotherapy Experts and Longtime Friends.* https://podcasters.spotify.com/pod/show/talking-therapy/episodes/Dont-Blame-the-Patient-e21k7tb

McWilliams, N. (2011). *Psychoanalytic diagnosis: Understanding personality structure in the clinical process* (2nd ed.). Guilford.

Mondimore, F. & Kelly, P. (2011). *Borderline personality disorder: New reasons for hope* (p. 182). Johns Hopkins Press.

Paulhus, D.L., Fridhandler, B., & Hayes, S. (1997). Psychological defense: Contemporary theory and research (Chapter 22, Abstract). In R. Hogan, J. Johnson, & S. Briggs (Eds.) *Handbook of personality psychology*. Academic Press. https://doi.org/10.1016/B978-012134645-4/50023-8

Smith, A.D. (2023, August 11). Paranoia may not be what you think it is. *Psychology Today*. https://www.psychologytoday.com/us/blog/up-and-running/202307/paranoia-may-not-be-what-you-think-it-is

Shahrokh, N.C. & Hales, R.E. (2003). *American psychiatric glossary* (8th ed.). American Psychiatric Publishing.

Vaillant, G.E. (2011). Involuntary coping mechanisms: A psychodynamic perspective. *Dialogues in Clinical Neuroscience, 13*(3), 366–370.

Chapter 32

Approach Trauma Lightly

Trauma intervention has aggressively gained momentum over the past few decades (Kleber, 2019), but beware of approaching it without a gingerly touch.

Since the upsurge in trauma awareness, it seems sufferers are more forthcoming with the chief complaints ranging from sexual assaults to war trauma to witnessing something horrifying. Despite divulging a traumatic event, it does not mean they'll be comfortable providing details about it or that therapists should dig about to learn more.

Regardless of a therapist's approach to treating trauma, the patient will inevitably be required to provide some level of detail. Traumatized people realize this and, to summarize several people I worked with, admitted avoiding treatment for a long time for fear of talking about "it" in detail. This isn't surprising given a chief symptom of trauma is avoidance of reminders (American Psychiatric Association, 2022). Thus, it makes sense that substance abuse is highly correlated to trauma (Brady et al., 2021), as many sufferers may naturally seek relief where it can be found. Many prison inmates I worked with were involved with the drug world, subsequently incarcerated for said involvement, and admitted they began using substances to cope with traumas.

With this delicate dynamic, therapists must take care not to scare off trauma patients by prematurely or zealously sifting for details.

This mistake can arise in the first session when taking a history. While the trauma is oftentimes acknowledged, that doesn't mean the patient wants to unpack it so fast. Is it not enough to know that something unpleasant occurred in the person's life? Though well-intended, requesting details may just serve as an impetus to quit before therapy begins.

Instead, it can be best to give the patient breathing space and let them feel they have control over divulging details. It's important to realize that comprehensive trauma details are not necessarily required for successful therapy. Perhaps the most important part of trauma therapy is the relationship between patient and therapist (Ormhaug et al., 2014; Norcross

DOI: 10.4324/9781032631400-37

& Wampold, 2019), where a safe space is created to explore how to move forward and to work on the inter-relational complications that are so often engendered by traumas.

Some patients might, in short order, provide a cathartic "confession" about something that happened to them. Being asked by a therapist if they have experienced anything traumatic could provide permission to release the pressure caused by years of internalizing, say, sexual abuse they were told never to mention or was ignored by caretakers. Others might provide a few details in their first session or two in an effort to see if the therapist can handle it when they're ready to share more.

While the patient's details could suggest they are willing to share, respecting their vulnerability and asking questions carefully is important. When a person mentions a trauma, it might seem opportune to inquire about particulars. However, focusing on the here-and-now could be more helpful in building the alliance that will see therapy through. What allowed them to disclose it? How has sharing the material with the therapist affected them? Exploring the person's perception of how the therapist perceived them, or what it was about the setting that led to willingness to share can provide the therapist with valuable knowledge of the patient's concerns and needs going forward.

If it seems appropriate at the time of the patient's revelation, asking "What more can you tell me about that experience?" or "Is there anything else you think I should know about this right now?" are gentle ways to explore. Both questions also indicate the therapist is not averse to hearing about something that others might have invalidated, or the patient might assume is "too much" for someone to hear. This sets the stage for willingness to engage with the therapist.

Others' trauma might not be the central complaint, but is nonetheless important. The patient in such cases might prefer to keep details scant because they have learned to constructively manage and don't want to risk unnecessarily reliving and retriggering. In these cases, leaving the details alone and making more strength-based/solution-focused inquiries may be much more helpful. For example, a patient who says they feel they have dealt well with a trauma could be asked, "What was helpful in dealing with it?" and exploring their resilience. If nothing else, it softly opens a discussion about their experience so the therapist might gain a better understanding of their background. Further, understanding the patient's innate capability to deal with stresses might come in helpful elsewhere. This isn't true only of trauma; solution/strengths-oriented interviewing skills can be applied trans-theoretically across presenting concerns. Solution-oriented interviewing skills books are often found useful by supervisees.

It must be realized, of course, that there will be people so persistently and acutely affected by their trauma that nothing short of niche trauma specialists or programs will do, and it is a therapist's ethical duty to realize when a referral is required. However, many patients have endured traumas, but a trauma specialist might not necessarily be required to treat them. Perhaps, for instance, the patient "clicks" with the therapist and feels safe, something they have not felt before, and allows work to commence on emotional concerns that were the result of some traumatic relationship.

While not confronting the trauma directly, assisting someone to overcome the emotional fallout of the event can be trauma resolving without ever going into detail about "it", which might engender ambivalence about therapy.

It's not unusual that helping patients take control of panic or anger, things that have come to symbolize the trauma and keep it alive, is enough for good progress. "The panic began occurring in my abusive relationship. I can't control the panic and therefore it seems that so-and-so still controls me," was the interpretation a patient once gave of their panic experience. Gaining control of panic can be very freeing in itself, but imagine how much more freeing it might be if it is viewed as "trauma reincarnate" and they learn to control it.

In the end, trauma is about not being able to come unstuck. With this in mind, therapists cannot go wrong inquiring into what life will be like when things have improved as a method of entering into trauma-related material. It also helps formulate treatment goals. Asking a patient what will be happening differently when they again feel empowered is a good example of using the future to resolve the past, as made famous by Viktor Frankl in *Man's Search for Meaning* (1985) and adopted by solution-oriented practitioners (O'Hanlon & Bertolino, 1998).

The patient, feeling so helplessly stuck, might honestly not even know what a better existence would look like. Some have told me all they know is, "I don't want to live like this anymore." Giving someone permission to daydream about something better, even if it seems like a mere pipedream at that point, can be therapeutic in itself. Helping them cultivate the vision and dwell in possibilities for change is a huge step. If someone doesn't have a vision, they have nothing to work towards.

Such safe and simple exercises alone can begin to light the path and help dilute the effects of the trauma. There is no need to immediately talk about "it."

Suggested Resources

For a thorough introduction to the mechanisms and pervasiveness of trauma and a review of numerous intervention approaches, Bessel van der Kolk's *The Body Keeps Score* (2014, Viking) should be seminal reading. My favorite trauma intervention book, however, is Bill O'Hanlon and Bob Bertolino's *Even from a Broken Web* (1998, Norton). While a solution-oriented therapy volume, the chapter on permission, validation, and inclusion (meaning here that there are broken parts, not entirely damaged patients) is transtheoretical and foundational for respectful intervention.

References

American Psychiatric Association. (2022). Trauma and stressor-related disorders. In *Diagnostic and statistical manual of mental disorders* (5th ed., text rev.).

Brady, K.T., McCauley, J.L., & Back, S.E. (2021). The comorbidity of post-traumatic stress disorder (PTSD) and substance use disorders. In N. el-Guebaly, G. Carrà, M. Galanter, & A.M. Baldacchino (Eds), *Textbook of addiction treatment*. Springer. https://doi.org/10.1007/978-3-030-36391-8_93

Frankl, V. (1985). *Man's search for meaning*. Pocket Books.

Kleber, R.J. (2019). Trauma and public mental health: A focused review. *Frontiers in Psychiatry, 10*. https://doi.org/10.3389/fpsyt.2019.00451

Norcross, J.C. & Wampold, B.E. (2019). Relationships and responsiveness in the psychological treatment of trauma: The tragedy of the APA Clinical Practice Guideline [Abstract]. *Psychotherapy, 56*(3), 391–399. https://doi.org/10.1037/pst0000228

O'Hanlon, B. & Bertolino, B. (1998). *Even from a broken web: Brief, respectful solution-oriented therapy for sexual abuse and trauma*. Norton.

Ormhaug, S.M., Jensen, T.K., Wentzel-Larsen, T., & Shirk, S.R. (2014). The therapeutic alliance in treatment of traumatized youths: Relation to outcome in a randomized clinical trial [Abstract]. *Journal of Consulting Clinical Psychology, 82*(1), 52–64. doi:10.1037/a0033884

Chapter 33

Learn About Self-Injury

Self-injury is a common clinical occurrence. It is also a stigmatized and misunderstood phenomenon by people in general, including therapists (Slesinger et al., 2019; Hasking et al., 2022). For new therapists, first encounters with someone who self-injures can be particularly trying, especially if their only reference is from popular culture portrayals, which have a tendency to be inaccurate (Transue & Whitlock, 2010). One of these inaccuracies is that self-injury is about manipulation, which, of course, can raise negative reactions from any audience.

Self-injury, to be clear, implies non-lethal inflictions, otherwise known as non-suicidal self-injury (NSSI). For some, it might conjure stereotypical images of someone with borderline personality disorder cutting their forearms after an argument, an ostensibly manipulative gesture. Others might see it as something trendy that teens learn from social media. However, self-injury is rarely mere manipulation and hard to consider "fashionable." The reasons people begin NSSI are varied but, as explained by self-injury expert Steven Levenkron (1998), it often comes down to psychological pain relief.

It would be erroneous to say that sometimes the fact someone self-injures is not used as an attention-getting tool. Readers might be familiar with a patient who cuts and, when mad, tries to use that as leverage: "Fine, I'm going to cut up!" However, if the phenomenon is only conceptualized through such a reductionistic lens, danger lies ahead. It could be easy to reduce them to a "manipulator" and act dismissively and try to intervene with confrontation, letting them know you're onto them. "Is this really the best way to get attention?" a therapist might ask. If only it were so simple.

The first thing to bear in mind is that self-injury can be a language in itself, not a mere activity (Smith, 2021). Often, when asked why they self-injure, especially juveniles, people reply, "I don't know," or, perhaps, "I was stressed." They honestly may not know why they do it, and chances are it's influenced by emotional stress. Wagging fingers or making assumptions of attention-getting just dampens the chances of any collaboration to correct

DOI: 10.4324/9781032631400-38

the behavior. The self-injurer sees the person is upset with them for it, so why should they bother trying to make them understand?

Consider that putting one's emotional landscape into words is not an easy task for many. Therefore, because internal experiences need to be expressed somehow, they are acted out instead. Perhaps cutting is a form of self-flagellation in reaction to the guilt of depression or trauma, quite literally bleeding the guilt and shame from oneself. The action speaks for them, and the degree of acting out/self-injury can be thought of as proportional to the degree of emotional turmoil. The more often and more painful the actions, the more severe the emotional struggle.

That said, it does not mean there is intention of death, no matter how much one self-injures. This doesn't give permission to take NSSI lightly, for it *could* lead to severe injury, such as if the self-injurer accidentally cut too deep. It should be noted that people who self-injure *are* more willing to hurt themselves, which can be a suicide risk factor, especially in adolescents, where up to 70 percent of those self-injuring have attempted suicide once (Grandclerc et al., 2016). Despite this, it must be remembered that this is not the case for every episode or period of self-injury, and therapists would do well not to become alarmist, as discussed in Chapter 30.

I'm always perplexed when a parent or partner says, "So-and-so tried to kill themself, I called the ambulance" and when I ask to see the evidence, it's a barely noticeable scar. For others it's a regular ritual, indicating that it is not meant to be terminal. "Do you use a clean razor?" I inquired of one young woman. "Of course," she said. If someone was planning to die from their cutting, the sterility of the instrument would not matter. Rather, here we have someone who is applying surgical precautions and precision to their procedure. Not trying to understand their experience and rushing to conclusions about suicide, leading to crisis evaluations and unwanted attention, may only escalate the emotional state of the self-injurer, engendering more desire to injure.

Another thing to keep in mind about NSSI is that it can serve as a grounding technique of sorts. More than once a person has explained that they cut or burn when depressed or dissociated in order to feel *something*. Describing his emotional numbness, a man once told me, "I get to literally feeling hollow. The physical discomfort distracts me from the emotional pain. Bleeding is a sign I'm still alive. The pain brings me into focus on something outside of me." As maladaptive as this may sound, it works, and may continue even when the person otherwise stabilizes. It could be conceptualized that it is maintained as a way of keeping numbness from seeping back in, but there may also be a physiological explanation to it.

Believe it or not, there is a self-injury-endorphin connection that hints at an addiction process (Worley, 2020; Johnson et al., 2022). Some self-injury experts have suggested that the person becomes addicted to the endorphins released during self-injury. Thus, the self-injury is an addictive behavior in that the person is essentially self-medicating. If this is true, it makes it clearer why some find it so difficult to discontinue the behavior. Some researchers (Blasco-Fontecilla et al., 2016) suggested an addiction model of treatment could be successful in treating self-injury.

Regardless of the roots of NSSI, it's hard to ask someone to discontinue something that works for them without having an alternative, but the specific function of the activity must first be understood.

A productive way to enter that conversation is by inquiring, "If those cuts (or burns, bruises, etc.) could talk, what would they tell me?" Other helpful conversation starting questions include:

- What is it like for you while doing that?
- Describe for me the after-effect. How do you feel?
- How does it affect you?
- How do you know when it's time to injure?
- Is it something you'd like to change? (This question can be a critical one for therapy).

This kind of questioning opens a dialogue about the *experience* of the self-injury and is much more productive than "Why do you do that?" or "What happened?" which can seem judgmental and distancing. Further, it may kindle a feeling of partnership in the therapeutic relationship. This is because the therapist and patient are exploring something together that the patient doesn't quite understand and others have shunned them for.

Once understanding is established, the sessions may venture into motivating the patient to explore alternatives or maybe discover exceptions, such as in situations when they usually would have injured but refrained. Examining what made that possible, perhaps their own alternative they had already constructed, can be invaluable if it can be capitalized on.

Lastly, NSSI doesn't always indicate psychiatric crisis intervention. However, it must be considered there may come a time when someone can't stop cutting because of the ongoing acute symptoms they use it to control. Maybe they have a history of suicide attempts, or escalating risk/warning factors, or tend to self-injure while abusing a substance. Therefore, safety planning, no matter how minimal the self-injury might be, must be a complete conversation.

Suggested Resources

Perhaps the best introduction to working with non-suicidal self-injury is a continuing education course on the topic. In addition, I urge those interested in self-injury treatment to invest in Steven Levenkron's *Cutting* (1998, Norton). In a compact but thorough and easy-to-read style, Levenkron dissects taboo, examines factors causing the act, including its attractiveness, and intervention strategies, including managing setbacks. *Non-Suicidal Self-Injury Throughout the Lifespan* by Kelly Emelianchik-Key and Amanda La Guardia (2019, Routledge) takes the topic further with additional focus on the cultural considerations of risk assessment.

References

Blasco-Fontecilla, H., Fernandez-Fernandez, R., Colino, L., Perteguer-Barrio, R., & de Leon, J. (2016). The addictive model of self-harming (non-suicidal and suicidal) behavior. *Frontiers in Psychiatry, 7*(8). doi: 10.3389/fpsyt.2016.00008

Grandclerc, S., De Labrouhe, D., Spodenkiewicz, M., Lachal, J., & Moro, M.R. (2016). Relations between nonsuicidal self-injury and suicidal behavior in adolescence: A systematic review. *PLoS One,11*(4). doi:10.1371/journal.pone.0153760

Hasking, P., Staniland, L., Boyes, M., & Lewis, S. (2022). Adding insult to injury: The accumulation of stigmatizing language on individuals with lived experience of self-injury [Abstract]. *The Journal of Nervous and Mental Disease, 210*(9), 645–649. doi:10.1097/NMD.0000000000001524

Johnson, B.N., McKernan, L.C., & Bruehl, S. (2022). A theoretical endogenous opioid neurobiological framework for co-occurring pain, trauma, and non-suicidal self-injury [Abstract]. *Current Pain & Headache Reports, 26*, 405–414. https://doi.org/10.1007/s11916-022-01043-9

Levenkron, S. (1998). *Cutting: Understanding and overcoming self-mutilation* (p. 32). Norton.

Slesinger, N.C, Hayes, N.A., & Washburn, J.J. (2019). Nonsuicidal self-injury: The basics. In J.J. Washburn (Ed.), *Nonsuicidal self-injury: Advances in research and practice*. Routledge.

Smith, A.D. (2021, July 8). Talking about self-injury: Combatting 2 myths that get in the way of therapy. *Psychology Today*. https://www.psychologytoday.com/us/blog/and-running/202107/talking-about-self-injury

Transue, L. & Whitlock, J. (2010). *Self-injury in the media* [Fact sheet]. Cornell Research Program on Self-Injurious Behavior in Adolescents and Young Adults. www.crpsib.com/userfiles/mediafactsheet.pdf

Worley J. (2020). Self-injury as an addictive disorder [Abstract]. *Journal of Psychosocial Nursing and Mental Health Services, 58*(6), 13–16. doi:10.3928/02793695–20200513-03

Safety Plan Document for Self-Injury/Suicide Prevention

The therapist can complete this sheet with the patient, who should keep the document in an easily accessible place and a photo of the document in their phone. If *in* crisis, it should be agreed that the patient will call 911/local police (local police #:   ).

Situations correlated with self-injurious behavior/suicidal thinking (e.g., relationship stress, dissociation, onset of depressive episode) indicating I should engage skills/seek support:

_____   _____

_____   _____

Thoughts correlated with self-injurious behavior/suicidal ideation (e.g., an increase in hopelessness, low self-worth, worry, traumatic ruminations, vengeance [using SIB to guilt others, "Look at what you made me do!"], preoccupation with thoughts of the relief self-injury has historically provided) indicating I should engage skills/seek support:

_____   _____

_____   _____

Helpful things I've done before to maintain safety when experiencing the above that I can do again:

_____   _____

_____   _____

Support names and phone numbers to contact when experiencing the above:

Family: _____

Friends: _____

Therapist: _____

Psychiatrist: _____

Caseworker: _____

Warning signs I am feeling out of control and might self-injure or attempt suicide (e.g., feeling 5 or more out of 10 [most likely to harm], feeling

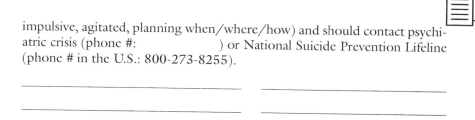

impulsive, agitated, planning when/where/how) and should contact psychiatric crisis (phone #:   ) or National Suicide Prevention Lifeline
(phone # in the U.S.: 800-273-8255).

_____   _____

_____   _____

Chapter 34

Exploring Therapist Self-Disclosure

Self-disclosure is not synonymous with becoming personally intimate or social with patients. Self-disclosure is a simple concept, but an art in itself as to how and when to apply this potential therapy accelerator, for it is not without risks. Consider the case of Judy, a newly minted art therapist.:

Judy was meeting with her patient, Mark, a talented sketch artist. At the end of a session, Mark shared his sketch through which he tried to express a variety of feelings that overtook him in the session. He was frustrated he could not quite draw what he was experiencing. Judy, also a sketch artist, and someone who sometimes struggled with her own moods, thought she could use this as a rapport/bonding moment. Recalling a sketch that she made of compartmentalized weather making up her body, she showed Mark. He was notably impressed, and was going to do his own spin on the drawing for the next session.

The next few sessions were more talk about art and technique than achieving any pointed therapeutic goals. Judy saw this as a good sign, since Mark was becoming more conversational. In the course of these sessions, Mark naturally inquired about Judy's artistic inspiration. Her inspiration was usually rooted in her own struggles with anxiety, which she reflexively shared given the casual tone of the recent meetings.

In supervision, Judy confessed treatment goals were not being met and she was stuck. She felt, for some reason, Mark showed up to check on her each week. Upon dissecting the experience, it was clear that roles were rapidly becoming reversed. In this case it was not very damaging, and actually became grist for the therapy mill. It became apparent that Mark needed someone to care for, which gave direction to the therapy.

Self-disclosure has its place in the treatment setting, but as in Judy's case, it can become perilous. Reflecting on the above, it is always satisfying to share a tale of triumph that could help another, and even more satisfying when another identifies with one's story. For Judy, that sharing, initially intended to be helpful to Mark, crept towards taking on importance for her, engendering a role reversal. Clearly, self-disclosure requires care.

DOI: 10.4324/9781032631400-39

Self-disclosure can be conducive for accelerating treatment in that it lends therapists credibility. It also reinforces that the therapist understands where the patient is coming from, which can be motivating.

Of course, patients are often curious about their therapists, and may see this sharing of something personal as a sign the therapist is willing to indulge their curiosities, and thus push for more. Most people like talking about themselves, and even with professional boundaries, it's easy to let personal material slip if someone signals sufficient interest in what the therapist is sharing. This is especially true if a therapist is somehow attracted to a patient or over-identifying with them, also known as positive countertransference.

Left unchecked, this kind of dynamic tears at the fabric of the therapeutic relationship; once a therapist feels these kinds of connections to a patient, it is hard to be objective. Sessions may become social, and while modeling good relationships is part of what therapists should do in treatment interactions, being a "paid friend" is unethical.

Over the years I have more often than not been comfortable with self-disclosure, though indeed found it an art in itself. It did seem to help get patients interested in sessions, but at times I caught myself feeling compelled to share a bit more, and then again. I once over-sympathized with someone in a similar break-up situation and caught myself about to share more than I should, a commiserating of sorts. As the man asked me if my ex-girlfriend had acted in a particular way, I realized it was becoming too personal. Despite these learning curve follies, it's generally been a positive experience for the patient and accelerated treatment. I'll never forget Monica's response to my self-disclosure.

Monica was a 14-year-old girl presenting with OCD, depression, and compulsively picked her skin and hair. Further, Monica was adopted, but the parents divorced, and she lived between them, and her biological sibling was killed in a car accident. Not long after our first meeting she tried cannabis and developed transient derealization states.

Despite this plethora of problems, she was one of the most resilient individuals I ever met. She continued to perform well academically despite ritualizing for hours with homework, and remained active in arts, socializing, and outdoor activity.

With all this, she was perhaps the poster child for strength-based interventions. Nonetheless, I wasn't getting anywhere with Monica until I heard a comment made by her mother, sitting next to her, "You think nobody understands you, Monica. Give him a chance." I stored this comment away until the next session. If I put it to use at that moment, it would have looked as if I was working too hard to gain her trust. I wanted it to be more spontaneous and when her defenses were possibly not quite as high.

The next week, Monica lamented the disturbing nature of one of her obsessions. She explained that it made her feel as though she was a disgusting person even though she did not voluntarily create the thought. I took it as my chance to show her we were aligned and I understand her experience. "It's just a reminder of what you know isn't true," I commented. "That's the way a very helpful therapist had described my similar obsessions," I finished. Monica quickly engaged eye contact and it was a turning point in our ability to collaborate. We were speaking the same language now, and having had successful OCD treatment myself, she started to consider that I just might be safe to work with.

Periodically, I would offer humorous self-disclosure about a shared tendency to need a "just right experience" regarding symmetric arrangements, another OCD symptom. This not only kept us aligned, but by demonstrating trivialization of the OCD symptoms, Monica came to do the same. How can someone take something seriously that they make fun of? Joking about, singing about, and otherwise being silly about something that has been so bullying discredits its power and can defang the obsessions and rituals.

It must be noted that certain populations lend themselves to avoiding therapist self-disclosure. Otherwise put: sharing with anyone the therapist has felt boundary-pushing from, or who may somehow use the information against them should not obtain insight into the therapist's personal life, no matter how small.

These populations include cluster B personality disorders, especially borderline and antisocial; anyone in a correctional setting; anyone the therapist knows has a history of being litigious with providers; and patients they know are attracted to them. The reasons here need little explanation, but, in short, these are populations who may take advantage of the therapist or misinterpret the sharing as something special, ultimately causing damage when they learn the therapist is not interested in a romance.

With that in mind, to keep liability low, before self-disclosing, therapists might wish to consider:

- What is my goal in sharing this?
- Am I sharing because I feel some affinity with the patient?
- Is there any reason this could backfire?
- Keeping it brief and details minimal if sharing does occur.
- Reviewing the self-disclosure in supervision before applying it.

A final word on self-disclosure pertains to when patients make a personal inquiry. So many therapists I've spoken about this topic with say they tell the patient they are not there to talk about themselves, or may even say, "that's inappropriate." I learned the hard way that such a blunt response is at the detriment of therapy.

I had been meeting with an enjoyable young couple who was making good progress. A couple of weeks prior to Christmas that year, at the end of the session, they asked if I knew if there were any nearby Christmas tree lots. They wished to pick one up on the way home and decorate it with the kids that night. As I mentioned a few local possibilities, the woman commented, "You know the area well. Did you grow up around here?"

I'm convinced that my response, an explanation of how it was my policy not to talk about my personal life with my clientele, saw to it that they never returned.

Likely part product of working in a jail at the time, and part product of the common idea patients shouldn't know about the therapist, I immediately regretted my reply as the tone of the conversation cooled and I sensed a hurt as the couple exited the room. What would it have harmed if I just acknowledged I was from a nearby town? They weren't asking for my address or anything intrusively personal. It was not even something necessarily related to therapy; it was mere small talk.

While it is correct that therapy sessions are for the patient, the therapist is part of the patient's world, and thus, it's only *appropriate* that at some point they are curious about the therapist. Pointedly deflecting the inquiry might not only weaken or even break the alliance, but there is possibly a gold mine of therapeutic material being missed. Consider a patient with social angst or deficits who attempts to make conversation by asking if the therapist has any weekend plans.

This is not intrusive, its progress, and delicate at that. A quick, "nothing planned," can signify disinterest in engaging them, ruining any confidence they mustered to make the small talk. "Thanks for asking," followed with a little detail about, say, the amount of yardwork that must be accomplished, and asking about their plans can be an incredibly meaningful exchange. The interaction might then be used to get them to be more willing to share in the next session. "So, how did your plans play out for last weekend?" This signifies others find them interesting, which, if continuously cultivated, could well lead to their willingness to reveal themselves more to people outside of the office. Imagine what could potentially be lost by trying to remain a blank slate.

While it's been my experience most personal inquiry of the therapist is of the nature of the above examples, there is an endless array of possibilities. These include asking the therapist, "What would you do?" to "Do you find me attractive?" The latter, by the way, isn't always because they are trying to seduce the therapist as on TV.

Take, for instance, someone with body dysmorphic disorder (BDD). People suffering from BDD perceive a particular physical characteristic as an inordinately magnified flaw. For example, someone possessing a couple of acne scars could literally perceive themselves as disfigured. In turn, their life revolves around hiding the "disfigurement," including frequently examining themselves in mirrors to be sure scars are hidden, and asking people close to them for reassurance. This, of course, might be interpreted as a gesture of acceptance, providing relief to one who struggles to accept themself.

Thus, such a patient, asking the therapist if they find them attractive, could be indicative of how important the patient finds the therapist, for they wish to be acceptable to them. Responding to the patient with, "My opinion seems important to you; before I answer, if you don't mind, I'm curious about that question. Tell me about what gave rise to it." It could be opening the door to next-level discussions about self-acceptance. At the very least, it is exploring the therapist-and- patient relationship, which always holds value as modeling willingness to share and disclose.

As for the decision to answer, uncensored, a patient's inquiry about such personal things can be a difficult choice. I once attended a training by the notable psychoanalyst Glen Gabbard, MD, where he addressed the topic as it pertains to working with borderline personality disorder. Dr. Gabbard explained that, at that time, he preferred to say, "That's a question I can't answer. If I say I do find you attractive, the climate in the room could change quickly. If I say I don't, you could be devastated. I am interested, though, why you'd like to know this, and why in today's session?"

This respectful approach protects both the patient and therapist, and I've found a modified version helpful to keep on hand: "It seems like you really value my opinion. I don't want to seem elusive, but it's been my experience that directly answering these kinds of questions can give rise to ethical dilemmas. No matter how I answer, someone could construe a troubling perception of my sentiments towards them."

Rather than shutting down the moment, these approaches allow perhaps the best of both worlds by attending to their question within an ethical safety net. There is always corollary conversation to come of it, however. Much can be gained by exploring the patient's wonder if the therapist finds them attractive. Perhaps the lack of direct answer engenders frustration towards the therapist that will encourage examination of interpersonal conflict resolution and managing ambiguity.

Before drawing a hard line and not answering patients' personal inquiries, consider what might be lost and how the moment could be used as therapeutic. I can't help but recall a favorite chapter from Irvin Yalom's *The Gift of Therapy* (2003). It is entitled, "All is Grist for the Here-and-Now Mill."

Suggested Resources

The magazine *Psychotherapy Networker* has a robust database of articles on the pros and cons of self-disclosure that readers are encouraged to peruse. My preferred reference on the topic, which all of my supervisees read, is in Irvin Yalom's *The Gift of Therapy* (2003, Perennial). The brief chapters on the topic serve as a very practical crash course in therapist disclosure.

Yalom not only examines the usefulness and potential hang-ups of sharing personal information, but discusses it further through the lens of therapist transparency and how to therapeutically disclose "here-and-now" feelings about the patient in the sessions. For readers inclined to podcasts, Alan Frances and Marvin Goldfried's episode of *Talking Therapy* (August, 2022) entitled "Therapist Self Disclosure" contains an introductory educational discussion about the topic between two esteemed, veteran practitioners.

Reference

Yalom, I. (2003). *The gift of therapy: An open letter to a new generation of therapists and their patients* (Chapter 22). Harper Perennial.

Chapter 35

There's No Need to Rescue

It is easy to get caught up in wanting to quickly relieve someone's suffering. Therapists are helpers, they entered the field to provide relief. Thus, some therapists may feel compelled to be available for patients at all times, even providing same day appointments if they call with an issue that sprung up that day. While it is sometimes necessary to see a patient the same day – perhaps a relative died or they need a risk assessment – providers may be doing more of a disservice if their modus operandi is to rush in each time someone is in distress.

First, we're not therapists to be anyone's savior. As Freud pointed out, the goal of therapy is to guide patients to be their own father and mother, i.e., help them gain insight and skills to live more optimally. If a therapist runs to each upset, they can build an expectation that they're a patient's unconditional rescuer. This does nothing but foster dependence on the provider and defeat the point of therapy. This is especially so with certain personality disorders who may "therapist shop" for such providers or groom others into fitting a rescuer mold. I recall working with a supervisee whose patient informed them what they needed and that the therapist must perform in that manner!

Dissecting the matter of keeping availability boundaries, we discover that not rushing in provides a rich therapeutic opportunity. The patient must engage skills already learned in treatment, or become otherwise creative to cope. The elapsed time having to manage can be therapeutic in itself.

To illustrate, we'll finish the story of Marla, from Chapter 15, who was having significant trouble with her boss, Karen. Once friends, Karen felt double-crossed by Marla because she did not take her in when her relationship floundered. To make matters worse, Karen was promoted, making her Marla's boss. The power differential fueled an opportunity for vindictiveness on the part of Karen. Within weeks, Marla developed significant panic attacks and began sessions with me. Being a minimally assertive person, she neither confronted Karen nor retreated, fearing equally problematic consequences from either action. So anxious was Marla, she barely got through the day with her racing thoughts and jaunts to the bathroom to vomit despite being

DOI: 10.4324/9781032631400-40

prescribed a take-as-needed antianxiety medication. She couldn't sleep, her course work suffered, and panics continued.

In therapy, she gained some ground in controlling the panic attacks and examining ways of managing the personnel debacle that led to them. After several weeks, so literally sick was Marla that she fantasized about just leaving and being free of Karen's wrath. This, however, would entail losing her education benefit and a job she felt purposeful in. "Analysis paralysis" enveloped her.

Marla tried reasoning that she could just try to tough it out for the next year until she got her degree, but feared serious illness from the stress. Alternatively, Marla could try confronting Karen directly, but this likely would lead to another level of hell. She thought about approaching human resources but feared a fallout at work or outside, once Karen knew she had reported her. She felt "talking it out in therapy" would lead to a decision. At times she admitted hoping I would tell her what to do, but then said that even if I did, she would still have to do it. Sometimes she'd make a decision, but then say she could not pull it off.

One Wednesday between sessions, Marla called requesting to come in quickly for assistance in making a decision. She said she was ready to leave but didn't want to act impulsively. On the phone, Marla was the same circular flurry of ideas. I knew it was going to be a matter of chasing tails again, and would reinforce her idea she had to vent the ideas in front of me to make a decision, which really just perpetuated her hesitation to make one. Realizing that given enough discomfort even the most passive person usually makes a move, I explained I'd see her on Monday and assured her we would work through what follows. I suggested that perhaps it would do her good to spend time with friends that weekend. Up until then, Marla not only feared burdening friends with her problem, but refrained from seeing them, saying it was a really busy semester, because she was embarrassed about her condition.

On Monday, Marla still seemed anxious, though shared that she had submitted her problem to human resources. Even though there was no guarantee this would resolve her problem, she felt there was at least momentum in doing something about it. Further, after finally talking to a friend over the weekend, who happened to be a law student, she realized the anticipated fallout might not be an issue, given the retaliation laws.

This session was a goldmine for Marla's growth. We examined what had made it possible for her to do something that scared her so. In an impressive feat of self-guided exposure therapy of sorts, once Marla felt sufficiently supported, she felt increasingly empowered. Also, I learned that Marla usually avoided others when she needed support, which opened a new topic in therapy.

When it's judged that a patient who calls does not have a crisis situation and the therapist maintains the original appointment, in the next session how the matter called about was handled is an important activity. Examining and cultivating anything productive, even if it was simply keeping the matter from worsening, is essential to patient growth; in effect, they brought about "being their own mother and father." If the solution was not as constructive, this will also be helpful to examine, as it can give insight into decision making, supports, and how to help them plan for future roadblocks.

The psychiatrist Milton Erickson explained that people know what they need to know, they just might not know that they know it. Essentially, he believed, effective therapy is a harnessing of the patient's own strengths and resources (Duncan et al., n.d.). How empowering! Sometimes, having patients on the couch robs them of the opportunity to discover things that will be useful in the therapeutic process.

Reference

Duncan, B.L., Miller, S.D., & Coleman, S.T. (n.d.). Utilization: A seminal contribution, a family of ideas, and a new generation of applications. Milton H. Erickson Foundation blog. https://www.erickson-foundation.org/blog/utilization

Chapter 36

Why Therapists Must Be Salespeople

I've been asked more than once about why a patient won't "buy" the therapist's intervention. Like making any sale, it's all in the marketing, as my supervisee, Lacey, discovered.

"I told them that exercise is a really important part of feeling better, and it would be a good idea if they thought about getting into a routine. I've suggested it the past three sessions, but they never follow through!" Lacey explained.

"Listening to yourself tell me about how you conveyed the importance of exercise to your patient, does it sound like it's something they need?"

"Well, I guess not, but shouldn't they try it if I'm suggesting it? I mean, I'm trying to help them!" she continued.

"Ideally, I suppose," I replied. "But there's no evidence conveyed they need it. Where's the appeal? The selling-point?" Thus, we worked on helping Lacey develop a more convincing component to her suggestions.

As illustrated, therapists need to make interventions appeal to patients. This can range from getting them to engage in some activity like journaling or exercising, to considering meeting with a nutritionist or psychiatrist, reading a book we recommend, or even, perhaps, the therapeutic process in general. Why should they do it just because we suggest it? It's got to have *appeal*; they need to understand *why* they need it, and *how* it will benefit them. Would you walk onto a car lot and purchase a new vehicle just because the salesperson suggested it?

Over 20-plus years, I've experienced that, almost invariably, if a patient is provided with detailed information on why and how something can be helpful, they're more likely to at least try it.

I continued with Lacey, "Here's an exercise sales pitch for a patient who might benefit from exercising. 'You know, I can't help but remember how you told me you used to really enjoy going to the gym and being active. It's really interesting what they've found about the effects of exercise on mood. A few years ago, I was at a continuing education seminar and the psychologist told us that back in 2000 researchers did a meta-analysis on the effects

DOI: 10.4324/9781032631400-41

of exercise on mood from 1950 to 2000; this essentially means they boiled down the results of all the research on the topic.

What they discovered was that people who exercised 3–5 times per week for 20–30 minutes at moderate intensity, which they defined as being able to talk but not sing, over the course of one month, had the same decrease in depressive symptoms as people in psychotherapy and on antidepressants, but all they did was exercise. I can't help but wonder what it might do for you to ease back into working out, given you're also in therapy and prescribed Wellbutrin?"

"That makes *me* want to go exercise!" Lacey said.

"So, you get my point."

We discussed how therapists need to educate themselves on the things they're suggesting. The more detailed therapists can be, the more informed and then, perhaps, interested the patient will be. With university resources, Google Scholar, and many reputable psychology sites with articles and blogs on expansive topics, there is no reason it should be difficult to get the information necessary for a perfect sales pitch.

Chapter 37

Learn to Reframe

Psychotherapy, at its heart, could be said to be a conduit to new ways of thinking that improve the way people perceive, feel, and respond to themselves and their environment. Reframing is a potent tool in that it provides an often immediate and powerful shift in perspective of a situation, perhaps even breakthrough moments that accelerate treatment.

To be clear, reframing isn't challenging someone to reconsider their view. For instance, a person who laments not finding a partner might be told, "Look, you're only 20 years old. Most people don't settle down until their 30s these days." This response is more of an attempt at rationalizing the situation, and it's unlikely any major shift in perspective will occur given it is only a statement of "consider this …"

Moreover, reframing has different faces that therapists can learn by getting trained in, say, narrative therapy or motivational interviewing. In the latter, for instance, reframing is a positive counterpoint to non-change language. For example, someone talking about how frequently they failed at something might be met with a comment about their impressive persistence in spite of their difficulties. Learning this ability to shift perspectives in fluid conversation is clearly a useful skill. In the above example, it could open discussions about motivation and strengths, moving towards more "change talk" as it is called in motivational interviewing.

The most striking reframes, however, seem to happen when a therapist is able to spontaneously strike a chord with the patient. In a quick-witted, reflexive response, striking when the iron is hot, the therapist just might be able to provide the patient with a new perspective on the topic. Consider the following illustrations.

John, a young man I worked with who had a penchant for worry, told me he had met a woman and was going on a third, and this time more formal, date with her after the therapy session. John described how much he liked her and why, and his admiration was palpable. He commented, "I'm so anxious, it's a good thing I came here before the date!" He went on to describe

DOI: 10.4324/9781032631400-42

feeling butterflies in his stomach, how his mind was flooded with thoughts of seeing her again, and that he was restless all day.

"John," I began, "let me reflect back to you what you just told to me. You can't stop thinking about her. You can't wait to see her tonight, and just the mention of her gives you butterflies. If *I* was describing having that same experience to you, how would you say I was feeling?" John replied, "You seem excited." "Yes," I finished. "There's a fine line between anxiety and excitement. In both situations we can say we get butterflies or fear we'll wet our pants. Given you're gushing, which one of these most accurately describes you?" John smiled broadly; he understood the lesson.

John continued, "I'm so used to feeling anxiety I never thought those feelings could be experienced in a good light. You're right, there's nothing wrong here, I'm very much looking forward to meeting her again. If I was worried and anxious about it, I'd have a sense of fear."

This was a poignant teaching moment when John realized how quickly he could sabotage himself with negative thinking and that he had some control over how he viewed things. It led to productive discussions about being more mindful, and proved to John that he was capable of emotions other than anxiety, which unfortunately had shaped his view of himself and the world. "There's a fine line between anxiety and excitement" defanged a decades-long neurotic process, making John feel more confident going to the third date.

Another patient I worked with, Tobias, had overcome significant social anxiety. At the time, we were working on depressive symptoms and life dissatisfaction. Though Thobias had become rather social in recent years, he was still prone to some backslide and fearing he would be deemed inept, especially if put on the spot.

At one point, he started a new job as an assistant probation officer. During the first couple of weeks, he noticed an attorney who, on a few occasions, smiled at him from across the courtroom. After proceedings she was always talking with colleagues or clients. Eventually, Tobias was able to cross her path on the way out of the Court and introduce himself. Not knowing if he'd have the opportunity again, he asked her for coffee.

Not long after, Tobias shared in a therapy session that a nosy colleague overhead this and told their supervisor the new guy was "making quick work" of trying to get with women at the courthouse.

Tobias found himself in the hotseat, being accused of giving the probation department a bad reputation by "working the ladies in the courtroom." He explained the course of the matter to his supervisor and was nonetheless met with, "Women smile at me all the time, that doesn't mean I go asking them out at work." While more assertive these days, he also was not about to tussle with his new boss and make things more difficult. Tobias swallowed his pride, apologized for the "mistake," and went on, but stewed on the interaction and being put on the spot.

Tobias explained that he berated himself for getting into trouble, was irritated with his new colleagues, and frustrated that he couldn't do anything more to defend himself. Knowing there was a time that Tobias rarely spoke, never mind asked for a date or defended himself, I offered, "You're no longer that shy kid playing video games all alone, are you?" Tobias's view of the situation quickly shifted, realizing all the progress he had made, and that he had handled the matter just like he should have.

Lastly, there is the case of Viola, a bereaved patient. She had recently lost her spouse and had the common complaint of emptiness, lamenting that she would never see him again. The absence of her husband's presence assailed her. "Viola," I said, "I can't help but notice you described the situation in a way that makes it seem like you no longer have a relationship with Eddie," to which she nodded in agreement.

"Are you sure of that?" I inquired, commanding her attention. "You tell me you reminisce about your life together; that you believe he went on to another life; that you continue to talk to him and have even felt that certain events since his passing were his communication. Is it that you don't have a relationship with him anymore, or is it that the *nature* of the relationship has changed?" Viola stared tearfully, taking in the idea.

Steering her away from the idea there was no relationship because he wasn't physically present allowed her to see that she was proving herself wrong because she was still interacting with him. This allowed her to evolve her thinking on the matter, and once again feel close to Eddie, instead of just "something out there."

These examples provide ideas on how to think about and incorporate reframing in the therapeutic discussion. To be successful, it's important to not only have a reframe, but to know when and how to deliver it. Ideally, it punctuates the session; if it is not heard, it is a wasted opportunity. The therapist needs to create the moment.

To accomplish this, it's imperative the therapist conveys they have something important to say. It can be engaging in a Socratic exchange, as in the example of John, making them a participant in the reframing revelation. Perhaps the patient's attention is heightened by turning the reframe into a question they have to respond to, like Tobias. Other times, creating a moment of intrigue or curiosity engages the person, as when I asked Viola, "Are you sure about that?"

While therapists might be apprehensive about delivering the reframe, for it is a skill requiring a knack, remember that even seasoned therapists' attempts don't always resonate with patients. This doesn't mean it is a total failure. If a patient disagrees with your suggestion or is quizzical, exploring their reaction to the reframe can supply further grist for the therapy mill.

Chapter 38

Getting Friendly with Metaphors

"You're two people who were on trains headed in opposite directions, and happened to get off and be on the same platform for a while," offered Dr. G. He was the psychologist I happened to be meeting with during a difficult breakup.

I had just finished lamenting to Dr. G that the relationship was no more. I found it impossible to imagine the woman no longer being in my life; that our lives sped away from each other so quickly. Zeroing in on, "lives sped away from each other," Dr. G reframed the situation in a way I might envision and make different sense of the situation. As researchers tell us, metaphors better convey nuance (Tay, 2020), which I felt in Dr. G's metaphor. It was implied, as in travel, a metaphor for life of which relationships are part, one must keep moving.

In essence, metaphors are like word pictures, and pictures are worth a thousand words. Offering a new way of envisioning a situation can lead to better understanding, or it can reframe someone's thoughts around a maladaptive thinking process. This is perhaps best explained by Frances and Goldfried (2023) who suggested that metaphors are poetic; people tend to think poetically, and it's often easier to recall poetry than prose.

Think about how often throughout the day or a session metaphorical or symbolic language is used. How frequently do people say, "picture this …" in order to make a point? Learning to use metaphors takes advantage of humans' natural propensity to understand meaning through the mind's eye and symbolism. Thus, metaphors in therapy can be exceptionally magic moments, punctuating a learning experience and creating a therapeutic encounter more likely to be remembered, as in the following examples.

Fred was a 25-year-old graduate school student studying earth sciences. He sought therapy with me because, according to his girlfriend, Heather, he was "in a funk again." Heather also pointed out that Fred never spoke to her about how he was feeling during these episodes and it strained their relationship. Overall the couple had a lovely relationship, but periodically, like when school and work stress billowed, Fred brooded on emotions, which

DOI: 10.4324/9781032631400-43

could last days. Fred's explanation was, "Why should I let my crap bother other people? I'll deal with it." This is common "logic" exposed in couples' work. Although he told himself that keeping his negative emotions to himself was protecting Heather, she became increasingly stressed.

During an early session, Fred looked particularly tired and commented he "felt like deadwood" that afternoon. Noting his "dead" reference, a metaphor that took advantage of Fred's interest in earth sciences took shape that could illustrate the benefits of communicating emotions.

"Surely you've had a class studying the world's great bodies of water," I began, getting his attention. "You know, the Dead Sea and the Red Sea are both fed by rivers teeming with life, but nothing survives in the Dead Sea. Do you know what makes the difference?" Fred sat quietly thinking it over, and shrugged. "The Dead Sea has no outlet," I finished.

"It isn't flushed out, so stuff stagnates and dies," he reflected. The message was clear. Fred was able to reframe the consequences of his internalized emotions and why communicating them was important. Stagnating like the Dead Sea, because he was not expressing his emotions, he contributed to his "deadwood" feelings.

Another instance involves Jeannie, a long-term patient. She arrived at a session describing her week as "a filthy mess" after a serious argument with her significant other. Jeannie was frantically trying to get a hold of her boyfriend after a heated disagreement in which both made regretful comments. She wanted to work on clearing the air, but her calls were not returned. Naturally, if upset enough, people may need to take space; it doesn't mean the relationship is terminated or they won't come around. Sometimes, like Jeannie, people can be so desperate to fix the problem that they're making it worse by essentially harassing the other person.

After we talked about this, I acknowledged that the situation did indeed seem messy and the air wasn't very clear, to keep with her term. This was followed by, "Jeannie, you point out the air isn't clear, but isn't it easier to clean up dust after it's had a chance to settle?"

Lastly, Brit, the father of a college-aged son he was close to, once complained about the strife his son was putting him and his wife through because he wanted to move away to college. The emotional sensitivity was palpable. Despite technology being able to keep them in touch by the minute and his son having vacations during which he could visit home, the father still ruminated on it being selfish and cruel of the boy to want to move away.

It was, of course, pointless to attempt to argue over who was being selfish, so I decided to try and alter his vision of the situation. "You know," I began, "the fox doesn't enter the hen house because it hates chickens and has the intention of being cruel and making a mess, it is something he has to do for survival, is it not?" After realizing it is a matter of perspective, Brit's father began to reconsider. His son may be making waves, but it isn't personal and it is something he needs to do to learn to be independent and survive. It did not erase the struggle, but it softened the blow and allowed more understanding to begin to transpire between the family members.

The above examples considered, metaphors cannot only accelerate therapy, they can also be effective in understanding the nature of someone's problem and in bringing diagnostic clarity. My colleague, Joseph Shannon, a psychologist specializing in personality and mood disorders, once told me that, at his initial meeting with a patient, he finds it useful to ask them for a metaphor to describe their lives.

Anyone familiar with personality disorders will know why this is so helpful. Personality disordered individuals are troubled because of the lens through which they view the world, which leads to problematic interactive styles and emotional complications. This activity not only helps obtain clues to diagnosis, but can guide the therapist to what the patient's view of the problem is.

Someone referred to a therapist by an employer because of their haughty and entitled office behavior, for example, may give a metaphor such as, "I'm a superhero when it comes to taking care of business, but nobody wants to listen to me. We could do things so much better, but everyone just dismisses me. Someday they'll see I had the answers to bettering the place." Comparing oneself to a superhero and believing their brilliance is being dismissed is rather grandiose. Couple this with the fact the patient acts haughty and entitled in the office, and it becomes clearer they harbor characteristics of narcissism.

Using metaphors can also help patients better relate the nature of their diagnosis or struggle. For example, ask a depressed person for a metaphor for their mood to ascertain the *nature* of their depression. If a patient complains of sadness, insomnia, and low motivation, they may tell me, "A grey cloud has been following me for years." Sticking with the metaphor, I ask, "Does it ever rain or get stormy?" Perhaps the patient answers, "No, it's like it's always on the brink of rain, there might be sprinkles, but that's it." Therapists familiar with dysthymia, a type of "low grade" chronic depression, would know this is an appropriate metaphor. Like a plant deprived of direct sunlight, people with dysthymia can survive and be productive, but not optimally.

If the patient instead replied that their moods "can be like hurricanes," asking about the duration and characteristics of the storms will be telling. If the weather changes for days, with winds and thunderstorms when it does, the therapist should wonder about mania, as in bipolar disorders.

Clearly, metaphors are a powerful tool in the therapist's arsenal. Some therapists, though, might be wondering how to develop an appropriate metaphor or, should one form, how to best convey it. Like many things, *how* material is delivered is just as important as what's delivered.

Thankfully, developing a skill for metaphors is something that can be practiced in everyday interactions. An exercise that could prove helpful is to start trying to make sense of your own thoughts or everyday observations in a metaphorical way.

Also, when hearing others' experiences, pay attention to any metaphors that are being used. Can you expand their metaphors to convey what is being perceived? For instance, if someone says how they would really like to do this and that, but laments, "I've always just been a dreamer," one could say, "That sounds like a nightmare." Such a comment puts the lack of ambition into perspective, and perhaps spurs a confession that it's "hard to sleep at night, just letting life go by." Obviously, this opens the gate to examining conflicts and goals. In everyday conversation, one needn't express the metaphor, but it is an exercise in thinking about how effective it might be. Allow it to be a playful experience.

Lastly, therapists new to metaphors in treatment need not fret about their inability to evolve a well-formed, appropriate metaphor and deliver it on the spot. While sometimes striking when the iron is hot is most effective, the therapist could also think about a metaphor between sessions, as topics can always be returned to. Using the above example of the "dreamer," if they were a patient, in the next session the therapist could offer, "I was thinking about how last time you mentioned you're 'just a dreamer' when it comes to your wants. Afterwards I thought about how frustrated you seemed with yourself, that being merely a dreamer might seem like a *nightmare*. How does that strike you?"

Even if the patient disagrees or is not taken by the metaphor as hoped, it can open the activity of developing a more meaningful, constructive or workable understanding of a troubling situation.

References

Frances, A. & Goldfried, M. (2023, January 23). Metaphors: The poetry of therapy. In *Talking therapy: An ongoing conversation between two psychotherapy experts and longtime friends*. https://open.spotify.com/show/6OpdUxppI3QsZxz2dTaDKA

Tay, D. (2020). Surveying view of metaphor versus literal language in psychotherapy: A factor analysis [Abstract]. *Metaphor and the Social World, 10*(2), 273–291. https://doi.org/10.1075/msw.00007.tay

Chapter 39

What if Someone Implies, "You'd Never Understand"?

It is natural that birds of a feather flock together, and we may feel we can only be understood thus. Therefore, some patients feel they need a therapist who has been in their shoes if they're to get any benefit from sessions.

This is especially true if it involves something unique. Anyone who has worked with soldiers may have discovered that some don't even talk with their peers about what they witnessed or did in war. Imagine, then, what it might take for that soldier to try to settle in with a therapist who has never been in the service, never mind combat?

One "how would you understand" scenario I've encountered numerous times is with parents. I can't recall the number of times patients struggling with concerns involving children say, "Do you have kids?"

Childless, I'd answer in the negative. Some of these earlier interactions led to, "Then I'm not sure if you're going to understand (or be able to help me)," followed by a seemingly fruitless discussion trying to convince them I could.

Maturing as a therapist, I figured out that many such patients simply needed reassurance I could be useful, not a debate as to my ability. During a continuing education training I recall the presenter talking about a therapist they supervised who encountered this very same situation. The therapist replied, "Well, I don't have my own children, so I can see how you might be concerned about my ability to empathize with that struggle. However, I've done a lot of work with families, and am always interested in learning their unique situation so that my work with them is tailored and comes from a well-informed place." This answer may not convince everyone of the therapist's ability, but lets them know they've worked with others in similar situations, providing some credibility.

My earlier work included a lot of treatment with people suffering from schizophrenia and other severe mental illnesses. As many of them stabilized from the acute stage of the disorder, they confessed to embarrassment or fear of talking about the unique experiences they had with hallucinations or delusions and understanding the meaning of them. Understandably, they

DOI: 10.4324/9781032631400-44

could be tacit about their internal experiences of encountering the stigma of schizophrenia or simply realizing their unique experiences might be difficult for most to relate to.

Aside from demonstrating unconditional positive regard, it was useful to acknowledge the difference or concern they felt. If a therapist attempts to reassure the patient by denying they're like others the patient has encountered, it can just deepen the defense. The patient must be *shown* they can trust the therapist and that the therapist is interested in understanding and knowing them.

If challenged, the therapist can use this as an opportunity to show their intent. For example, responding, "I hear what you're saying. From what you've mentioned, you've had your share of misunderstanding and being discounted because of your experiences. I've not been in those shoes, but when I work with people like yourself, I'm always interested in how those encounters have affected them." Again, the goal is to establish credibility. The therapist starts by letting the patient know they hear their concern. They then establish that they have worked with similar people, and they're willing and able to invest in helping them.

Should the therapist be new to working with people with schizophrenia, inviting a discussion about their experiences with stigma and others and learning about what they have encountered could go a long way in showing investment and willingness to work with them.

Other times, patients can be more frustrating, and even insulting, in their exchanges about how the therapist does not understand them or cannot help them. I can't help but recall an elderly woman, Kay, I worked with, concerning her dissatisfying family relationships. Being more than double my age, Kay would follow up things she shared with, "But I don't know why I'm telling a little squirt like you about my problems."

After hearing this a few times, I mentioned I was curious about the comment. What did she mean by it, especially if she continued to attend the sessions? Kay explained she liked coming because I listened to her, unlike many others, so there was a chance I could end up offering something helpful. However, being so much younger than her, she was cautiously optimistic at best, despite my already having spent 15 years in the field at the time.

"Can a male doctor deliver a baby?" I inquired. "Of course," said Kay. "What's that got to do with anything?" I replied, "So, what you're saying is, is that even if someone hasn't experienced something themselves, they can still be helpful to someone who is experiencing it, right?"

Chapter 40

Pay Attention to the Role of Culture

In the past several years, cultural/identity sensitivity has become an expansive topic. The tide of graduate school courses, continuing education programs, and journal articles and books makes it clear it's more than ever a required area for professional competence.

Despite the flood of information and heightened awareness and increase in culturally sensitive intervention, considering the innumerable cultural matters, from race to religion, that can be encountered, it's impossible to be globally versed in cultural-related clinical encounters. This is not, of course, born of any voluntary idleness pertaining to the matter, but that people tend to work within familiar cultures, or a practice location is within a region with one concentrated cultural minority.

Regardless, omniscient cross-cultural competence is not required, for the therapist can still act competently in their navigation of new cultural encounters. The following three illustrations pertain to cultural niche factors and how they were navigated or resolved, in the hopes of inspiring readers to consider if a presentation has a cultural significance, and how to work with it.

Nothing to Say

Have you ever sat with a patient who is frustratingly quiet and non-relational? On the surface, it may seem part of a pattern of disinterest, but there's usually more than meets the eye (Smith, 2020). As part of my court-related work I once evaluated a teenager, Joel, who was of an Orthodox Jewish background. He was pleasant in demeanor and articulate in small talk, but remarkably terse as the discussion became more personal. This, despite the fact that the purpose of the evaluation, which was explained to Joel, was to help the court understand and thus effectively work with him.

When I spoke to Joel's parents, I inquired if he made any mention of his interview with me. They said he had not, but that's not unusual, as his frustrations and court involvement were things that he preferred to

DOI: 10.4324/9781032631400-45

keep to himself. "It's the nature of our heritage, keeping your problems *your* problems," explained his mother. Later, while talking to a Jewish colleague, I was informed that despite the toll that keeping so internalized may take, it's often viewed as carrying on tradition and showing strength.

In this case, I asked Joel's parents what their feelings were about him participating in the court-related psychological assessment. Acknowledging it could be helpful to his case, they saw it as a necessary order by the court. Therefore, I asked Joel's parents if they could let him know I enjoyed meeting with him, and would like to follow up in the near future. In the meantime, I asked them to talk to him about his experience with me and share their thoughts about the process, which might give him a sense of permission to be less defensive that could lead to better outcomes for him.

Joel returned and was a bit more informative. He did explain his tendency to remain internalized, and that it was difficult not having an outlet, so he naturally exploded at times, "releasing the pressure." Ultimately, it was clear Joel suffered from depression. Knowing more about the cultural factors at play, I asked him how it was speaking with me that day. Joel explained that "it was OK."

"Would it have been easier to talk with another person of Jewish background about this stuff?" I asked. He nodded. We then had a discussion about his willingness to perhaps work with a congregational rabbi or chaplain versed in pastoral counseling to manage his emotions.

Hard to Believe

In relation to details about some out-of-control experience they had had, Hispanic patients have explained to me, "I blacked out." Given the first presentations of this I encountered was in a correctional system, it seemed like an alternative to "convenient amnesia" or another excuse to not have to take responsibility. Early on I would challenge inmates who said this, or internally roll my eyes. While some might have been trying to fool me, ethnic psychopathology researchers have long known that the phenomenon is real.

The *DSM* includes several disorders under Cultural Concepts of Distress. Among these is "Ataque de Nervios," (American Psychiatric Association, 2022) or Attack of Nerves, unique to Hispanic populations. Symptoms include intense, acute anxiety, anger, aggression, and may include dissociative episodes like dissociative amnesia. This means the person, under immense emotional stress, experienced an alteration in consciousness that led to an inability to recall the event.

Not knowing about "culture-bound" diagnoses at the time left me feeling cynical, which obviously was not helpful to the patient. It was only after I heard a Puerto Rican colleague describe someone on their caseload having the same "black out" that I learned it is unique to Hispanic people.

This led to my researching the topic and investing more in understanding inmates' experiences with it. Being exposed to the culture-bound diagnoses was helpful going forward in that it opened my eyes to how different backgrounds experience mental illnesses in unique ways.

Just as therapists familiarize themselves with general mental health diagnoses, studying culture-bound varieties could help in establishing rapport with ethnic clientele more quickly. This obviously could make for a better therapeutic relationship in that they see you have familiarity and thus they might be more willing to share. Reflecting on my own early experiences with the "black outs," how could I be helpful working on something I didn't believe existed?

Overworked

Xiang explained that months before he and his wife, Jackie's, appointment, he experienced an insidious onset of stomach pains and headaches. Their primary care doctor found no physical complications, opined that Xiang was over-worked and stressed, and suggested some extra rest and a better diet. And extra rest soon followed, as Xiang napped at work during his lunch break, and he sometimes barely made it through a work day. At home, the couple were not nearly as active as they once were. Jackie spoke to Xiang's mother, a nurse, who suggested he was depressed, though Xiang denied any emotional concerns. This is when Jackie called for a couple's consultation.

In the meeting, Xiang, holding Jackie's hand on the couch, appeared fatigued and a bit nervous. He commented he feared he was disappointing his wife, and that she might eventually leave him. "I don't feel well anymore," said Xiang. Given his mother's report of his possible depression, I asked Xiang to complete a depression inventory so I could try to gain some insight into his thoughts and internal experience. Xiang indeed experienced a depressive thought process but his most prominent complaints seemed to be physical symptoms. After some discussion, he agreed to meet with an Asian psychiatrist who could confirm both clinically and culturally whether or not Xiang was depressed.

After the psychiatric consultation, the couple returned and Xiang explained that the doctor offered an insight that made sense to him. What began a couple years ago as an ostensibly heightened interest in his career leading to working more hours was likely Xiang's way of distracting himself from feeling dissatisfied about where he was in life at age 30. It also increased his income, which provided a sense of accomplishment. Further, the doctor told him, it's culturally acceptable, and even expected, to work long and hard, providing a sense of virtue that assuaged his sinking self-image, and something to hide behind in his denial of depression; "It's just my culture."

In Asian experiences, depression often manifests with significant physical symptoms (Novick et al., 2023) and may not include the obvious sad or irritable expression that Western populations are used to (Yeung & Kam, 2006). One possible reason for this is that in a culture that substantially frowns upon lack of emotional control, it makes sense that depression is expressed as physical symptoms, which are much more acceptable than mental defects.

During a subsequent session, Xiang asked if he could meet with me privately. Feeling some alliance building, he explained that he was starting to allow himself to be vulnerable, and knew he had a lot to explore and work on. I explained how it would be unethical for me to meet with them privately and as a couple, but Jackie jumped at the opportunity, for Xiang wanting to meet for therapy was a breakthrough. Over the next year, with much curiosity on my part about his cultural influences, we explored the cultural-clinical nexus of Xiang's existential crisis, eventually resolved some shame, and discovered a better sense of purpose, which benefitted both him and his relationship with Jackie.

In each of these cultural encounters, maintaining intentional awareness to the presence of ethnic diversity paid off in that it encouraged listening for clues to assist in culturally sensitive navigation. It can be helpful for therapists facing similar situations to integrate heightened attention to ethnic awareness, along with bearing in mind that perhaps the most helpful thing is *wanting* to get to know the patient and *showing* the therapist wants to understand.

Showing a desire to understand and allowing the patient to guide the therapist demonstrates interest in collaborating for the patient or loved one's wellness. This approach, coupled with consulting with colleagues of similar cultural or identifying backgrounds can be invaluable in keeping as respectful and effective as possible.

Suggested Resources

With the increase in diversity awareness in clinical settings, it is suggested that students take a course in multicultural counseling, and new therapists start to get into a habit of annually attending a diversity-related continuing education program. Meanwhile, perhaps the most-accessible resource for culture-based diagnostic considerations is the cultural formulation chapter in section 3 of the *DSM 5* and *DSM-5 TR* (American Psychiatric Association, 2013, 2022). Further, reviewing the glossary of cultural concepts of distress, an appendix in the *DSM*, can be helpful if one finds oneself working in a very ethnically diverse setting.

Regarding psychotherapeutic interventions, Lilian Comas-Diaz's *Multicultural Care* (American Psychological Association, 2011), is a sound introduction and reference for therapists wanting to feel more cross-culturally competent. Alan and Mary Ivey and Carlos Zalaquett's *Intentional Interviewing and Counseling: Facilitating Client Development in a Multicultural Society* (2022, Cengage) offers guidance on adapting one's interviewing and counseling skills for unique multicultural encounters.

References

American Psychiatric Association. (2013). Culture and psychiatric diagnosis. In *Diagnostic and statistical manual of mental disorders* (5th ed.).

American Psychiatric Association. (2022). Culture and psychiatric diagnosis. In *Diagnostic and statistical manual of mental disorders* (5th ed., text rev.).

Novick, D., Montgomery, W., Aguado, J., Kadziola, Z., Peng, X., Brugnoli, R., & Haro, J.M. (2013). Which somatic symptoms are associated with an unfavorable course in Asian patients with major depressive disorder? *Journal of Affective Disorders, 149*(1–3), 182–188. https://doi.org/10.1016/j.jad.2013.01.020

Smith, A.D. (2020, September 9). Cultural sensitivity in mental health care: Getting to know your audience. *Psychology Today.* https://www.psychologytoday.com/us/blog/and-running/202009/cultural-sensitivity-in-mental-health-care

Yeung, K. & Kam, R. (2006). Recognizing and treating depression in Asian-Americans. *Psychiatric Times, 23*(14). https://www.psychiatrictimes.com/view/recognizing-and-treating-depression-asian-americans

Chapter 41

Talk About Medications

While therapists are not psychiatrists, they can be viewed as acting gatekeepers to medication efficacy or complications. Thus, there is still a need for therapists to have more than a superficial knowledge of psychiatric medications. However, it's unethical and a significant liability to give any medication directives. Because of this, there seems to be an implication that it's just safer to steer clear of medication discussions other than, "Do you think they work?" and "Are you taking them?"

It is no secret that psychiatry appointments are short. They are just long enough to check in and make a change if required; they average 15 minutes (Miller, 2021). This can be even less in "med clinics" in institutions like jails and nursing homes. When I worked in correctional environments, I recall psychiatrists seeing 20 people in three hours. Further, the short appointments limit the amount of detail a psychiatrist can provide about medications, and thus patients might not be informed about side effects other than the most common or serious possibilities.

Psychiatrists also tend to meet with patients less frequently than therapists. Given these considerations, it's easy to see that therapists are more likely to notice efficacy of medications and/or side effects before the next psychiatrist appointment. Thus, they encounter questions like, "Why isn't this working yet?" from patients.

While therapists do not instruct patients about managing their medications, they have a duty to be able to recognize side effects, know what can be generally expected in terms of effectiveness, and have a basic knowledge of how they work.

Of these duties the most important is noticing significant side effects and instructing the patient to alert their physician, or perhaps the therapist might contact the physician right away about the concern. A few more examples of instances that should lead to an immediate consultation with the physician are:

- Onset or increase in suicidal thinking after beginning antidepressants.

DOI: 10.4324/9781032631400-46

- Increased agitation and racing thoughts after starting to take certain types of antidepressants, which could indicate onset of medication-induced manic symptoms.
- Movement complications like restless legs or muscles that don't move properly (extrapyramidal side effects) after starting antipsychotic medications.
- A feverish, delirium-like state with movement complications called neuroleptic malignant syndrome (NMS), occasionally induced by antipsychotic medications, which can be fatal (Berman, 2011) and needs immediate medical intervention.

Another matter involving medication knowledge is working with patients to maintain prescription compliance. Many patients' treatment experiences are minimized by lack of pharmacotherapy because they discontinue taking the medications not because of the side effects, but because there is no immediate, expected gratification (Jung et al., 2016). In these instances, a little psychoeducation can go a long way.

Consider that 4–6 weeks is a long time to wait for results if someone is suffering from serious depression or anxiety. It's therefore not unusual for patients to prematurely discontinue a newly prescribed common antidepressant (e.g., Prozac, Trintellix, Cymbalta, Wellbutrin, etc.) within the first few weeks because they feel it isn't working fast enough. Even older ones like tricyclic antidepressants (e.g., Elavil, Anafranil) might have a quick effect on sleep and appetite, but still take a while to have the full effect. A therapist who knows what to expect from antidepressants can explore whether expected improvements, no matter how small, like clearer cognition or more energy, have materialized. They can then explain that such seemingly small gains are normal early results at three or four weeks, and a sign the medication is gaining traction, which could encourage the patient to persist with the trial.

On another compliance factor, it's been documented that patients who do not understand the relationship between their illness and the medication prescribed might be less apt to be compliant (Semahegn et al., 2020). Indeed, I've observed that if patients understand how or why a medication works, they seem more willing to entertain it. This was the case with Cliff, a person with schizophrenia who I worked with.

Cliff did well after several months of carefully following his psychiatrist's prescription regimen. Like some patients who, once improved, feel they no longer require the medication, during one session Cliff confessed he had not been taking it as prescribed "and I still feel OK." He described that the medication "calmed me, and I'm good now." This was concerning, as most people who discontinue taking antipsychotic medication experience a reinstatement of symptoms within a year or sooner (Perkins, 1999; Emsley et al., 2013), and Cliff was quite impaired when symptomatic.

"Cliff," I began, "you know from our discussions that when you're not feeling well, there are a number of factors at play. There's biology, stress, and a resurgence of some old conflicts about stuff in your past that we've been working on. I just wanted to let you know that following the doc's prescription can help protect against struggling again if you encounter stressors or those old wounds get triggered. The medication makes sure that neurochemical activity stays in check, notably one called dopamine. It seems that people prone to your kind of symptoms have a dopamine system that can misbehave. This can get triggered, especially under stress, and it's believed to be a big contributor to the intensity of the voices and your feeling disorganized."

Explaining to Cliff that part of his symptom picture arises from a biological process that needs an internal check and balance allowed him to re-conceptualize the importance of following his doctor's directions, and therefore, for the time being, he continued his medication.

Therapists who work with people like Cliff or others with chronic/severe mental illnesses, like bipolar disorders and severe depression, will know that there is a tendency for patients to have "on again off again" relationships with their medications for various reasons. While psychopharmacology is only part of an intervention, given the strong biological component of these illnesses, medication can be vital to general stability, the long-term benefit of which is priceless. This is because some illnesses, especially bipolar disorders, can produce a "kindling effect" (Weiss et al., 2015). This means that each episode sets the stage for the next to come on faster and perhaps be longer and more severe. Clearly, an ounce of prevention is worth a pound of cure.

Even more common than medication non-compliance once the patient is feeling better is non-compliance due to side effects. From sexual inhibitions on antidepressants to weight gain and movement complications on neuroleptics and mood stabilizers, patients struggle to weigh the benefits of the prescription. Provided the potential for serious side effects like NMS or suicidal thinking, therapists would do well to regularly check with the patient whether there have been any medication changes. They might also ask the patient to sign a release of information form for the psychiatrist to share a progress note after each appointment.

If there is a medication alteration, its useful to ask questions like, "What have you noticed since adding that medication?" or "Any changes in how you feel since the dose change?" Therapists are not only seeking news of (hopefully) symptom improvement, but also of any side effects. Being knowledgeable about what to expect in terms of efficacy and timeframes for effects can help therapists see burgeoning benefits and encourage compliance.

Knowing about the side effect profiles of the classes of medications, therapists can be observant for development of such concerns. For example,

Parkinsonian shaking (akathisia) or painful/stuck muscles (dystonia) are not uncommonly generated by older antipsychotic medications such as Haldol, Mellaril, or Trilafon, which are still utilized. The newer, "second generation" antipsychotic medications like Zyprexa, Abilify, and Saphris hold some potential for these unpleasant side effects (Divac et al., 2014), but more particularly a proneness to weight gain and metabolic/endocrine issues (Chokhawala & Stevens, 2023).

Concerning the latter, some males, for instance, can experience gynecomastia, or the development of breasts. Even in nothing is observable, it can be helpful to ask patients if their psychiatrist explained to them what side effects might occur, and inquire if they've been experiencing any of them. If so, they can then be informed something is possibly a side effect and referred to the psychiatrist sooner rather than later, hopefully before they discontinue the medication of their own volition and potentially regress.

Consider someone who says their psychiatrist told them they might have loss of appetite while taking stimulants for ADHD. The patient explains to the therapist that they take it twice daily, and have little appetite at lunch and dinner. The therapist asks, "How does that affect you?" The patient reports they feel weak or moody as they day wears on, which can inhibit their ability to function optimally, though the ADHD symptoms are better. This should spur collaboration with their psychiatrist sooner rather than later.

The therapist's role, here, is to help educate the patient and collaborate with the psychiatrist to keep the patient safe on the medication, and hopefully compliant. The sooner medication problems are discovered and addressed, the less likely a person is to experience severe side effects that may make them wary of medications.

There is one last observation about the importance of talking about medications with patients. Medication isn't just a biological component of intervention. It has, as so eloquently presented by psychiatrist David Mintz, *meaning* (Mintz, 2022). While seemingly a psychoanalytic idea, it is relevant across theories, as the need to consume medication can shape one's image, either in one's own eyes or those of others. Chances are, readers have encountered responses to asking who prescribed a medication such as, "the crazy doctor," indicating the patient's self-perception after seeing a psychiatrist.

Therapists can open the medication meaning discussion by simply asking about the medication's effectiveness. For example, the therapist might offer, "I'm glad the new dose seems to be working better. While we're on the topic, sometimes people tell me that medications are more than something that works on symptoms, like there's a relationship with the medication, or meaning given to their being prescribed. What can you tell me about your take on that?"

Perhaps, for example, the patient shares that medication makes their mental health struggle "real," and is an objective confirmation of a handicapped image. This then creates a dilemma in that, while helping some symptoms of depression, there may be shameful cognitions about requiring the prescription that require exploration and intervention, as they contribute to keeping depressive thoughts stoked, hindering optimal recovery.

Exploring the full medication experience, from effectiveness to the meaning assigned to it can clearly open therapeutic doors. Though therapists are not physicians, their place in helping patients understand and navigate their medications for better outcomes is in the therapist wheelhouse and can be practiced ethically.

Suggested Resources

It is easy enough to internet search medication basics like how long they take to work, side effects, and what they are used for. Despite this basic knowledge being readily available, therapists should consider a periodic continuing education training in psychopharmacology to keep updated and have a forum to ask questions.

To gain a full appreciation of psychopharmacology, therapists are invited to read Wallace Mendelson's *The Curious History of Psychopharmacology* (2020, Pythagoras Press), an account of serendipitous discoveries that led to psychiatric relief and set the stage for modern medications. For the therapist wishing to gain insight into the clinical implications of the meaning of being prescribed medication and how it contributes to whether someone is medication compliant or not, David Mintz's *Psychodynamic Psychopharmacology* (2022, American Psychiatric Association) is a first-of-its-kind publication.

References

Berman, B.D. (2011). Neuroleptic malignant syndrome: A review for neurohospitalists. *Neurohospitalist, 1*(1), 41–47. doi:10.1177/1941875210386491

Chokhawala, K. & Stevens, L. (2023, February 26). Antipsychotic medications. In StatPearls [internet]. https://www.ncbi.nlm.nih.gov/books/NBK519503

Divac, N., Prostran, M., Jakovcevski, I., & Cerovac, N. (2014). Second-generation antipsychotics and extrapyramidal adverse effects. Biomed Research International. doi:10.1155/2014/656370

Emsley, R., Chiliza, B., Asmal, L., & Harvey, B.H. (2013). The nature of relapse in schizophrenia. *BMC Psychiatry, 13*(50). doi:10.1186/1471-244X-13–50

Jung, W.Y., Jang, S.H., Kim, S.G., Jae, Y.M., Kong, B.G., Kim, H.C., Choe, B.M., Kim, J.G., & Kim, C.R. (2016). Times to discontinue antidepressants over 6 months in patients with major depressive disorder. *Psychiatry Investigation, 13*(4), 440–446. doi:10.4306/pi.2016.13.4.440

Miller, J.J. (2021). The 16-minute med check. *Psychiatric Times, 38*(2). https://www.psychiatrictimes.com/view/16-minute-med-check

Mintz, D. (2022). *Psychoanalytic psychopharmacology: Caring for the treatment-resistant patient.* American Psychiatric Association Publishing.

Perkins, D.O. (1999). Adherence to antipsychotic medications. *Journal of Clinical Psychiatry, 60*(supplement 21), 25–30. https://www.psychiatrist.com/wp-

Semahegn, A., Torpey, K., Manu, A., Assefa, N., Tesfaye, G., & Ankomah, A. (2020). Psychotropic medication non-adherence and its associated factors among patients with major psychiatric disorders: A systematic review and meta-analysis. *Systematic Reviews, 9*(17). doi:10.1186/s13643-020-1274-3

Weiss, R.B., Stange, J.P., Boland, E.M., Black, S.K., LaBelle, D.R., Abramson, L.Y., & Alloy, L.B. (2015). Kindling of life stress in bipolar disorder: Comparison of sensitization and autonomy models. *Journal of Abnormal Psychology, 124*(1), 4–16. doi:10.1037/abn0000014

Chapter 42

Personality Disorders Are Important

It's been estimated that up to 20 percent of the world's population experience a personality disorder (Gawda, 2018). Considering mental health treatment settings harbor concentrated representations of diagnoses, there is a greater than 20 percent chance therapists will encounter them in patients. In fact, it's been estimated that prevalence in the mental health care setting is at least 30 percent (Fariba et al., 2023).

Are you prepared?

Unfortunately, it seems that unless a therapist develops a specific clinical interest in them, personality disorders get little attention in academic and early career experiences. The ones that are given attention tend to be borderline, narcissistic, and antisocial, perhaps the most vexing, which can ingrain a fear of anything "personality disordered" in therapists. In fact, personality disorders are among the most stigmatized diagnoses in mental health, including by practitioners (Sheehan et al., 2022, Masland et al., 2023).

Aside from the aforementioned, do you recall there are seven other personality disorders included in the *DSM*? Further, it would be remiss not to recognize the work of unparalleled personality researchers like the late Theodore Millon, PhD (2011), who reminded us there are actually several more, such as the exuberant, passive-aggressive, self-defeating, and depressive. While each of these was at times recognized in the *DSM*, the American Psychiatric Association felt they were better accounted for by other *DSM* diagnoses and created undue diagnostic confusion.

For instance, the depressive personality was said to be too difficult to differentiate from dysthymia, a form of persistent depression. However, interested therapists will likely find value in understanding that a depressive personality refers to enduring personality dynamics, and not a mood state (Shedler, 2022). Of course, troubling personality dynamics can lend themselves to depressive episodes and will need addressing if the tendency for depression is to be resolved.

DOI: 10.4324/9781032631400-47

These "non-*DSM*" personality diagnoses can introduce tricky diagnostic situations for billing purposes. However, the "Other" and "Unspecified" personality disorder categories may suffice if a therapist is inclined to recognize them.

Clearly, personality has a plethora of considerations and clinical implications, and popular misunderstandings about personality disorders keep the waters opaque. In particular, the idea that personality disorders are impossible to treat and that if it is someone under 18 "you can't diagnose that" are particularly troubling, perhaps even unethical. Consider that, if nothing else, therapists should be able to identify whether or not personality complications are present and make appropriate referrals to providers who can adeptly treat them.

Given the unique flavors and significant pathology of personality disorders, it is not enough to know how to treat the anxiety, moodiness, or relationship problems inherent in them, which may be the initial presenting problem(s). The long-standing, incredibly pervasive, inflexible, maladaptive thinking and behaviors of people with disordered personalities requires a special skill set, especially with the level of transference that can occur.

Early in my career I often heard colleagues say, "She's just a borderline," or "He's just a narcissist" and I was warned to steer clear of such patients. "Those people will just manipulate you," I was told. Finding this intriguing, and curious how I was supposed to steer clear of someone with a personality disorder if they were on my caseload, I felt I had no choice but to develop an interest in personality disorders if I was to work effectively among them.

This pejorative stance against personality pathology is not unusual to hear in the clinical world, and some researchers are investigating whether personality disorder stigma amongst professionals is correlated to their training (Lindell-Innes et al., 2023). Indeed, based on my early colleagues' opinions, despite my budding interest in personality disorders, I often found myself minimizing and thinking pejoratively about this population. All the while, however, I couldn't help but think, "The person didn't ask to be that way." This empathic idea is what spurred me to be educated about them and how to best work with such diagnoses. It would be foolish not to recognize these are difficult disorders to work with and some, especially borderline personality disorder, can be simply taxing.

This does not, however, give therapists license to cull them or deny the person has the problem because they are incapable of skillfully treating them. I am increasingly convinced that some therapists, through their own unconscious defenses, may deny a personality disorder is present in order not to fail at treating it, and save face. It makes sense that this could be the case early on as one gains confidence and is trying to establish clinical prowess.

Unfortunately, this could well lead to frustration and some *loss* of confidence because the real issue at hand is not getting addressed; the patient's challenges escalate and the clinician feels increasingly powerless and frustrated. Meanwhile, the patient suffers when they could have been in proper care.

It took some time to learn to work effectively with personality disorders, and I eventually realized how, at times, I duped myself into seeing borderline personality as "bipolar" and antisocial personality as "intermittent explosive." Upon reflection I believe it was because I better understood those personality disorder euphemisms as less-threatening and less vexing, and thus felt I could better work with the individual.

Pretending the personality-disordered patient primarily suffers a different diagnosis, for whatever reason, is a disservice, no matter how well-intended. Period.

Remember, even though symptoms like moodiness, poor impulse control, and avoidant behaviors are present in many diagnoses, it is erroneous to think therapists simply treat symptoms and not the disorder. In personality disorders, the moodiness, poor impulse control, and avoidance is driven by a machine more sophisticated than low frustration tolerance, thrill seeking, or performance anxiety. Thus, when addressing personality, it is necessary to understand there are long-ingrained, maladaptive core schema about relationships and the world driving the behaviors.

Someone with a dependent personality, for example, cannot only be given anxiety coping skills for when alone and weekly tasks of independence to show them they can manage on their own. Their life revolves around the idea that "I'm incompetent and incapable, so rely on fastening myself to others so they can care for me and make my decisions" (Smith, 2022). Insight will need to be developed into how their clinging behaviors actually push away the intimacy they desire, in the hope of motivating them to gain a sense of independent self. Other issues can quickly arise, like becoming dependent on the therapist, who must in turn recognize this and help them feel connected but autonomous and capable. It is much more labyrinthine maneuvering than symptom reduction. A completely new way of learning to relate is required if the therapy is to be considered successful.

Another reason therapists pull back on diagnosing personality disorders is age and wanting to spare youth the diagnosis. There is a specious belief that "you can't diagnose a personality disorder under 18." With this in mind, readers are encouraged to read the "Development and Course" portion of the personality disorder chapter in the *DSM 5-TR* (American Psychiatric Association, 2022) where it is stated that, except for antisocial personality, diagnosis of personality disorders in juveniles is indicated at times. Be clear, however, it is not to be taken lightly and it must be established that the behavior is a years-long, maladaptive, inflexible pattern.

Therapists can be doing teens a great disservice if a personality disorder is recognized and not diagnosed, especially borderline. I've been told by colleagues for years that the main reason the diagnosis isn't applied is because it stigmatizes the youth. I cannot keep track of how many juveniles I have evaluated who have received years of mollified diagnoses such as unspecified bipolar disorder, mood disorder not otherwise specified (*DSM* editions prior to *DSM 5*), or unspecified behavior disorder to account for what is a years-long pattern of behavior that clearly meets the criteria for borderline or narcissistic personality disorder. Interventions suited to the applied diagnoses, like parental boundary maintenance, coping skills, and medication, have little effect and the struggles continue to intensify until the youth has even sometimes been deemed treatment resistant.

This attempt to not stigmatize them clinically leaves the teen to stew in tumultuous relationships and a host of complicated emotions. They also can become the target of peers and adults as "the troubled kid" who is to be avoided. Is it not more ethical to diagnose, plan, and treat accordingly to spare the child a life of such interactions? It is an important consideration (Wall et al., 2021). In fact, recent researchers (Chanen et al., 2022) have suggested all mental health professionals working with youth should be attuned to accurately recognizing emerging personality disorders in order to provide early intervention given their pervasiveness. Theodore Millon (2011) provided comprehensive views of emerging personality disorders to assist with this particular process.

If further proof is required that not acknowledging a personality disorder does more harm than good, look no further than Kiera van Gelder's biography *The Buddha and the Borderline* (2013). The author discusses how she learned a personality disorder was in her hospital charts for years but she nor early therapists were informed about it, which set the stage for years of extra suffering.

To be most clinically effective, readers are encouraged to explore their own views surrounding personality disorders and how that might interfere with constructive practice. Reading accounts of work with these populations, or biographies, is a good start. Students in my Behind the Diagnosis course, for instance, have found reading detailed accounts of therapy with personality-disordered people, like Stuart Yudofsky's *Fatal Flaws* (2005), an inspiration for garnering empathy and interest in the subject.

Suggested Resources

Readers who desire a thorough, practical introduction to personality pathology are directed to Joseph Shannon's trainings on the topic. Dr Shannon delivers material about this stigmatized population in a compassionate and hopeful manner and provides 40 plus years of insight into what works for these patients. He has retired from touring the US with his training courses, but they are available through Institute for Brain Potential (www.ibpceu.com).

As for books, Stuart Yudofsky's *Fatal Flaws* (American Psychiatric Association, 2005) presents a wealth of developmental and diagnostic material on eight pathological personality styles. Each case Dr Yudofsky presents reads like a novel as he guides readers through conversational narratives of long-term patients, all the while explaining the patient's behaviors and his responses. *Disorders of Personality* (3rd edition) by Theodore Millon (2011, Wiley) provides a highly digestible, comprehensive review of disordered personalities, including the ten listed in the *DSM 5* and several others. Dr Millon considers historical perspectives, perspectives of different theoretical orientations, diagnostic components, childhood manifestations, and treatment approaches, complete with case vignettes.

Those interested in exploring childhood personality pathology are referred to psychiatrist Efrain Bleiberg's *Treating Personality Disorders in Children and Adolescents* (2004, Guilford Press), illuminating identification of, and treatment for, disordered personalities in youth.

References

American Psychiatric Association. (2022). *Diagnostic and statistical manual of mental disorders* (5th ed., text rev.) (pp. 00–00).

Chanen, A.M., Sharp, C., Nicol, K., & Kaess, M. (2022). Early intervention for personality disorder [Abstract]. *Focus, 20*(4), 402–408. https://doi.org/10.1176/appi.focus.20220062

Fariba, K.A., Gupta, V., & Kass. E. (2023). Personality disorder. [Updated Apr 17, 2023]. In StatPearls [internet]. StatPearls Publishing. https://www.ncbi.nlm.nih.gov/books/NBK556058

Gawda, B.U. (2018). Cross-cultural studies on the prevalence of personality disorders. *Current Issues in Personality Psychology, 46*(4), 318–329.

Lindell-Innes, R., Phillips-Hughes, A.L., Bartsch, D., Galletly, C., & Ludbrook, C. (2023). Attitudes of psychiatry trainees towards patients with borderline personality disorder: Does the stigma begin during training? [Abstract]. *Personality and Mental Health, 17*(4), 1–9. https://doi.org/10.1002/pmh.1587

Masland, S.R., Victor, S.E., Peters, J.R., Fitzpatrick, S., Dixon-Gordon, K.L., Bettis, A.H., Navarre, K.M., & Rizvi, S.L. (2023). Destigmatizing borderline personality disorder: A call to action for psychological science [Abstract]. *Perspectives on Psychological Science, 18*(2), 445–460. https://doi.org/10.1177/17456916221100464

Millon, T. (2011). *Disorder of personality: Introducing a DSM/ICD spectrum from normal to abnormal* (3rd ed.) Wiley.

Shedler, J. (2022). The personality syndromes. In R.E. Feinstein (Ed.), *Primer on personality disorders* (pp. 6–7). Oxford University Press.

Sheehan, L., Gaurean, B., and Corrigan, P.W. (2022), Debate: Stigma implications for diagnosing personality disorders in adolescents. *Child and Adolescent Mental Health, 27*(2), 203–205. https://doi.org/10.1111/camh.12556

Smith, A.D. (2022, January 23). 10 core beliefs of personality disorders: Understanding maladaptive schema helps make sense of the vexing behaviors. *Psychology Today.* https://www.psychologytoday.com/us/blog/up-and-running/202201/10-core-beliefs-of-personality-disorders

Van Gelder, K. (2013). *The buddha and the borderline: A memoir.* New Harbinger.

Wall, K., Kerr, S., & Sharp, C. (2021). Barriers to care for adolescents with borderline personality disorder. *Current Opinion in Psychology, 37*, 54–60.

Yudofsky, S. (2005). *Fatal flaws: Navigating destructive relationships with people with disorders of personality and character.* American Psychiatric Publishing.

Chapter 43

Ask for Feedback

Noel pondered if a newer patient was experiencing any benefit from their meetings. "Have you asked your patient for feedback on how they feel the sessions are going?" I asked.

"Won't that seem like I'm doubting myself?" he asked. "We're supposed to appear confident so they have faith in us, no?" I responded, "I suppose if you anxiously ask if they're comfortable or if they approve of your work, it certainly may. But let's look at it as more of a collaboration."

The truth is therapists are not always going to encounter visible improvements to know how things are going, especially at the outset. Patients likely won't give feedback on their own, either. This is perhaps due to not wanting to offend the therapist or, honestly, they just don't know what to expect. Even though they feel no benefit, they may simply believe that this is therapy and eventually something will come of it.

In the course of interviewing hundreds of people about their therapy experiences, I asked some why they kept with a provider for months or years despite little progress. "They're the doctor, they know what's best," is a frequent response, "so when they say to set up another appointment, I do."

Sadly, patients can perpetually and needlessly suffer in these circumstances. Asking for feedback can make sure that does not happen. It's a good practice to inform the patient at the outset they can feel free to offer feedback on how they are experiencing therapy, and that periodically the therapist will check in with them about it, too. This plants the seed for them to be vigilant for any concerns, and shows the therapist is interested in an honest relationship.

Collaborative evaluation of the sessions can be easily kneaded into the therapy work. I have found it can help pick up the next session where we left off, or it's a nice way to wind down.

Returning to Noel, I asked him if I did anything in our supervisory interactions that he might find useful for gathering feedback in his sessions with patients. "Sometimes you start off asking me how I digested the previous supervision. Sometimes when we wrap up, you ask what was most helpful

DOI: 10.4324/9781032631400-48

about our meeting, kind of like reviewing what we discussed," said Noel. "Precisely!" I continued, "Those questions might seem like a review, but is that not me checking in with you, asking for feedback, to make sure you're benefitting?"

"I see," finished Noel, "it's in the semantics and presentation, not point blank asking the patient to evaluate *me*."

"Yes, it helps me know you're profiting from our meetings and gives you a chance to review what we talked about. Sometimes, too, I notice your wrinkled brow and inquire if things make sense or if you want clarification, which you can do with patients," I ended. The route to tactfully, and therapeutically, obtaining feedback doesn't have to be awkward.

Opening or closing sessions with such material can be therapeutically rich. Patients process therapy material between appointments. Therefore, opening the following one by asking how they digested the previous one not only picks up where you left off, but provides insight into what might have been helpful or difficult, guiding the session.

Winding down a therapy hour by asking how the session was for the patient can also be helpful. This is especially so if time is getting short and you must find a tactful way to close down the session. Brenda, for instance, was very talkative and the session had only a few minutes remaining. Catching her eye, the therapist said, "Brenda, I'm not trying to cut you off, but today went by pretty quick; we've only got five minutes left. We talked about a lot of stuff, some of it not so easy for you, and I just wanted to take a few minutes and check in how it was for you today." Her feedback can provide not only her perception of the collaboration, but provide a potential place to restart next time.

Other times, I have found it helpful to carefully listen for opportunities to mine information about patients' therapeutic experience. Lenny, for instance, was a depressed and overall isolated young man. He worked a lot to avoid his father, who abused alcohol and who always wanted something from him. His mother perpetually wanted his handyman skills and to use him as a babysitter.

While independent and successful in his career, Lenny had little social/emotional support. One day, Lenny revealed he had been talking to a romantic interest who asked about his family. He shared that he recoiled at this inquiry, figuring the person would be afraid to involve themselves with someone seemingly sandwiched between two demanding parents. Lenny confessed he just did not feel he could be honest about his family without it somehow making himself look bad. "Talking to others about that stuff isn't like coming here," he explained. Therein was the opportunity to hear Lenny's thoughts on his therapy experience. "What *did* allow you to tell me about your family?" I wondered aloud. "You're incredibly easy to talk to," he replied.

Not only did Lenny give me feedback on his therapy experience, but I learned what worked for Lenny and what he needed more of. The ensuing discussion revealed that he found the therapeutic relationship, experiencing that he can learn to successfully interact with others and be accepted despite flaws he may see, more satisfying than any pointed therapeutic direction.

"Given your background, it makes a lot of sense that you'd find making a connection with someone supportive and open to *your* needs fulfilling. You can grow a lot from a healthy relationship." I finished, "I'm always curious about people's experiences here. What else can you tell me, good or bad, about what it's been like coming here for you?"

I was able to get Lenny's feedback, and, further, use the opportunity to provide exactly what he found helpful. By requesting his input, it showed Lenny he mattered; while inviting his honesty (i.e., thoughts, good or bad), it opened the door to working on his honesty with others about how they affected him.

There is much to be capitalized on by practicing sharp listening.

Section V

Professional Development

Chapter 44

Consider an Integrative Approach

What does one of the greatest martial artists of all time have to offer psychotherapists? The answer is stylistic flexibility. Bruce Lee did not become "The Little Dragon" by pigeonholing himself in one fighting approach. He saw that all traditions of defense had something to offer him. "Use no way as way. Have no limitation as limitation," Lee suggested (Lee, 2011).

During his early years in China, Lee studied a southern style of kung fu called Wing Chun, which focused on hand strikes and stand-up grappling. Given the southern Chinese are more compact people, their kung fu approaches relied on shorter strikes and "in fighting." In contrast, in the north, people are taller and have more leg advantage, so styles focus more on kicking and acrobatics (Martial Tribes, 2018).

Although Wing Chun was effective in general self-defense or fighting amongst other southern Chinese styles, it did not take Lee long to see the limitations. He realized, for example, that if he was taken down, he lacked solid ground fighting skills. While he was quick with his hands, he observed, it was not the fluidity required to encounter a Western boxer. Lee thus began studying a palette of fighting approaches to integrate into his Wing Chun foundation. He even studied fencing, for he admired the footwork to develop skill in dodging opponents. "Take what is useful," Lee touted in *The Tao of Jeet Kune Do* (2011).

In graduate school and while developing my skill as a therapist, I couldn't help but recall Lee's writing. I was overwhelmed by all of the different therapy styles I was introduced to, and the people I learned about them from seemed to be dogmatic practitioners. There were person-centered (Rogerian) professors, cognitive-behavioral supervisors, psychoanalysts, and those touting solution-oriented/ultra-brief therapy styles.

Sometimes the style seemed preached, and I felt it must be followed like a religion if I was to be an effective therapist. Was I to devote myself to one approach despite feeling I could use material from each? My supervisees over the years have asked similarly.

DOI: 10.4324/9781032631400-50

As I matured, I felt like a dilettante because I never subscribed to one approach as I felt I was "supposed to." However, I began noticing that I was effectively using skills from this or that modality, even though I was not an expert in those modalities. A supervisor eventually told me this wasn't wrong, and, "You just have an integrative style."

"Integrative" has become an umbrella term (Benito, 2018) but you may also hear the term "eclectic style" used, and there are technical differences. Eclecticism regards selecting convenient techniques from various styles (Kratochvíl, 1994), perhaps akin to developing an expansive toolbox. This isn't synonymous with "throwing something until it sticks," but, like a mechanic, one must be familiar with how and when to use these tools. On the other hand, integrative psychotherapy occurs when a therapist successfully merges two or more systems which they find complimentary.

Researchers have told us that this is not a new phenomenon in psychotherapy. In fact, it's believed that the first reference was from a practitioner in the 1930s who urged that Pavlov's classical conditioning be incorporated into analysis (Stricker & Gold, 2008).

The mingling of styles blossomed some more in the 1960s as new styles arose to integrate. No longer was it only Neo-Freudians and Gestalt therapists, but entering the scene were Aaron Beck's cognitive therapy, Albert Ellis's rational-emotive behavioral therapy (REBT), and Carl Rogers' person-centered approach. In the following decades, Steven Hayes' acceptance and commitment therapy (ACT), Marsha Linehan's dialectical behavioral therapy (DBT), and Richard Schwartz's internal family systems (IFS) gained success and therapists had more tools and theories to unify.

One approach that unfolded over those years that remains successful and popular is cognitive analytic therapy (CAT). Combining the analytic practice of understanding how past relationships influenced present problems and providing correction with cognitive interventions, CAT delivers a sort of shorter-term, but in-depth, integrative approach.

Integrative psychotherapy gained enough interest for Stony Brook University-based psychologist Marvin Goldfried and his associates to organize the Society for Exploration of Psychotherapeutic Integration in 1983 (Stony Brook University, 2023). SEPI, as it has become known, is active to this day, complete with an annual conference. Students and supervisees, as they search for their therapeutic identity, have found it helpful to peruse SEPI's training courses and newsletters.

Readers may be wondering what integrative psychotherapy looks like in action. To illustrate, let's examine the case of Alice, for whom my personal integrative approach worked well. She was a college-aged adult, who was referred by her primary care doctor. In the previous year, Alice's visits to the doctor had steadily climbed to almost weekly visits. She always seemed to have a variety of symptoms she interpreted as signs of serious illnesses.

CT scans, blood work, and specialists she was referred to never uncovered anything alarming.

Despite the assurance from the doctors, Alice nonetheless continued to worry if maybe they just were not picking up on the problem. Perhaps, she wondered, she had a very rare disease that needed to evolve until it could show up on tests. Alice had WebMD bookmarked, along with online forums for diseases she believed she could have, in turn working herself up and bringing herself back to the doctor. Alice's presentation is classic illness anxiety (hypochondria).

As we began to examine her concerns, we met some success working in a solution-oriented psychotherapy method. This approach capitalizes on exceptions to the problem. Alice realized she had days that were less anxiety-provoking, such as when she had more structure and therefore less time to worry about illness. She agreed that getting more consistent structure could be helpful, and started to profit from this helpful realization.

More classic CBT work like exposure therapy came into play when we worked on keeping her from WebMD, or limiting her to two visits to the doctor a month. Alice learned to sit with the anxiety of not running out for second and third opinions after being examined by her primary physician. She eventually saw that regardless of whether or not she got those opinions, the original complaint never got worse, and it dawned on her how much time and money in copayments she had been wasting over the years.

When the severity of Alice's symptoms began to dull, and the therapeutic relationship became more intimate, she revealed that she has always had an overwhelming fear of death. Alice explained that she needs to do whatever it takes to make sure she does not perish prematurely. This, she noted, was why it was always imperative she be on top of any potential illness.

Such a revelation is fertile ground in therapy, and not to be ignored. This ingrained belief was clearly the catalyst of the anxious behaviors. Treatment shifted to not only focusing on combatting specific symptoms, but to wrestling, via a more existential psychotherapy approach, with the death anxiety she harbored. Alice discovered she felt her life had little substance, and she needed to live as long as possible in order to hopefully try and find meaning. If we had continued to only categorically check off symptoms and send her on her way, Alice would never have been able to work towards filling this major void in her life, and most likely the pathology would have returned.

Suggested Resources

Talking Therapy: An Ongoing Conversation Between Two Psychotherapy Experts and Longtime Friends, a podcast by Alan Frances, MD, and Marvin Goldfried, PhD, presents a variety of relevant thought-provoking discussions. The topics covered include therapy style, commonalities amongst all therapies, and, in "Ending the Psychotherapy Wars" episode (March, 2022), the need to provide cross-theoretical training for clinical flexibility. *The Handbook of Psychotherapy Integration* by John Norcross and Marvin Goldfried (2019, Oxford University Press) is a comprehensive reference on research and application of integrative psychotherapy.

My favorite book featuring successful psychotherapy style integration, considering the perennial bickering between the psychodynamic and cognitive-behavioral guilds, is psychiatrist Michael Garrett's *Psychotherapy for Psychosis: Integrating Cognitive-Behavioral and Psychodynamic Approaches* (2019, Guilford Press). Lastly, exploring the Society for the Exploration of Psychotherapeutic Integration will prove useful in answering questions about integrative approaches. This can be found at www.sepiweb.org.

References

Benito, M.J. (2018). The fine line between integration or eclecticism and syncretism in new therapists. *Dual Diagnosis: Open Access, 3*(308), 1–5. doi:10.21767/2472–5048.100042Kratochvíl, S. (1994). Eclectic, synthetic and integrative psychotherapy. *Ceskoslovenska Psychiatrie, 90*(6), 305–314. Lee, B. (2011). *The tao of jeet kune do* (exp. ed.). Black Belt Communications.

Martial Tribes (2018, June 17). *Disciplines: North versus south kung fu.* https://www.martialtribes.com/north-vs-south-kung-fu

Stony Brook University (2023). Marvin R. Goldfried, Ph.D. *Department of psychology: Faculty profiles.* https://www.stonybrook.edu/commcms/psychology/faculty/faculty_profiles/mgoldfried

Stricker, G. & Gold, J. (2008). Integrative therapy. In J.J. Lebow (Ed.), *Twenty-first century psychotherapies: Contemporary approaches to theory and practice.* Wiley.

Chapter 45

Limiting Liability

If you have never thought about what it means to be held liable, now is a good time to start. Liability means being held responsible, usually from a legal standpoint. While therapists might not be surgeons, they still have people's lives in their hands.

Consider, for example, instances where patients harm themselves or others. Could the therapist have intervened or otherwise halted the action(s)? "Was the therapist negligent?" an attorney might ask. Consider, too, that a vindictive patient might allege therapist abandonment if the therapist didn't call back within a particular timeframe. The attorney could question, "Did the therapist provide clear guidelines about what their clientele should expect in terms of availability, response timeframes, and what to do in the event the therapist might not be immediately available for an acute matter?"

The above are just two of the kinds of questions a therapist could find themselves answering in the legal arena if they do not pay attention to liability risk management. Consider today's world of teletherapy and texting, and it might seem therapists' liabilities are ever-expanding.

Without constantly monitoring one's risk, a therapist opens themselves to ethics board complaints, licensing board discipline, civil and even criminal suits. Even if a therapist is not found guilty of a complaint, there is collateral damage to consider:

- A reputation may be sullied based on the accusation becoming known.
- The stress and cost of board/legal procedures.
- Lost income while a license is suspended pending investigations/trials.
- Increased liability insurance premiums.

It must be remembered that a therapist's liability and board defense insurance is not impenetrable armor. While insurance does offer a level of protection, it cannot prevent the bullet items. Rather, liability insurance is largely for covering attorney consultation/representation fees and punitive settlements. Some psychotherapist liability insurance providers also offer a

DOI: 10.4324/9781032631400-51

set number of annual hours of legal/ethical consultation per year regarding things like best practice procedures in the therapist's jurisdiction.

Since liability insurance is not a magic eraser, what's a therapist to do to limit liability and corollary damages? Readers may be thinking, "Don't have personal relationships with patients" or "Don't try to treat something you're not qualified to." While both are correct, there are three big things *to do* that provide a wealth of protection for the patient and therapist.

1. Invest in quality liability and board defense insurance, *even if* your employer provides coverage. This is because their coverage could be the bare minimum and, for instance, not cover certain types of conduct or board complaints (Landau & Reamer, 2022).

   While insurance cannot erase the situation, it offers protection from vast legal fees, and there is the possibility of obtaining additional legal consultation. Attorney Robert Landau (Landau & Reamer 2022), an expert in ethics and risk management in behavioral health, recommends therapists obtain insurance with the maximum aggregate available, coverage for depositions/subpoenas, Health Insurance Portability and Accountability Act (HIPPA), and cyber liability. It is also possible to find plans that assist in compensating for lost wages during an investigation. As therapists mature in their career, they may wish to add other coverage, such as issues related to having supervisees on site.

   Obtaining sufficient coverage probably sounds like an expensive endeavor. However, readers might be relieved to learn that my personal insurance needs are less than $200 annually for $5 million aggregate. Further, professional associations sometimes have partnerships with insurance providers that reduce the cost, and some insurance providers give additional discounts if the therapist has attended an ethics training in the past year.

2. Document, document, document! Ostensibly, documentation probably seems to be a fairly dry subject. That is, until one is audited by an insurance company or has a complaint waged against them (Wiger, 2021). It is the only record of what occurred, and therefore perhaps a therapist's most valuable tool in defense. Thus, it is not only ethically appropriate (American Counseling Association, 2014), but common sense, to document in a timely fashion. Ideally, this occurs immediately after the session. If documentation must occur later, making a quick note post-session of what to include will help the therapist recall appropriate details and not confuse patient information.

   At a basic level, documentation, from diagnostic assessment to treatment plans to session notes, conveys not only mental status and risk material, but patient progress or lack thereof despite the therapist's best efforts, and shows the practitioner is maintaining standards of care. It is also a place to note any concerns, like a patient's sexual suggestion or threat, how the therapist responded, and who they conferred with about managing the matter. Without documentation, it never happened.

Thus, documentation is essential to both patient and practitioner. Volumes have been written on documentation, and readers will benefit from reviewing the titles in Suggested Resources. To help with session notes, a worksheet is included at the end of this chapter.

3. Maintaining confidentiality might sound easy, but there are plenty of opportunities to slip up. Readers are surely familiar with not discussing identifying information when discussing a case, or, say, talking about patients with someone who is discovered to be a mutual acquaintance. But what about:

- Encountering a patient in the community.
- Attending to a patient's call outside the office.
- Patient information storage for mobile providers like in-home therapists.
- Internet searching one's patients.
- Deciding when a deliberate break in confidentiality is required.

In the words of a late colleague, a psychiatric attorney, the answers to each of these questions starts with, "It depends." It is one thing, for example, to reciprocate a patient's "hello" on the sidewalk. It is another to decide what to do if the patient says "Hello," then points to people exiting a store and says, "I'd like you to meet my family." In each situation, the risks and benefits to patient welfare must be weighed. Perhaps the therapist chooses to meet the family, fearing it would hurt the patient's feelings and ruin rapport if they didn't. Then the patient's spouse says, "X tells me they're feeling much better since talking to you. What's your approach to treating them?"

How would you respond?

Clearly, liability provides plenty of food for thought. Each of the above is worthy of preemptive conversations in clinical supervision. They also illustrate the importance of knowing who to contact for consultation in everyday practice. If there is an acute situation, and a supervisor is not immediately available, conferring with a nearby colleague, and documenting the encounter, can mitigate risk by showing the therapist did not act in haste and they tried to make the best decision possible.

Aside from heeding the above and maintaining supervision, therapists will find it helpful to attend an annual training on ethics or clinical risk management to keep abreast of general best practices. A checklist of actions to limit liability is included at the end of the chapter.

Suggested Resources

Other than taking a regular ethics seminar, my recommended resource for keeping liability limiting practices in sight is the "Avoiding Liability" blog from liability insurance provider CPH & Associates. Each month showcases a particular issue that might have associated liability, and how to mitigate the risk. Therapists do not need to get their insurance though CPH in order to access the blog, which is available at https://cphins.com/blog.

For those working in correctional facilities, with cluster B personality disorders, divorce, or custody populations, or are generally concerned about legal backlash, Bill Eddy's *High Conflict People in Legal Disputes* (2016, Unhooked Books) is an indispensable reference for navigating situations with potentially litigious clientele.

References

American Counseling Association (2014). *Code of ethics.* https://www.counseling.org/docs/default-source/default-document-library/ethics/2014-aca-code-of-ethics.pdf?sfvrsn=55ab73d0_1

Landau, R. & Reamer, F.G. (2022). *Ethics and risk management in behavioral health: What every clinician needs to know about mental health and the law* [Webinar]. Professional Education Systems Institute.

Wiger, D.E. (2021). *The psychotherapy documentation primer* (4th ed.). Wiley.

Liability Limitation Checklist

☐ Even if my employer offers liability insurance, do I purchase my own?

Does my liability insurance:

☐ Have at least $3 million, and, ideally, $5 million aggregate coverage?
☐ Include some form of general legal/ethical consultation?
☐ Cover cybersecurity-related concerns, especially if practicing telehealth?
☐ Provide support for depositions/subpoenas?
☐ Cover HIPPA-related complaints?

Do I:

☐ Only practice within my scope (e.g., not giving medication advice, not treating disorders for which the therapist has no experience/training)?
☐ Attend an annual ethics training?
☐ Keep up with continuing education required for licensure?
☐ Maintain appropriate boundaries with patients, especially refraining from anything sexual, or any form of social relationships?
☐ Bill *only* for services provided that are allowed by the respective contracts with managed care companies?
☐ Engage in the supervision required for my pre-licensure requirements/ obtain adequate supervision for post-licensure requirements?
☐ Keep records of supervision, including material discussed and how the supervisor responded?
☐ Obtain therapy for personal concerns that could jeopardize patients (e.g. substance abuse, bias)?
☐ Carefully document any concerns that arise in the therapy and how they were addressed, including supervision sought (e.g., patient sexual advances or threats and how they were managed; a patient decided to discontinue treatment).

Psychotherapy Note Checklist for Thoroughness and Limiting Liability

At the most basic level, a psychotherapy note should include:

- ☐ Brief notation of progress/lack of, keeping patients' personal details limited in case records are obtained by another party.
- ☐ Mental status, including commentary regarding changes in mental status.
- ☐ When the next appointment will be.

Other material that therapists encounter should be added to the above, as required, including:

- ☐ Risk assessment. This should not only occur when someone is clearly presenting risk factors/warnings. Patients with a risk history, even if they are currently stable, should be monitored and asked when their last incident (thoughts and/or actions) were, how they managed it, and what they will do should they feel risk mounting.
- ☐ If a risk to others occurs and there is a duty to warn, details of whether the person was able to be contacted and/or what other action was taken to try to protect the individual.
- ☐ Notation of medication changes/complaints/effectiveness, and if the patient was referred to their prescriber or the therapist was going to reach out for them.
- ☐ Notation of accusations towards the therapist or boundary concerns towards the therapist (sexual advances, touching, request for social contact, threats, indication a patient has followed the therapist, aggression) and how they were addressed. This should include who the therapist sought supervision/consultation from, if needed.
- ☐ If a patient has been consistently late, no-showing, or not paying on time and how this was addressed with them and their response.
- ☐ If the patient required an alteration in providers to address something outside of the therapist's scope and how this was coordinated.
- ☐ If the patient wished to terminate therapy against the therapist's advice and how this was addressed, including informing the patient how to contact them if they changed their mind.
- ☐ If a patient is deemed to require a physician's assessment for an ailment or non-psychiatric medication re-evaluation that is possibly causing/exacerbating the patient's presenting psychotherapy concerns.
- ☐ If the patient needed a referral to a social service or advocacy assistance (such as for school or work), and how the therapist helped in the situation (providing guidance on whom to contact, coordinating someone to contact the patient, etc.).

Chapter 46

Clinical Supervision Is Vital for Therapist Growth

New therapists can feel overwhelmed and crave guidance. Starting clinical work can be anxiety-provoking, never mind if the therapist has fears about supervision, like Jane. A second-year graduate student in a psychology program, Jane was apprehensive about beginning clinical work and participating in supervision because in her prior career meeting with a supervisor meant performance criticism and micro-managing.

An adept clinical supervisor will be sensitive to the likelihood that supervisees might be anxious about supervision, especially at the start (Smith, 2021). Clinical supervision is not meant to be about wholesale criticism. Therapists do not receive supervision because it is assumed they lack competence. This might be hard to take in when a therapist has just finished school and feels like they've been force-fed years of information. They just want to prove themselves now and meeting with someone about their work could seem an on-the-job equivalent of having a term paper corrected.

Looked at in another light, however, supervision is what *allows* therapists to go prove themselves. Under the watchful eye of an appropriate supervisor, therapists become refined and cultivate strengths, improving patient outcomes and therapist confidence. It also mitigates liability, because the supervisors guide their supervisees to best practice.

To be clear, supervision is not "therapy for the therapist," but, like therapy, a supervisor will help the supervisee explore matters and navigate their clinical growth. It is also not just for head-scratching diagnostic situations and new techniques to try. Perhaps the best definition of supervision is from the late Ann Alonso, PhD (1985).

Dr Alonso explained that clinical supervision is "not quite teaching, but not quite therapy," and that a clinical supervisor acts more like a mentor and model. They can give the supervisee guidance on theory, technique, and cultivating the special skills of therapists while sharing their experiences and perspectives, she suggested. Herein the supervisor is "not overprotective or controlling," said Dr Alonso (1985, pp. 19–20), but rather encourages the supervisee to explore, and thus grow, under the security of their consultation.

DOI: 10.4324/9781032631400-52

As for what supervision looks like in practice, a supervisor will probably ask about specific items such as how the therapist is feeling about their work, or for an update on a previously discussed patient. It is essential, however, that supervisees present any struggles they are encountering. The supervisor does not know what the individual might need. It isn't like practicum where there are recorded sessions the supervisor reviews.

With this in mind, therapists ideally will keep track of frustrations and stumbling blocks. When I first meet students and supervisees, our initial conversations are about what strengths they bring to work as a therapist, and what may be challenges. As they progress, I watch for these in their recordings or listen for them as they tell me about work with particular patients. It is an ongoing discussion throughout our work to keep focused on maintaining strengths and shoring up deficits. At the start, it may be a good exercise to think of these as your basic supervision needs, and review these with your supervisor regularly.

Inevitably, more complicated matters will arise. These include issues of working with certain diagnoses, feeling defeated, managing a case where a patient is pushing boundaries, or encountering a patient the therapist over-identifies with. There is also the ineradicable counter-transference, or the therapist's partly conscious or entirely unconscious emotional reactions to patients at times including feelings, associations, and fantasies.

Thus, it can be helpful for therapists to admit to strong negative or positive feelings about a patient or that they are harboring a bias. Perhaps the therapist is bothered by feeling allure, sexual and non, like deep admiration for a patient for their status in life. Naturally, revealing something of this nature may cause apprehension in the therapist; it could seem that just thinking it already crossed a boundary. An established supervisor will have empathy and explore the concerns, especially with regard to how they are affecting the therapy work.

Concealing such conflicts is likely to cause harm, both in ineffective work with the patient or even put the therapist at risk. There is a phenomenon called "downing of the duck" in correctional environments. Charismatic inmates, over a few months or years, can groom staff to the point they are taken advantage of. This may be sexually, for contraband (drugs, cigarettes, pornography, weapons, special food, etc.), or even assistance with escape.

Patients are capable of similar feats. Sensing a therapist's weaknesses is a strength for some patients, especially those with certain personality disorders. Perhaps the therapist embodies everything a patient wants in a relationship. They're kind, encouraging, smart, and exhibit the unconditional acceptance of Carl Rogers. It is noticed the therapist doesn't seem overly assertive and the patient tries pushing a boundary for special treatment by, say, squeezing a few extra minutes out of a session.

Interpreted as a gesture of admiration, they probe further. "Can you help me with my coat? My shoulder is stiff and I can't quite get it on," is the next request, bringing physical contact. "Please, there was a mugging on the news the other night that happened in a parking lot near here. It's gotten dark since I came in, could you walk me to my car?" Reasoning it is a justifiable request, the therapist obliges. Each new request gathers thunderclouds but resistance seems futile. Perhaps the therapist does not feel good about their work with this patient, and these actions feel redeeming, or maybe the patient's seduction fills a romantic void. Left unchecked, the duck always comes down.

If a therapist's work is creating internal drama of any sort, it's a cue to seek assistance and where supervision is worth its weight in gold. Supervision offers a chance to resolve the matter by therapists learning about themselves, which will protect them and provide better responses to similar trying circumstances.

Readers are encouraged to use the sample supervision log included at the end of this chapter to keep track of material to discuss and what guidance the supervisor provides.

References

Alonso, A. (1985). *The quiet profession: Supervisors of psychotherapy*. Macmillan.

Smith, A.D. (2021, September 2). What is supervision for psychotherapists?: A successful clinical supervision relationship is deeper than "checking in." *Psychology Today*. https://www.psychologytoday.com/us/blog/and-running/202109/what-is-supervision-psychotherapists

Supervision Log

Name of supervisee:_____

Name of supervisor/location: _____

Date: _____ Duration of supervision: _____

Topics and patients I would like to discuss:

1. _____
2. _____
3. _____
4. _____

Supervisor's feedback on topics, patients, other material discussed:

1. _____
   _____
   _____
2. _____
   _____
   _____
3. _____
   _____
   _____
4. _____
   _____
   _____

What I plan to do differently after this supervision session:

_____
_____
_____
_____
_____

☐ How did supervision feel and did I get my needs met?

_____

_____

_____

_____

*If feeling supervision was lacking, the therapist is encouraged to broach this in supervision.

Prior to next supervision

☐ Did I follow through with acting on feedback?

   If yes, what were the results? If not, what was the challenge?

_____

_____

_____

_____

Chapter 47

Take Continuing Education Seriously

The obligation to formal education doesn't stop once someone graduates. This might seem daunting when one has recently been freed from years of education to become a therapist. However, this activity isn't mere licensing body bureaucracy; it is to ensure that practitioners stay up to date with information important to their practice. As one researcher described it, continuing education is critical for mental health professionals "to not only maintain their competencies but to also evolve them" (Washburn et al., 2023).

Thus, once licensed, depending on the state and licensure type (counselor, clinical social worker, psychologist, etc.) licensees are required to fulfill a certain number of continuing education hours every two years to renew the licensure. While some states make it compulsory for therapists to have a certain amount of continuing education units (CEUs) in particular domains, particularly ethics, therapists are usually free to choose their areas of interest.

One might imagine that the fact therapists can largely decide what continuing education topics they engage in would lead to actively seeking opportunities for such trainings of interest. However, I've been amazed at the number of colleagues who avoid trainings until the last minute and then scramble to obtain the required amount of CEUs to renew their license. Ultimately, neither the professional nor their patients benefit because the trainings were a topic the therapist has little interest or use for other than credits.

Several factors can bring about this chain of events. Though there is no definitive research on the matter, it's not hard to conclude that full caseloads, cost, and lack of interesting topics being presented locally have traditionally been barriers. With the advent of webinars and recorded presentations, however, excuses dwindle. This is especially so since many employers offer tuition remission for CEUs nowadays, and recorded trainings can be completed piecemeal.

DOI:10.4324/9781032631400-53

Since newer therapists are often curious about everything, but may not have settled into a specialty population or treatment modality, it might be overwhelming at the outset to decide what trainings to attend. However, it can also be helpful to focus on attending trainings regarding material from supervision or get recommendations from your supervisor. Common areas of focus at this career stage include diagnoses or populations prevalent in the therapist's setting, the diagnostic process and differential diagnosis, learning about psychiatric medications, gaining cultural competence, understanding the effects of trauma, and risk assessment.

Locating relevant CEUs is made particularly easy given CEU providers send mailings to counseling centers and practices. Simple internet searches reveal what topics will be lectured on nearby. Should a therapist discover an expert they admire, keeping track of their speaking circuit ensures they can be updated annually by someone admirable, making it a globally enjoyable experience.

Further, if a therapist wishes to not only be updated, but is interested in maintaining an edge, reading journals and newsletters in one's areas of interest is indispensable. If one finds reading research tedious, joining organizations specific to one's interest, such as the Anxiety and Depression Association of America, can keep professionals up to date on relevant material without the pages of technicalities. In the same vein, publications such as *Harvard Health Online* offer seemingly endless up-to-date articles on both psychological and medical topics.

If it is to better understand diagnoses or situations of interest that someone seeks, reading biographical accounts of individuals with the particular experience is indispensable. Students in my Behind the Diagnosis class always seem to enjoy reading biographies about bipolar disorder, OCD, or other diagnoses that are misunderstood due to popular culture misconception, and learn what the condition is really like.

Reading biographies also expands the understanding from a collection of symptoms to how it affects the person's being, the people around them, and even society. Therefore, reading biographies is also a great way to expand empathy. The more empathy therapists possess, the better providers they will be. The psychiatrist Irvin Yalom (2003, p. 18) explained that patients benefit enormously just from being fully seen and fully understood.

Being an informed provider not only better helps one's patients, it makes the task more enjoyable. Learning new and effective skills and conceptualizations will keep the therapist's confidence buoyed. They will meet like-minded practitioners at conferences and develop professional peer relationships for consultation and motivation, and may even be inspired to expand their career to provide trainings or writings of their own.

References

Washburn, J.J., Teachman, B.A., Gaudiano, B.A., Penberthy, J.K., Peris, T.S., Davison, G.C., & Hollon, S.D. (2023). The central role of lifelong learning and humility in clinical psychology. *Clinical Psychological Science*, *11*(4), 744–756.

Yalom, I. (2003). *The gift of therapy: An open letter to a new generation of therapists and their patients.* Harper Perennial.

Chapter 48

Have Clinical Heroes

Who doesn't recall having a childhood hero that somehow inspired them? Maybe it was a parent, sports star, or caregiver whose interests, ability, and values resonated with you, and they influenced some of the early paths you took. Later, it could have been a professor whose class you enjoyed and they encouraged your specialty interest.

One does not have to be a child to have heroes. Taking oneself to the next level requires inspiration, and more often than not it burgeons from admiration of others' work or activity. Funnily enough, in the professional world we may have mentors, supervisors, or even celebrity figures in the field that we admire, but we don't usually hear colleagues discussing people within their clinical interests at the rock star level. Perhaps this is an attempt to maintain a professional appearance, but *why not* have childish enthusiasm for a professional figure? If someone inspires you, tap into it and let it work for you.

This is not suggesting one becomes a clone. Rather, it's more about inspiration and incorporating that betterment into the therapist's professional identity.

Emma Redfern (2021, pp.15–19), a British psychotherapist, explained:

> My sense is that some of us need role models like us who we can emulate as we train. Others of us can push against or reject such larger-than-life yet approachable figures, and grow and develop by doing so. Also, as my choices say as much about me as they do about those I have chosen, I can reflect on myself, my current style of being a therapist … Something else I recognise is that by thinking of these individuals in this way, I allow myself some small portion of earned secure attachment.

If you feel struck by someone's message, explore the influence. It could also have career-altering potential. My first encounter with a clinical hero was instantly profound.

DOI: 10.4324/9781032631400-54

Early on, working in a correctional setting, I discovered that it was difficult to practice existential psychotherapy, which was my foundational framework, given the acuity of many mentally ill inmates' difficulties. Further, inmates could transition to areas of the facility in which I didn't work, and given the high caseloads and the service model the jail followed, there was minimal contact. Given these variables, I often only had a few months of once or twice-per-month contact. While I developed well-honed crisis intervention and diagnostic assessment skills, I struggled to provide something more than supportive for those requiring "outpatient" intervention.

At the same time, I was just licensed and needed to begin accumulating continuing education credits. Given the level of trauma in inmates' lives, it seemed appropriate to attend the well-known solution-oriented therapist Bill O'Hanlon's "Resolving Trauma without Drama" seminar. Bill taught about trauma interventions using the solution-oriented approach, a treatment theory I only knew in name. Bill educated in an entertaining and easily comprehensible manner, and I effortlessly absorbed everything he had to say. This short-term approach was exactly what I needed for working with the inmates and I immediately felt empowered. Later, as I honed my solution-oriented practice, it proved essential to my integrative style. I found it complimented my existential framework nicely, allowing me to help patients rapidly reduce symptom acuity while wrestling with the underlying conflicts that engendered them.

Further, Bill was an unstoppable writer on the subject, and I read everything I could by him. Enjoying writing myself, and beginning to feel I had something to share as I matured into the field, the contagious enthusiasm of his books imbued in me an impetus to try writing newsletter columns and magazine articles, which, upon reflection, sowed a seed of interest in teaching. Corresponding with Bill over the years and following his newsletters was like riding a wave into the next professional dimension.

Later, while cultivating my understanding of borderline personality, I was similarly struck by psychologist Joseph Shannon, a well-known personality expert. Not only did I enjoy Joe's approach to working with this type of personality, but his empathic stance towards disorders of personality sparked in me a curiosity about the patients I was taught to avoid in my earlier years. This curiosity about personality enhanced my understanding of the importance of examining how someone relates to themselves, others, and the world, which, as noted in Chapter 42, affects a variety of clinical matters.

Joe had a nearly continuous speaking circuit, and his enthusiasm for teaching was equivalent to Bill's for writing. I thus felt encouraged to try teaching, which I have come to enjoy as much as clinical work. Joe has since become a friendly colleague, and someone with whom I can discuss mutual interests.

Isaac Newton said, "If I have seen further, it is by standing on the shoulders of giants" (Chen, 2003). Newton, of course, meant this in a way of studying and emulating the greats, the people before him he found heroic, as his foundation, just as a therapist might Freud or Rogers or Beck. But giants need not be vestigial. Anyone whose stature impresses us to look up, to want to stand on their shoulders and see what they see, can be our giants, our clinical heroes. Let them know your admiration. They just might lend a hand and take you even higher.

References

Chen, C. (2003). On the shoulders of giants [Abstract]. *Mapping scientific frontiers: The quest for knowledge visualization.* Springer. https://doi.org/10.1007/978-1-4471-0051-5_5

Redfern, E. (2021). Dark and light: What our psychotherapy heroes reveal about ourselves and our profession. *Irish Journal Counseling and Psychotherapy, 21*(4), 15–19.

Chapter 49

Improve Your Clinical Skills After Hours

The therapeutic foundation is grounded in forming solid connections. Many of the things that make successful therapists are also key components of good socializing. While it would be unethical to practice treatment or diagnosing anyone outside of the office, given psychotherapy is based in interpersonal exchange, everyday social interactions are ripe with opportunities to hone therapists' abilities.

Taking an inventory of one's social strengths and deficits can help decide what to focus on. Chances are, for example, if one is prone to interrupting in conversations, one is predisposed to following suit with patients.

The range of possibilities of things that could be practiced are expansive, but the following are some illustrations that have stood out.

Undoubtedly, the therapist's most valuable tool, from which all other interaction springs, is listening skills. When discussing listening skills with supervisees that feel pressured to talk, I often refer to a former patient's observation. He summarized that, as he saw it, no one in his family listened to each other, they only wanted to say their piece, then wondered why no one got along. He explained, "They doesn't understand that's why we have two ears and one mouth. We're supposed to listen twice as much as we talk."

Whether at home or in the office, this is a sound reflection. Naturally, people want to say what they feel is important or otherwise have to offer. However, if someone has a tendency to be the dominant talker, it can suggest they aren't interested in listening. Surely, you have had such interactions where the conversation is more a case of "listen to the other person." Imagine sitting across from a therapist who is such a person? People don't necessarily develop this kind of communication habit because they are selfish, but patients don't know this, and working on this tendency could help improve interactions.

Another pillar of social/therapist skills is observation. Being attentive to behavior can be an immense help in work with patients. Does someone tend to glance away when talking about certain topics? Cross their legs during others? Perhaps in a family therapy session, two parties who usually sit across

DOI:10.4324/9781032631400-55

from each other happen to sit next to one another. Each of these observations is something to mine. Learning to look for language nuances and subtle changes in dynamics in everyday life can pay big dividends in the office.

Speaking of looking, some students confess they struggle to maintain eye contact, as they feel it's too intense and become distracted by it. It is no secret that eye contact has a lot to do with confidence; someone feeling subordinate will often avoid it. It can be challenging to provide reassurance or to be taken seriously if confidence is lacking. Depending on the person they're interacting with, this might also signal disinterest, which can negatively affect the working relationship. I can speak from experience.

As a young adult, I had an inflammatory illness that left my eyes full of dead inflammatory cells, or "floaters." I discovered that if I darted my eyes around, it would briefly clear my visual field. I did not realize this action was so obvious to others until a patient remarked that it was hard to focus on talking to me when my eyes would intermittently dart. It was as if they were asking if I had trouble focusing on them. Upon asking those close to me about the matter they agreed it could appear that I was looking around, but they also understood the situation. Nonetheless, I began learning to sit with the nuisance while talking and only darting my eyes if the person looked away or if I made a situation to break eye contact.

Someone who has noticed they tend to avoid eye contact might practice socially by the same process that exposure therapy occurs, and is also something a supervisor can practice with a struggling supervisee. Deciding to look up more regularly for a few seconds of eye contact can help signal that one is not trying to be distant, and a desensitization effect begins to take place that allows the gaze to be held longer and longer.

Another action that takes a little confidence is interjecting and redirecting. This is not the same as being a sentence finisher or interrupter. Patients can get off track and therapists must rein them back in to stay focused. It's not a matter of cutting them off, but learning the art of taking opportunities.

Chances are you know someone who can be tangential or a conversation domineer. Developing the skill of sensing opportunities to seize the conversation will help corral sessions where a patient's tangent, for instance, is gravitating away from the original topic. Learning this skill may begin by watching for when they take a breath and say, "I'm following along, but can you hold that thought? I'm curious about something you said back there ..." and the conversation can't help but be rerouted.

Asking for clarification is another indispensable tool to make a habit of. Assumptions can be dangerous roads to go down. I recently was interviewing a young man who kept referring to himself as "antisocial." While I assumed he meant he was somehow socially avoidant, given how the word is used by non-clinical people, inquiring, "what does antisocial mean?" provided a rich return on him diagnostically and interpersonally. He actually didn't mean it as a form of asocial behavior. The young man explained that he likes to be interactive, but, as a result of his traumatic history, he is extremely vigilant and careful about who he interacts with and how.

Even if we think we know what someone means, reflecting back our understanding and seeing if it is correct, or asking for an example are easy ways to get into regularly asking for clarification.

Lastly, it can be especially therapeutic to help someone understand what their diagnosis means. Unfortunately, it seems therapists are trained to understand diagnoses as checklists of symptoms and not experiences. As discussed in Chapter 28, the key is to relate to them what the experience means, and that they're not reduced to a pile of symptoms.

Unfortunately, as made clear in Section III, unless one is in the psychology field, understandings of mental health diagnoses are frequently wrong, and perpetuate stigma. One of the objectives of my Behind the Diagnosis course is for students to learn more deeply about mis-portrayed mental illnesses and to then educate others about them as an avenue to destigmatization.

One of the exercises is to interview three people who do not work in mental health about their understanding of a particular diagnosis. Frequently, the person interviewed says that those suffering from the condition are dangerous and can change on you at any moment, and they'd be hesitant to associate with someone like that. The student's job is to then explain to the interviewee what the life of someone with the condition is like and what it actually means to have the diagnosis.

Whenever someone uses, for example, diagnoses as adjectives ("He's so 'schizo'," "She's so OCD," "They must be bipolar," etc.), the encounter can be capitalized upon to ask if the speaker really knows what those terms mean and used as an opportunity to practice one's psychoeducational skills.

Chapter 50

Do Therapists Need Therapy?

Up until 40 or 50 years ago, it was a given that students wishing to be psychotherapists, particularly psychoanalysts, attended their own therapy.

One reason was it provided an opportunity to instill empathy in therapists for what it's like "being on the couch." The second, and perhaps more important reason in the psychoanalytic tradition, was that learning about one's own conflicts and defenses was considered essential in effective therapy that relied heavily on relating. This would not only help therapists recognize and work with such conflicts in patients, but have an awareness that their own subconscious could help them be an "unbiased clinical observer because their own countertransference has been mitigated" (Schwartzman & Muir, 2019).

These days, outside of some European countries and psychoanalytic programs, it is rarely compulsory that therapists-in-training attend their own therapy (Malikiosi-Loizos, 2013).

It's easy to see how the reasons psychoanalysts encourage personal therapy would be valid and useful for therapists in general. Regardless of whether one practices psychoanalysis, researchers tell us that psychotherapists having their own therapy plays a role in cultivating empathy, genuineness, and other characteristics helpful to patient growth (Macran & Shapiro, 1998). One might also come to appreciate the power differential and how a therapist can be idealized.

The psychiatrist Irvin Yalom (2003) drove the point home well when he noted that the therapist's most valuable instrument is themself. Engaging in personal therapy helps therapists "be familiar with their own dark side and be able to empathize with all human wishes and impulses" (pp. 40–41). Further, explained Yalom, personal therapy helps new therapists learn to accept feedback (and thus what it's like to receive feedback and the importance of empathic delivery), discover their own blind spots, and appreciate the impact they have on others.

At the very least, personal psychotherapy for students and trainees, explained one researcher, "enhances their understanding about their

DOI: 10.4324/9781032631400-56

profession through personal experience/learning ..." (Edwards, 2018). In effect, a therapist who has not been in their own therapy might be akin to a mechanic who has never driven a vehicle. It can make it difficult to fully appreciate what one is working towards, and what the clientele really needs.

Of course, many therapists were inspired by their own therapy and can empathize with being the one on the couch. That said, there's a difference between having had therapy in middle school and being in therapy while practicing. For one thing, chances are, attention was not being paid to the therapeutic process, which could be useful to the therapist's own practice. Two, conflicts relevant to being a better psychotherapist, such as, for instance, feeling incompetent, or harboring negative feelings based on personal experiences about certain clinical populations, probably weren't being addressed.

Based on personal experience and discussions with colleagues, a general, longer course of psychotherapy, where the trainees can examine and take control of their anxieties, moods, and existential conflicts, is ideal. A consistent, long-term experience not only provides an opportunity to explore many facets of self-improvement, it can also be especially helpful in learning about the therapeutic process. Readers engaging in personal therapy are encouraged to reflect on their experience as a patient and what translates to their practice.

Despite the likely benefits, students and supervisees sometimes still hesitate when it surfaces in supervision, and that is usually not without good reason.

Students and supervisees have shared that they would like to engage in personal therapy, especially given the stress of work/life balance in graduate school. The barriers tend to be cost, insurance coverage, and/or time when they're carrying a full caseload, perhaps have a family, and work. It has also been noted that some psychotherapy program students said they fear for their confidentiality given they are limited to campus counselling center services because of transportation or college insurance coverage (Schwartzman & Muir, 2019). This is of particular concern on smaller campuses.

Others have acknowledged therapy would be wonderful, but the time isn't right. There is a real concern that old issues which have been satisfactorily compartmentalized or dissociated from for the time being will leak out. The ensuing emotional toll might then sabotage their ability to maintain equilibrium in the program or early career work.

After the Covid lockdown of 2020, supervisees offered a new reason to not bother with personal therapy: therapists are hard to come by, period, never mind one they mesh with. There was a fear of a revolving door of wasted time awaiting one, only to not feel a fit, and start all over again.

I would be remiss if I did not encourage ongoing consideration of personal psychotherapy despite the concerns and barriers, as they are not as insuperable as they might seem. The following four ideas might be helpful for readers navigating the aforementioned concerns:

- Many employers have employee assistance programs (EAPs) available to the employee and their family. An EAP generally does not cost anything to utilize, and, while usually no more than ten sessions can be attended before the managed care plan must be used, they can provide an understanding of the therapeutic experience and be used to work through some acute concerns.
- Teletherapy options have created numerous alternatives. Among these is that, if time is limited, patients can meet with therapists from home, office, or even their car, saving drive time. Further, a student worried about being seen or heard in the campus counselling center could utilize a teletherapy option by arranging session times for when their roommate is out, attending from their vehicle, or scheduling it for when they visit home on the weekends.
- For the person concerned about unintentionally surfacing suppressed conflicts, to gain some experience as a patient, they could consider seeking more pointed therapy to address, say, insomnia, communication with a partner, or becoming more mindful.
- Locating a suitable therapist in a timely fashion can be quite difficult today. Instead of internet searches and cold calling, asking a trusted professor, adviser, or clinical supervisor can yield surprising results. Many therapists do not advertise, prefer vetted referrals, and are happy to do favors for their associates.

Lastly, therapists experiencing some particular conflicts are highly encouraged to seek even short-term therapy, given the potentially fatal consequences in therapy. These include:

- Substance use that renders one using, craving, or withdrawing on the job.
- Impatience/low frustration tolerance, especially with regard to patients' progress.
- Feeling incompetent/fearful of failure (not to be confused with angst of a normal learning curve).
- "Imposter syndrome," usually evidenced by asking oneself, "Who am I to be providing care to these people?"
- Consistently feeling the weight of patients' material, especially in the form of secondary or vicarious trauma. Signs of the latter two include experiencing intrusive thoughts of patients' material, heightened anxiety about the specific trauma or when meeting with the patient, and the material seeping into the therapist's dreams. Secondary trauma is a

more immediate onset of such symptoms, perhaps triggered by material that was particularly difficult for the therapist. Vicarious trauma is insidious, usually the accumulation of years of work with traumatized people. It tends to have a more pervasive effect, coloring the therapist's self-perception, world views, and even spirituality, along with damaging their feelings of safety, intimacy, and trust (Jimenez et al., 2021). This not only harms their personal lives, but the potential effect on patients can be devastating if the therapist cannot provide the basic materials to cultivate intimate relationships in the office.

• Bias towards particular clinical populations. For example, a supervisee recently expressed strong negative feelings toward people who abused substances. This is concerning because, even if the patient is not presenting for substance abuse concerns, substance abuse rates are high in mental health care. Any patient confessing to drug or alcohol use stands the risk of not being treated fairly by a therapist with such a conflict.

• A self-defeating, or masochistic tendency, as evidenced by a need to cater to, and even suffer for, patients. This behavior can encourage patient dependency, the therapist being taken advantage of, and opens therapists up to liability. Some signs of this problem include maintaining 24/7 availability; taking on tasks the patients should manage, such as calling their psychiatrist for appointments or getting clarification from their managed care organization; and arranging unnecessary meeting frequency, not because of a wish for more reimbursement, but for want of having someone to care for.

While any such concerns should, of course, be brought to clinical supervision, a clinical supervisor is not in the role of therapist. The supervisor can provide support by helping find assistance for such a struggling therapist, while helping navigate risk management for the patients of such a struggling therapist.

In the end, consider it's a standard stipulation in codes of ethics (American Counseling Association, 2014; American Psychological Association, 2017) that it is imperative that therapists monitor personal struggles to gage if they are impeding professional competence. Obtaining personal psychotherapy may not only be career enhancing, but, in some cases, could save a therapist's career.

References

American Counseling Association (2014). Therapist responsibility. *2014 American Counselling Association ACA Code of Ethics* (p. 8). https://www.counseling.org/resources/aca-code-of-ethics.pdf

American Psychological Association (2017). Ethical principles of psychologists and codes of conduct. Competence (section 2.06). https://www.apa.org/ethics/code

Edwards, J. (2018). Counseling and psychology student experiences of personal therapy: A critical interpretive synthesis. *Frontiers in Psychology, 21*(9). doi:10.3389/fpsyg.2018.01732

Jimenez, R.R., Andersen, S., Song, H., & Townsend, C. (2021). Vicarious trauma in mental health care providers. *Journal of Interprofessional Education & Practice, 24* https://doi.org/10.1016/j.xjep.2021.100451

Macran, S. & Shapiro, D.A. (1998). The role of personal therapy for therapists: A review [Abstract]. *British Journal of Medical Psychology, 71*(1), 13–25. https://doi.org/10.1111/j.2044-8341.1998.tb01364.x

Malikiosi-Loizos, M. (2013). Personal therapy for future therapists: Reflections on a still debated issue. *The European Journal of Counselling Psychology, 2*(1), 33–50. https://doi.org/10.5964/ejcop.v2i1.4

Schwartzman, C.M., & Muir, H.J. (2019). Personal psychotherapy for the psychotherapist in training. *Psychotherapy Bulletin, 54*(4), 15–21.

Yalom, I. (2003). *The gift of therapy: An open letter to a new generation of therapists and their patients.* Harper Perennial.

Chapter 51

Protecting Your Own Mental Health

One of the hazards of the occupation is exposure to sad or otherwise disturbing situations. Hearing trauma stories, sitting with severely depressed people, evaluating people after self-injury or suicide attempts, or working with families that are falling apart can take its toll. Working in forensic populations might add another layer.

A good friend once said to me, "You just sit there and listen to people's problems all day. How do you not just absorb it all?"

The uninitiated have a vision that the mental health profession is akin to sitting in a constant rain of woe, that therapists are just sponges to soak up patient complaints and somehow wring themselves out to start all over again. While therapists surely realize it's more involved than my friend's assumption, it is well-known (Posluns & Gall, 2020; Rokach & Boulazreg, 2020) that they often neglect their self-care in the name of helping others, and if they are not careful, certainly could absorb too much. This seems even more likely if practitioners work with highly traumatized populations (Lanier & Carney, 2019; Roberts et al., 2022).

Coupling constant exposure to difficult material with difficult administrators and working in a demanding hospital or clinic setting can lead to burnout. Add to this that the demand for therapists is not being met (Amenabar, 2022) and some may feel obligated to pick up slack. Given all this, burnout is not likely to vanish.

It was noted in one recent study that 62 percent of 327 therapists met burnout criteria (Spännargård et al., 2023). This worn-down state has been correlated to onset of poor mental and physical health of therapists, decline in clinical effectiveness, and even misconduct (Nissen-Lie et al., 2021).

Provided this has all been in the news, students and supervisees entering the field during or post-Covid pandemic not infrequently ask, "How do you do it?"

The first thing that comes to mind is that the correctional environment I began in demanded that I allowed a "healthy callus" take form. Within a couple of years, I began to feel the pressure and friction of the environment

DOI:10.4324/9781032631400-57

made a psychological callus, as manual labor encourages on the hands. It was just like the callus finger padding that helps one's grip.

While "callus" may conjure ideas of insensitivity, there is a semantic nuance to "callousness" that must be acknowledged. I didn't become cold and unempathic. It was quite the opposite. It was exactly like the protective layer on one's hands through which one can still feel, something that provided me with the protective layer that was necessary to continue working with very ill inmates, in turn, cultivating further empathy for them.

Anyone feeling that they're having a similar evolution might want to objectively review the experience in supervision, or at least engage in self-reflection. This is because there is a difference between work engendering a dissociation of sorts, leading to indifference, and the therapist experiencing a protective layer that allows them to continue to enjoy their work.

The aforementioned aside, as trite as it seems, I must stress the importance of practicing what one preaches and engaging in self-care and boundaries. It is especially important to establish this early on, as burnout is associated with younger age and less experience (Simionato & Simpson, 2018). Many health care employers offer work-life balance management through trainings and employee assistance programs that can be taken advantage of if someone needs help navigating life balance.

Undoubtedly, this advice has sustained many who continue to enjoy and grow in their career. Joseph Shannon, a psychologist who has spent 40 plus years working with personality disorders, shared with me that he found helpful advice from the trailblazing cognitive-behaviorist Aaron Beck, MD. Dr. Shannon said that Beck explained therapists who engaged in a depression treatment strategy he favored tended to be the ones who warded off burnout. This involved incrementally increasing non-career-related activities that conduct a sense of mastery, are purely pleasurable, and provide some spiritual/existential satisfaction (Beck et al., 2015).

As I found my way, I noticed that I was fortunate that these three items have long been interwoven into the fabric of my days and likely what has kept me from coming undone. Music and comedy provide me joy and accompany me in all of my commutes; the evenings find me decompressing by tying fishing flies, and 35 years of doing this has given me a sense of mastery; while I can't always be hiking or backpacking, otherwise cultivating a strong appreciation of the world around me by admiring what's new in bloom, the quality of sunlight, or the behavior of the birds brings me a constant micro-dosing of earth-driven spirituality.

Any time a therapist is veering toward burnout territory, to regain equilibrium it would be beneficial not only to look at reducing pressure with the help of supervision, but also to examine which of the three items has been neglected.

References

Amenabar, T. (2022, November 16). Therapists say they can't meet high demand as anxiety, depression linger. *Washington Post.* https://www.washingtonpost.com/wellness/2022/11/16/therapist-high-demand-mental-health

Beck, A.T., Davis, D.D., & Freeman, A. (2015). *Cognitive therapies for personality disorders* (3rd ed.). The Guilford Press.

Lanier, B.A. & Carney, J.S. (2019). Practicing counselors, vicarious trauma, and subthreshold PTSD: Implications for counselor educators. *The Professional Counselor, 19*(4). https://tpcjournal.nbcc.org/practicing-counselors-vicarious-trauma-and-subthreshold-ptsd-implications-for-counselor-educators

Nissen-Lie, H.A., Orlinsky, D.E., & Rønnestad, M.H. (2021). The emotionally burdened psychotherapist: Personal and situational risk factors [Abstract]. *Professional Psychology: Research and Practice, 52*(5), 429–438. https://doi.org/10.1037/pro0000387

Posluns, K. & Gall, T.L. (2020). Dear mental health practitioners, take care of yourselves: A literature review on self-care. *International Journal for the Advancement of Counseling, 42*(1), 1–20. doi:10.1007/s10447-019-09382-w

Roberts, C., Darroch, F., Giles, A., & van Bruggen, R. (2022). You're carrying so many people's stories: Vicarious trauma among fly-in fly-out mental health service providers in Canada. *International Journal of Qualitative Studies on Health and Well-Being, 17*(1). doi:10.1080/17482631.2022.2040089. PMID: 35195506; PMCID: PMC8925925

Rokach, A. & Boulazreg, S. (2020). The COVID-19 era: How therapists can diminish burnout symptoms through self-care. *Current Psychology, 41*, 5660–5677. https://doi.org/10.1007/s12144-020-01149-6

Simionato, G.K. & Simpson, S. (2018). Personal risk factors associated with burnout among psychotherapists: A systematic review of the literature [Abstract]. *Journal of Clinical Psychology, 74*(9), 1431–1456. https://doi.org/10.1002/jclp.22615

Spännargård, Å., Fagernäs, S., & Alfonsson, S. (2023). Self-perceived clinical competence, gender and workplace setting predict burnout among psychotherapists. *Counselling and Psychotherapy Research, 23*(2), 469–477. https://doi.org/10.1002/capr.12532

Chapter 52

You Can't Save Them All

Therapists inherently harbor positivity. How else would they ever believe patients could change? They must also be realistic, however, and learn to recognize that, despite their ability, not every patient will improve, and it is no reflection of incompetence.

It's one thing to be persistent; another to indefinitely attempt to elicit any positive responsiveness. Approaching that juncture is a signal that perhaps it's time to review the lack of progress and discuss other possibilities or referrals.

It pays to learn when to pick one's battles. This, of course, begins with taking stock of what competencies, training, and clinical interests one has. If a patient or referral falls outside of the therapist's competency, it will not only be frustrating to both parties, but could be considered unethical. It's easy to see the inherent problems in, say, a therapist whose background is in treatment of phobias trying to work with someone with emerging psychosis.

Even within their niches and no matter how long they've practiced, a therapist only has so deep a bag of tricks and one personality. They may have the right tricks but the wrong interpersonal "click" with some patients, or vice-versa. It is also impossible to be adept at working with every issue a patient could bring to your office. You may be very successful at working with couples, but during the course of treatment it is discovered that both parties' substance abuse plays a big role in the relationship dysfunction. It is nice to think that you could continue to work with the couple because it is a relationship issue. Despite this, if the therapist is not skilled in addiction work, chances are they'll watch the couple continue to digress despite their efforts.

In my practice I carefully screened for patients with concerns that I was competent in working with. Periodically, however, they held hidden surprises, like the return of an eating disorder. Amelia, for instance, showed an improvement in the depression she came to therapy for. It wasn't long after her mood brightened that she started looking gaunt. Amelia explained that she was feeling stressed and was thus losing weight, but did check in with her doctor.

DOI: 10.4324/9781032631400-58

When I called her primary care physician to express my concern, it was explained to me that Amelia indeed has been dropping weight and seemed to have a reemergence of anorexic symptoms. Anorexia is a medically dangerous condition that I am not trained to work with. It would have been unethical, even with supervision, to try and work with Amelia on her eating disorder. In fact, the need for specialized care in eating disorders is taken so seriously that insurance companies might not reimburse non-eating disorder certified therapists as a check against inadequate treatment.

Given the medically dangerous condition takes precedence, and Amelia was only able to have coverage for one therapist, we worked to get Amelia into anorexia treatment, with the understanding that if she wished, she could return once the anorexia remitted.

Even if a therapist has a particular talent for a certain population, they'll no doubt periodically encounter exceptions that stretch their clinical wit and patience. It has nothing to do with losing their edge, and, if records are obtained from previous providers, there's a good chance it will be discovered they had similar experiences.

The psychiatrist Michael Stone wrote a book called *Personality-Disordered Patients* (2006) which includes a chapter entitled "Personality Traits at the Edge of Treatability." Dr Stone tells readers that there are some particularly troublesome traits/characteristics that tend to prove so pervasive they render treatment nearly impossible. These include patients prone to vindictiveness, spitefulness, being overly sentimental and self-pitying (maudlin), being untrustworthy/undependable/unreliable, laziness, procrastination, and being scatterbrained ("flakiness"). I would like to add pervasive pessimism to this list. It is easy to see how these qualities can keep a patient from going anywhere in treatment despite a therapist's best efforts.

Considering Dr Stone's list, I can't help but recall how after each session I had with two particular patients I invariably questioned my clinical skill. I'd successfully worked with severely mentally ill and personality-disordered inmates in solitary confinement and prided myself on reviving some "hopeless" cases in my practice.

However, these two people, who initially presented with depression, something that rarely felt burdensome to work with, always left me feeling defeated. The common thread was that they both harbored the most pessimistic mindsets I have ever encountered. It was not a matter of the glass being half empty or half full. Even if it was full, they'd complain about the contents of it. The following illustration makes clear the challenge.

A lonely, elderly lady, Janice, had been coming for help with sadness and anxiety. In a store one day, I saw a card that said, "Life isn't about weathering the storm. It's about learning how to dance in the rain." This was a nice metaphor for what we had been attempting to work on. I also figured it could strengthen the therapeutic alliance, bringing her something therapeutically relevant I thought she might enjoy, demonstrating that I thought of her outside the session.

Her response, with a disgusted expression, was, "Well, I'm certainly not going out and dancing in any rain."

Try as we might, we just can't get through to everyone.

Reference

Stone, M. (2006). *Personality-disordered patients: Treatable and untreatable*. American Psychiatric Publishing.

Index

active empathic listening (AEL) 29, 31
ADHD *see* attention-deficit
  hyperactivity disorder (ADHD)
Alonso, A. 203
anorexia 226
antipsychotic medications 76, 176, 178
antisocial personality disorder 183
anxiety 50; acute 56–58; co-occurrence
  rate 83; diagnosis for 83; and
  excitement 162; illness 14; pervasive
  57, 86; social 43, 75, 79, 83
asking: about meaning 39–41; for
  clarification 215–216; for feedback
  187–189; questions 45
assertiveness 12
attending skills 3, 17, 19–20
attention-deficit hyperactivity disorder
  (ADHD) 77, 80, 83; diagnosis
  101–102; diagnosis accuracy
  92–94; symptom checklist measure
  106; symptoms 101, 102, 178; *see
  also* bipolar disorder; borderline
  personality disorder (BPD);
  generalized anxiety disorder (GAD);
  obsessive compulsive disorder
  (OCD); personality disorder
autism 76; diagnosis accuracy 91–92;
  sensory peculiarities 91; social
  awkwardness 91, 96

Beck, A. 194, 213, 223
behavioral interventions 10, 80
"Behind the Diagnosis" course 72,
  184, 209, 216
bipolar disorder 10, 60, 77, 73, 99,
  108, 177, 183, 184; diagnosis
  72; diagnosis accuracy 94–95;

presentations 115; *see also*
  attention-deficit hyperactivity
  disorder (ADHD); borderline
  personality disorder (BPD);
  generalized anxiety disorder (GAD);
  obsessive compulsive disorder
  (OCD); personality disorder
body dysmorphic disorder (BDD) 153
body language 25; patients 26–27
borderline intellectual functioning 76
borderline personality disorder (BPD)
  14, 30, 77, 82, 118, 135, 144, 152,
  183, 184; *see also* attention-deficit
  hyperactivity disorder (ADHD);
  bipolar disorder; generalized
  anxiety disorder (GAD); obsessive
  compulsive disorder (OCD);
  personality disorder
burnout 222, 223

Cahalan, S. 111
callousness 223
chief symptom 71, 86, 88, 140
clinical: documentation 108; skills 214–
  216; supervision 203–205, 220
cognitive analytic therapy (CAT) 194
cognitive-behavioral therapy (CBT)
  skills 13, 14
cognitive interventions 10, 194
continuing education 208–209
continuing education units (CEUs)
  208–209
culture-bound diagnoses 171–172
culture, role of 170–174; depression
  172–173; ethnic diversity 173;
  overworking 172–173
cyclothymia 115

symptoms 86; ADHD 101, 102,
178; contextualization of 87–88;
generalized anxiety disorder (GAD)
88; none reported 108; panic
111; personality disorder 183;
presentation 114–115; reduction
13–15

teletherapy options 219
therapeutic presence 21–23
therapist: anxiety 28; approach
to treating trauma 140–142;
assertiveness 12; attending skills
19–20, 49–50; attention to
pertinent negatives 107–108;
characteristic of 11–12; conflicts
219–220; energetic 11–12; fidgety
27; good fit with patients 11; in
high-stress situations 23; initial
interaction between patient and
21; interventions appeal to patients
159; learn to reframe 161–163;
maintain eye contact 22; own
therapy 218; protecting own mental
health 222–223; psychoanalysis

217; relief of symptoms 13;
remain calm and relaxed 22–23;
self-disclosure 150–154; stress
management 89
therapy 9–10; relationship 17
third ear, listening with 42, 44
tinnitus 50
trauma: reincarnate 142; secondary
219–220; substance abuse 140;
therapist's approach to treating
140–142; vicarious 220
trust 17

validation 30
van Gelder, K. 184
vicarious trauma 220
voice-hearers 63, 65, 66

Wallas, L. 42
Wampold, B. 21
work-life balance management 223

Yalom, I. 4, 55, 154, 209, 217
"Young Schema Questionnaire" 14
Yudofsky, S. 184

For Product Safety Concerns and Information please contact our EU representative GPSR@taylorandfrancis.com Taylor & Francis Verlag GmbH, Kaufingerstraße 24, 80331 München, Germany

Printed and bound by CPI Group (UK) Ltd, Croydon, CR0 4YY
08/06/2025
01897005-0008